Financial Innovations and Market Volatility

To

Tom Donovan and *Leo Melamed*

Financial Innovations
and
Market Volatility

Merton H. Miller

BLACKWELL
Cambridge MA & Oxford UK

First published 1991
Reprinted 1991, 1992, 1995

Blackwell Publishers, the publishing imprint of Basil Blackwell Inc.
238 Main Street
Cambridge, Massachusetts 02142, USA

Basil Blackwell Ltd
108 Cowley Road
Oxford OX4 1JF
UK

Library of Congress Cataloging in Publication Data
Miller, Merton H.
    Financial innovations and market volatility / Merton H. Miller.
        p.   cm.
    Includes bibliographical references and index.
    ISBN 1–55786–252–4
    1. Capital market—United States.   2. Finance—United States.
3. Stocks—Prices—United States.   4. Stock Market Crash, 1987—
History.   I. Title.
HG4910.M52   1991   90–29036
332.63'2'0973—dc20   CIP

British Library Cataloguing in Publication Data
A CIP catalogue record for this book is available from the British Library.

Typeset in Palatino
Printed in the USA by Maple-Vail

This book is printed on acid-free paper

Contents

Part IV The Academic Field of Finance

List of Tables

List of Figures

Foreword

Merton Miller is a great economist.

He is also a fine warrior. In the 1950s he takes up finance and engineers a stunning campaign that, after a period of years, decisively undermines the Old Guard and installs Modern Finance.

That done, he brings his methods to the Real World, and becomes a strategist for Chicago's commodity crowd in their battles with New York's establishment and Washington's power brokers.

He does all this with such finesse, such humor, and above all, such devotion to economic principle that you reluctantly admire him even as he rides past you to victory.

Here you can learn by example as you study his strategies. You may even learn how to win the war, by adopting public policies that promise the greatest good for the greatest number of people.

Fischer Black
Goldman Sachs Asset Management
New York City

Author's Preface

This volume began, although I didn't suspect it at the time, with a phone call in the fall of 1983 from Thomas Donovan, then as now, the president of the Chicago Board of Trade. He invited me to become a Public Member of his organization's board of directors. Serving in that post opened for me an entirely new perspective on futures markets. The standard finance literature on futures focuses mainly on the demand side–on how the customers can use futures contracts to manage risk. At the board of directors' level, by contrast, the emphasis is on the supply side–on how to provide transactions, clearing, and settlement services to the customers at prices remunerative to the exchange's members. Futures exchanges are not just idealized Walrasian markets; they are business organizations. And they operate in a very competitive environment indeed, as I learned first hand during my two-year tour of duty at the Chicago Board of Trade, and have been reminded again since becoming a Public Governor of the Chicago Mercantile Exchange in January 1990.

The business side of US futures exchanges, and especially their effort to remain competitively viable, is the major theme running through and connecting virtually all of the essays in this book. The "financial innovations" of the title are seen as just so many competitive new products introduced for motives and with methods (including intensive market research) similar in all essential respects to those in more familiar industrial settings. And "market volatility" of the title is seen as just the banner under which retail stockbrokers and other competitors of stock index futures have sought to enlist first the Congress and later the Securities and Exchange Commission and the Treasury on their side of the competitive struggle.

A second running theme of the book, and one that serves as well as its organizing principle, is the great stock market crash of October 19-20, 1987. The three chapters in Part I all date from before the crash, though presentiments of the traumatic events to come show up clearly in the title essay "Financial Innovations and Market Volatility" (Chapter 3). The processes giving rise to the innovations themselves, and especially to financial futures (perhaps the most important of these innovations) are considered in this essay along with some specu-lation about why so much innovation was packed into so small a span as the past twenty years. The essay "Liquidity and Market Structure" (Chapter 2), excerpted from an article written jointly with Sanford Grossman now at the Wharton School, sets forth the basic theoretical framework of the demand and supply of immediacy that shows up in one form or another in all the remaining chapters of the book.

The Crash itself takes center stage in Part II, leading off in Chapter 4 with the Final Report of the Chicago Mercantile Exchange's Commit-tee of Inquiry for which I served as chairman. That report, understand-ably, focuses mainly on the role that index futures played, or at least are supposed to have played, in the events of the day. Views of the 1987 Crash, and crashes more generally, taken with a wider-angle lens, are offered in Chapters 5 and 6. Index arbitrage figures heavily in all these chapters as well as the earlier Chapter 2. Anyone needing a brush-up on the mechanics of index arbitrage can find it in Chapter 7.

Part III, the largest section of the book, deals with issues of com-petitiveness and public policy. Chapter 12 discusses these issues with respect to futures exchanges and Chapter 8, which was co-authored with Charles Upton, currently Dean of the School of Business at Kent State University, discusses them with respect to exchanges more gen-erally. One long-lived policy issue touched on in several chapters (especially Chapters 4 and 12), but one that may, mercifully, finally be approaching resolution, is that of private-sector versus public-sector control over stock index futures market margins. Chapter 9 deals with the empirical side of the controversy by vivisecting the only academic study claiming that public-sector control over margins could successfully dampen stock market volatility.

Another long-lived policy issue also overlapping several chapters is that of taxes on securities and futures transactions. Chapter 10 is a short "op ed" focusing entirely on that issue and written at a time when the controversy over the Securities Transactions Excise Tax was at its height. Chapters 11 and 13 take up some post-Brady Commission reforms such as "circuit-breakers" and the New York Stock Exchange's Rule 80A restricting index arbitrage on days with big market moves. Rule 80A was just coming into force as that chapter was being finished. Although the discussion of the rule in Chapter 13 has been somewhat outdistanced by recent market events and by new studies of the rule, I have here, and throughout, resisted the temptation to "revise and extend my remarks," as they say in the *Congressional Record*. The chapters are presented as originally written, warts and all.

Resisting the temptation to second-guess myself was hardest, understandably, for the book's final essay on the past and likely future of the academic field of finance. It was written some four years before Harry Markowitz, William Sharpe, and I received the 1990 Nobel awards in economics for helping found that field. The essay, reflecting as it does mainly my previous incarnation as a corporate finance specialist in the years before Tom Donovan called, may well seem out of synch with the rest of the book. I have included it here, nevertheless, largely at the behest of my two editors, Elizabeth Johnson of Basil Blackwell and Ida Walters of the Mid America Institute, who felt it would add a personal touch to the volume.

To the Mid America Institute and its executive director, Robert Kamphuis, I owe a special debt not only for the indispensable assistance of Ida Walters, but for much other encouragement and support over the years. Mid America Institute and its local sponsors have often served as the first critical forum for trying out the ideas and arguments presented here.

My thanks also to the many past and present fellow board members of both the Chicago Mercantile Exchange and the Chicago Board of

Trade who have so patiently tried to teach me the mysteries of their trade, and to the many staff members at both exchanges on whose technical expertise I have drawn so heavily in preparing these essays–notably Rick Kilcollin, Todd Petzel, and Ken Cone at the Chicago Mercantile Exchange and Scott Early, John Stassen, and Tom Coleman at the Chicago Board of Trade.

But above all, I must thank those two outstanding leaders of the futures industry by whose side I have been privileged to work (and fight) during these past hectic years: Tom Donovan of the Chicago Board of Trade and Leo Melamed of the Chicago Mercantile Exchange, the father of financial futures. To them, with great respect and affection, I dedicate this book.

One final word to readers. Because these papers were prepared for many different audiences and occasions, some repetition of themes and images was inevitable. Like everyone else, I have my favorite stories and I love to keep telling them. But since not all readers will want to read all the chapters, and certainly not in a single sitting nor in the order presented, I though it better to leave the stories just as originally delivered. The particular occasion for presenting each paper is indicated at its close.

Merton H. Miller
Chicago

Part I

Before the Storm

1 Financial Innovations: the Past Twenty Years and the Next

No word is more overworked these days than "revolution." Yet, in its original sense of a major break with the past, the word revolution is entirely appropriate for describing the changes in financial institutions and instruments that have occurred in the past twenty years.

As one small example of how far we have come, I can still recall the shock and incredulity of my Belgian colleagues at the University of Leuven in 1966 on learning that I, as an American citizen, could not then legally own monetary gold. Nowadays, of course, we can hold and trade not only gold coins, gold bullion, gold futures, and gold options but literally hundreds of other financial instruments that either didn't exist in 1966 or existed only in rudimentary form. A partial list of major novelties would include, in no particular order: negotiable CDs, Euro-dollar accounts, Eurobonds, sushi bonds, floating-rate bonds, putable bonds, zero coupon bonds, stripped bonds, options, financial futures, options on futures, options on indexes, money market funds, cash management accounts, income warrants, collateralized mortgages, home equity loans, currency swaps, floor-ceiling swaps, exchangeable bonds, and on and on. The mind boggles.

Can any twenty-year period in recorded history have witnessed even a tenth as much new development? As we review the list—and, remember, it is only a partial list—we can only wonder whether and when this unprecedented innovative surge will begin to lose its force. Are even more financial innovations in prospect and where are they likely to arise?

To organize our thinking about likely future financial innovations I propose first to look to the processes that produced the remarkable flood of new instruments and institutions. An understanding of the underlying driving mechanisms may give clues about where the machine is likely to go. But to keep this discussion from becoming too dull, let me restate the question as it was recently posed to me by a reporter from a leading financial journal. The journal was considering an award–in the spirit of Hollywood Oscars–for "the most significant and successful financial innovation" of the last twenty years. Several academic and industry finance specialists were to be invited to submit nominations and a brief supporting defense of the choice. I, too, have a candidate for the award. And I will get to it, in due course, after sketching out briefly the criteria I applied in making my selection.

Defining terms: What is an "innovation?" What is a "successful" innovation? And what is a "significant, successful" innovation?

For the term "innovation" and how it differs from just plain improvement, modern statistics provide some helpful distinctions. Time-series analysts break into two parts the change over time in the value of any series such as the gross national product or consumer prices. One part is the change that could, in principle at least, have been forecasted by extrapolating known past information. The other part is thus the unanticipated, unforecastable change–the "surprise," as it were. It is these surprises that have been aptly dubbed the "innovations" in the time series. And it is to their counterparts among the recent surge of financial instruments and institutions that I will be directing attention.

To say that financial innovations, like innovations generally, are basically unforecastable improvements is not to suggest that their emergence is merely a matter of chance or of artistic creative impulse. Such creativity does indeed occur in business; and, in the case of some of the financial innovations, the artist has even left us his signature. But that is certainly not always true. Many of the financial innovations on my earlier list already existed in one form or another for many years before they sprang into prominence. They were lying like seeds beneath the snow, waiting for some change in the environment to bring them to life.

What process stimulated the new and energized the dormant innovations in finance over the past twenty years? I wish I could say that it was the flood of MBAs out of our business schools over this period. That was certainly part of the story but not the decisive part. The major impulses to successful financial innovations over the past twenty years have come, I am saddened to have to say, from regulations and taxes.

Taxes and Regulations as Impulses to Innovation

The income tax system of virtually every country that is advanced enough to have one seeks to maintain (or perhaps I should say "has sought to maintain") different rates of tax for different sources (and uses) of income–between income from capital and income from labor; between interest and dividends; between dividends and capital gains; between personal income and corporate income; between business income paid out and business income retained; between income earned at home and abroad; and so on. At the same time, modern finance theory assures us, as practitioners have known, that securities can be used to transmute one form of income into another–in particular, higher taxed forms to lower taxed ones. These transformations are not without cost, particularly when pushed to extremes. Were any country actually to leave its tax system unchanged for a generation or so, an equilibrium might emerge in which no incentives were left for further shifting income. The gains from exploiting the remaining rate differentials would be exactly balanced by the costs of transformation at the margin. The total revenue raised would tend to stabilize, subject only to the inevitable slow attrition coming from the normal, extrapolative, trend-related flow of improvements in transactions technology. But, of course, we will never know that nirvana-like state of equilibrium. For a variety of reasons–including especially desire to blunt the force of previous successful innovations by taxpayers–governments (or, more properly, the shifting coalition of interest groups, that vehicle for protection and advantage) prefer to keep changing the structure, thereby altering the internal rate differentials and creating new opportunities for financial innovation. This endless sequence of action and reaction has been aptly dubbed the "regulatory dialectic" by Edward Kane of Ohio State University (see Kane, 1986).

Note that changing the tax structure both motivates and defines a "successful" innovation. Each innovation that does its job successfully earns an immediate reward for its adopters in the form of tax money saved. The government is virtually subsidizing the process of financial innovation just as it subsidizes the development of new seeds and fertilizers but with the important difference that in financial innovation the government's contribution is typically inadvertent. There are cases, particularly in the politically sensitive housing area, where the US government has been the major pioneer of new financial instruments. For the most part, however, the role of government in producing the pearls of financial innovation over the past twenty years has been essentially that of the grain of sand in the oyster.

Although I have chosen to emphasize tax changes as an initiating force in financial innovation, the same process can be seen at work in any financial area subject to government regulation, which is to say, still virtually everywhere. The pressures to innovate around prohibited types of profitable transactions, or around newly imposed or newly-become-effective interest-rate ceilings, are particularly strong but, as we have come to see lately, even what purports to be deregulation can sometimes trigger changes that go far beyond the intentions of the original sponsors.

We now have definitions for "innovations" and "successful innovations" and some insight about what produces them. But which ones merit the accolade "significant" innovations? Here again, we can get valuable clues from the language of modern statistics. Time-series analysts and economists distinguish between those innovations whose effects are "permanent" and those whose effects are only "transitory." Similarly with financial innovations. Some have a period of success and then disappear, or virtually so, once the specific tax or regulatory change that fueled their initial success has been removed. Their effects have thus been basically transitory, though they may well continue to sleep on under the snow, ready to spring up once again should favoring circumstances arise.

But a few innovations manage not only to survive but to continue to grow, sometimes very substantially, *even after their initiating force has been removed*. These are the truly significant innovations.

Many instances of such nontransitory, significant innovations can be found among those on my earlier list. The Eurodollar market, for example, owed its origin to a curious US restriction known as Regulation Q. The regulation, among other things, placed a ceiling on the rate of interest that commercial banks could offer on their time deposits. Over much of the post-war period, that rate ceiling was, if not actually above, at least not drastically below the market clearing level. But that changed in the late 1960s and early 1970s with the rise in US and world interest rates. The US money-center commercial banks soon noticed that the restrictions of Regulation Q did not apply to the dollar-denominated time deposits in their overseas, and especially Western European, branches. (These dollar-denominated accounts, in turn, owed their origin to still earlier sets of government restrictions; but that is another story. See, for example, Shaw, 1983.) The US banks and their foreign rivals could and did bid competitively for short-term dollar-denominated accounts; and they continue to do so on a huge scale today even though Regulation Q has long since become a dead letter.

The currently huge Eurobond market was set off by a tax rather than a regulatory change. It sprang up initially in response to the US government's institution in the late 1960s of a withholding tax of 30 percent on interest payments on bonds sold in the United States to overseas investors. The locus of the market for dollar-denominated bonds for non-US citizens thereupon moved from New York to London and other money centers on the continent. The withholding provision has since been repealed, but the Eurobond market it induced has continued to thrive, in part, no doubt, because it also served to bypass the cumbersome new-issue prospectus requirements imposed by the Securities and Exchange Commission on public issues of securities by even the best-known US firms. Another adaptation to that same withholding tax by some US banks and firms was the creation of a Netherlands Antilles subsidiary corporation as a treaty-protected withholding-exempt financing arm. That adaptation, however, appears at this time not to be passing the survival test for permanence and, hence, "significance" by my definition.

In singling out these two particular examples of the innovation process, I did not mean to slight the contributions to innovation of governments other than my own. There is plenty of glory to go around. The current vogue for "swaps," for example, was set in motion some years back by firms seeking ways to avoid British government restrictions on dollar financing by British firms, and on sterling financing by non-British firms. Other important innovations have involved the simultaneous inadvertent contributions of two or more countries. The ideal Miller example is the zero-coupon bond. No single innovation epitomizes so neatly the many strange and often unplanned elements that come together to produce a significant financial innovation.

The explosion in the issue of deep discount bonds by US corporations in 1981 was occasioned not strictly by a tax change, but by the recognition of a hitherto unsuspected technical flaw in the Treasury Department regulations that interpret the US tax law. Zero-coupon securities were already in existence, of course, notable examples being Treasury bills and even the Treasury's own Series E Savings Bonds. But long-term deep discount instruments had rarely, if ever, been issued by taxable corporations until the Treasury's blunder was appreciated. So gross was that blunder–which permitted a linear approximation for computing the implicit interest, and, hence, inflated the present value of the interest deductions–that a taxable corporation could actually come out ahead by issuing a zero-coupon bond and giving it away !

The Treasury reacted after a couple of years with legislation closing off the avenue, and the supply of new zeroes by US corporations abruptly ceased. But the demanders for zero-coupon instruments that the first innovation had uncovered were still there and begging for more. Much, though certainly not all, of this demand was sustained by the corresponding blunder of the Japanese tax authorities in treating all of the appreciation not as deferred taxable interest, which would have been advantageous enough to the holder, but as capital gains. And capital gains under Japanese law were exempt from tax. Zero-coupon bonds, moreover, were a neat way of blunting the force of Ministry of Finance restrictions on the value of foreign bond holdings by Japanese pension funds. Despite minor adjustments recently, these rules and the demand for zeroes they create still remain. Meanwhile, with the corporate supply dried up, our own innovators have been busily creating a synthetic supply of zero-coupon bonds for Japanese buyers (and for tax-exempt domestic pension-fund portfolio "immunizers") by stripping the coupons from US Treasury bonds and selling them separately as zeroes.

So much then for my criteria for defining significantly successful financial innovations. Now comes the hard part. Any surviving, successful innovation must have reduced dead-weight transaction costs and expanded the reach of the market, otherwise it wouldn't have been successful, let alone significant. But which of the many possible candidates merits the award of *most* significant? And how is relative significance to be scaled? Not, I think, just by sheer volume of business. On that score, the Eurobond and, even more, what is fast becoming the Euro capital market would be an easy winner. Size is part of the story, but not all of it. To qualify as most significant, an innovation must be important not only in and of itself, but must have stimulated substantial further innovations as well. It must have set off a chain reaction, as it were, if that is still a permissible analogy in the light of recent events. By this standard, my nomination for the most significant financial innovation of the last twenty years is financial futures–the futures exchange style trading of financial instruments.

Financial Futures: Origins and Early Development

You may be surprised that I did not single out options trading as the prime innovation. Options are certainly the darling of the academic finance community. They represent the one case in which we can translate our underlying theoretical notions into an exact pricing relation–the justly famous Black-Scholes formula and its numerous extensions. Options are also more basic and fundamental securities than futures contracts in that, with options (and Treasury bills), one can always create synthetic futures, but not the other way around. It can also be shown that many of the fancy instruments in my earlier listing are really just options in disguise. But my concern here is with innovation, and that requires getting events into the proper historical sequence. In that sense, financial futures come before options; only a few months ahead, it is true, but still, ahead.

That first truly successful innovation in financial futures can be pinpointed quite precisely, as can the name of its inventor, or, at least, its prime mover. He was Leo Melamed of the Chicago Mercantile Exchange, though Leo Melamed himself often modestly gives credit for the original inspiration to Milton Friedman who, at the time, was a member of the Department of Economics at the University of Chicago.

Milton Friedman, for some reason that I don't know but can suspect, came to believe sometime in 1971 or so that the British pound was overvalued. No Chicago bank, however, would accommodate him by allowing him to sell the pound short. He happened to mention this on some social occasion to Leo Melamed, who then, as now, had close ties to the University of Chicago. That mention registered with Melamed because the symmetry of futures contracts for short and long positions had always been one of the standard claims for advantage of the Chicago-style futures markets over the New York-style stock markets. No costly borrowing and escrowing of securities were needed to go short in Chicago; no senseless uptick rules had to be observed before a short sale could be executed. A short in Chicago was just the negative of a long.

This potential cost advantage of futures trading, however, was, at that point, of purely academic and polemical interest since only futures in physical commodities, and a rather small set at that, were actually being traded. But the Chicago commodity futures exchanges in their drive to diversify had, by the late 1960s, amply demonstrated their willingness to experiment with imaginative, new kinds of contracts even though most were doomed to fail. Some of these experiments, like iced broilers and plywood (and, going back still further, live cattle and pork bellies), actually presented far greater challenges to the ingenuity of the contract designers than did foreign exchange, which is, after all, already a highly standardized commodity.

So with some fanfare, though not an enormous amount, the International Money Market was inaugurated in 1972 as an offshoot of the

Chicago Mercantile Exchange and the era of financial futures trading began.[1]

Although I was in Chicago at the opening of the International Money Market, I was not caught up with any sense that an event of great historical significance was taking place. I let the occasion pass. One reason I failed to read major significance into the opening may have been my awareness of the already existing and well-functioning market for foreign currencies. It was not an exchange market, of course, with a single trading pit but, rather, a classic "upstairs" market with telephonic connections between the trading desks of the major banks and between the banks and the large foreign exchange brokers. Each trading bank received (or solicited) orders for foreign exchange from its own customers—either businesses with overseas transactions or smaller banks servicing their own customers. Small orders would be filled directly out of inventory by the desk; in the active currencies, incoming customer orders could be crossed. For large orders, for substantial order imbalances, for rebuilding dealer inventories, or perhaps just for purely speculative reasons, the trader could tap into the telephone market. The

---

[1] While the Chicago Mercantile Exchange justly deserves credit for being first off the mark with its foreign exchange futures contract, its crosstown rival, the Chicago Board of Trade, had actually proposed exchange trading of options on common stocks as early as 1969. Such options, however, fell under the jurisdiction of the US Securities and Exchange Commission, at that time a particularly heavy-handed regulatory agency. Setting to rest the SEC's professed concerns about speculation and insider trading in options managed to delay the opening of the Chicago Board Options Exchange for more than five years. The search for the origins of exchange-traded financial futures is complicated further by the exchange trading of options at the Chicago Board of Trade as far back as the 1920s. They were options on commodity futures, however, not stocks, and they were banned by Congress in one of its periodic anti-speculative convulsions in the late 1930s. That this previous incarnation of options trading is not more widely known may be simply a matter of unfamiliar terminology. What we now call options were then known as "privileges." What is perhaps even less widely known is that common stocks were also traded on the Chicago Board of Trade in the same era in ways that had at least some elements of futures style market arrangements. But, to borrow some terminology from historian David Landes of Harvard University (see Landes, 1983), these early, aborted episodes were "anticipations," perhaps, but not true innovations in our sense of the term.

trader had the choice either of identifying himself immediately to the bank counterparty on the other side of the trade or, as is the custom particularly in Europe, of maintaining initial anonymity by placing the order through a broker. Eventually, of course, the two parties must disclose their identities because both the spot and forward transactions have a credit component (and each bank trader will typically have a list of specific counterparty position limits that he must honor).

Knowing one's counterparty is one way of reducing the moral hazards of trading. And, by and large, it has been a successful way in foreign exchange, though some conspicuous examples of fraud (like the Herstatt affair) have occurred in the foreign currency market both before and after 1972. But it works only if the number of players can be kept small–small enough (which, in practice, means that the players themselves must be large enough) for each player to be able to monitor every other player.

The futures market, by contrast, as my colleague Lester Telser has so often stressed (see especially Telser, 1981), is an impersonal market in which there is no premium on knowing one's counterparty. The moral hazard of trading with strangers is solved by interposing an intermediary–the clearinghouse–between the actual traders. The clearinghouse guarantees that the terms of the contract will be fulfilled and protects itself, in turn, by requiring (and monitoring) the posting of collateral (the familiar "margins") by each party to the contract.

Leo Melamed's hunch that a futures contract (and its associated clearinghouse infrastructure) could substantially lower the costs of buying and selling the major foreign currencies proved to be justified by events. The International Money Market attracted a substantial volume of trading virtually from its inception–not all that common a result with new contracts. The sand in the oyster turned out to be the abandonment in the early 1970s of the Bretton Woods system of fixed exchange rates–fixed, that is, except for periodic convulsions. Floating rates create precisely the kind of price volatility and hedging demand that futures trading needs and thrives on.

The coming of exchange trading for foreign currencies did not displace the upstairs, interbank market, of course. The really big trades–

$2 or $3 hundred million or more at a crack are still likely to be routed upstairs. The International Money Market's comparative advantage would be in the handling of, say, 200 trades at around half a million each. This is not to say, however, that only traders in that range have benefited. Evidence gathered subsequently from other financial futures markets shows that spreads in the upstairs, big-player spot and forward markets are significantly smaller when the futures markets are open than when they are closed. And, at the other end of the order-size spectrum, even those whose transactions in foreign exchange are confined to airport kiosks are also presumably benefiting. Think how much more sizable the dealer's spread would have to be if he didn't have access to reasonably low-cost hedging for his own inventory. It is important to keep that source of benefits in mind because the financial futures I am extolling are not typically products that individuals consume directly. They are essentially industrial raw materials.

Instituting futures trading of foreign exchange, in sum, reduced transaction costs and provided thereby all the classical gains from trade. That alone, however, would not have earned it my award: nomination, or honorable mention perhaps, but not the big prize. What earns it that award is its having served as a model and exemplar for trading in so many instruments in addition to foreign exchange.

It is obvious enough now (though it certainly was not so obvious then) that the same conditions that opened the niche for foreign currency futures also were present elsewhere–to wit, a virtually standardized product already heavily traded but in specialized markets to which only a small set of players had direct access. The Chicago Board of Trade soon thereafter introduced GNMA (Government National Mortgage Association) futures–a contract that some regard as the first true *financial* futures in the strict sense of the term. Its claims for this honor may have to be filed posthumously, however, since current trading of even its much revised contract is down to fewer than 200 contracts a day, and falling. Shortly after the GNMA, the Chicago Mercantile Exchange introduced Treasury bill futures, a contract still very successful, with the initial sand in the oyster in that case being provided by some special features of our tax law that gave substantial unintended tax benefits (since removed) to futures trading in T-bills.

From short-term T-bills, it was an easy logical step to long-term Treasury bonds (though the practical step was far from trivial because of the greater difficulty of standardizing instruments with different coupons and maturities and with less regularity in the infusion of new supplies; the US Treasury, moreover, was anything but supportive). Long-term T-bonds, traded on the Chicago Board of Trade, have now become far and away the leading financial futures contract in terms of daily trading volume. From Chicago, government bond futures trading has now spread to foreign money centers such as London where, one suspects, its impact in lowering transaction costs is likely to be even greater than it was in the United States, given the more heavily car-telized trading structures there. In fact, financial futures must surely be given some of the credit for the wave of deregulation and decarteliza-tion now sweeping through the European (and, to some extent, even the Japanese) capital and money markets.

Had the impulse from the original financial futures innovation stopped at this point it would have been remarkable enough. But then came another extension that created enormous new potential applica-tions for financial futures, a potential that has only just begun to be tapped.

Cash Settlement and the Increasing Abstraction of Traded Commodities

The extension was "cash settlement." The typical commodity futures contract gives the holder the right to demand delivery of the com-modity at the agreed-upon price and the times, places, and quality grades specified in the contract. And the short, on the other side of the contract, has the corresponding obligation to deliver. In practice, rela-tively little physical delivery actually takes place. Most short con-tracts are liquidated by offset–that is, by going into the market and buying an equivalent (standardized) contract. But some physical deliv-ery does take place and it can be, all things considered, an unnecessary nuisance. Not only must the physical costs of supporting the delivery system be incurred, but the right to demand delivery at contract expiration can confront careless or unwary traders with delivery squeezes or corners when the time for contract closeout approaches. Maintaining a regulatory apparatus to deal with such closeout problems is one of the costs of futures trading.

Why then hadn't the delivery option been dropped in favor of cash settlement long ago? In part, and particularly for the traditional agricultural commodities, perhaps no spot prices were sufficiently tamperproof to serve as an accepted basis for settlement. Cash settlement in such circumstances would change only the form, not the substance, of the squeeze problem. But that surely cannot have been the case for instruments such as foreign exchange or T-bills, where large and active spot markets exist.

What prevented cash settlement in those instruments, even if it had been efficient to adopt it, was a provision of law. In many of the states in the United States, notably Illinois where the big exchanges are located, a contract settled by delivery, if only in principle, was a futures contract. But a contract that could be settled only in cash was a wager. And in most states (except for Nevada and parts of New Jersey) wagering, even between consenting adults, is illegal (unless, of course, the state owns the casino, as in the state lotteries, or is at least a major partner, as in pari-mutuel betting).

These restrictive state laws, however, were superseded in 1974 by the federal regulatory statute that set up the CFTC (the Commodity Futures Trading Commission) as a successor to the the Commodities Exchange Administration, and gave the CFTC sole jurisdiction over futures markets. Since there was no federal prohibition of gambling, cash settlement, suddenly, if inadvertently, became conceivable.

The notion that the CFTC could contribute, even inadvertently, to innovation in futures trading will, of course, bring a smile to the face of anyone familiar with its subsequent history and reputation. The contribution of the CFTC to progress and innovation in futures markets has almost always been to slow it down and impede it. All new futures contracts must have CFTC approval before trading can begin. Delays in granting approval often run to a year or more; and even when the end is almost in sight and the traders are virtually lined up waiting for the starting bell, contracts have been sent back for further low-order but, at that point, costly revisions. All this, mind you, for new contracts whose potential had previously been studied in depth by the exchanges whose members will bear the risks if the contract fails (as, indeed, most of them do). And the amounts involved in developing new products are too large for frivolity. In the case of just the two recently introduced, and still largely unsuccessful, Over-The-Counter Index contracts, the Chicago Board of Trade and the Chicago Mercantile Exchange invested a combined total of $5 to $6 million, an amount on the order of a quarter of the entire CFTC annual budget.

Although the original authorization of the CFTC in 1974 had the unintended side effect of displacing state restrictions on cash settlement of futures contracts, the legal steps that positively affirmed cash settlement were not fully in place until 1981. But once the CFTC had removed the major obstacles to this innovation (other than itself, of course), two major steps forward soon were taken by the industry.

The first, and by far the more important in terms of current volume of trading, was a futures contract in common stock–not of one particular company but of a whole portfolio of individual stocks. Since the settlement for the portfolio of stocks was to be in cash rather than by physical delivery, it was natural to focus on those portfolios most relevant for possible hedging purposes in the investment community, especially the institutional investment segment. And that suggested the major market indexes (and possibly also industry subindexes) of the kind already widely used in performance evaluation.

That judgment proved sound, but, in some other respects, there were major surprises. The problems associated with contract closeouts under the delivery system did not disappear; they only changed their form. The closeout on expiration days now involves not the shorts scrambling to deliver the spot commodity to the longs, but the so-called "program traders" scrambling to unwind their arbitrage positions–either short the index future and long the stocks or long the futures and short the stocks. On some days–the so-called "triple witching days"–the actions of the program traders are sometimes reinforced by the similar arbitrage-related actions of the options converters, and big fluctuations occur in the prices of some of the underlying stocks. If, say, the program traders and the option converters happen to have predominantly short positions in the stocks as the close approaches, then there will be a sudden surge in the demand for shares to cover those short positions. The same excess demand arising at the opening of trade or during the course of the trading day can often be accommodated without a large price change by delaying trade until enough potential sellers have been notified and solicited. But when the imbalances pile up unexpectedly just before the close, the time is sometimes too short to hunt up additional outside counterparties. Price concessions to those on site may be the only balancing mechanism left before the final closing bell is rung. Other closeout procedures that will obviate these occasional wide price moves (and yet not kill the arbitrage demand for futures and options) are currently the subject of much active research and controversy.

The closeout problems, though they have attracted much attention, should not obscure the important economic contribution of financial futures by directly and indirectly reducing the costs of transacting in common stocks. The accomplishment of cash settlement futures on that front has been major, but there was one even more startling contribution of cash settlement to come.

The stock index futures were at least based on potentially tradeable baskets of goods. And, indeed, the program traders and other arbitrageurs assemble just such baskets. But the next step in financial evolution was to indexes that were closer to being measures of abstract concepts than to deliverable bundles of commodities. There is futures trading now in ocean freight rates, and, more interesting yet, in "inflation"–at least as measured by changes in the US Consumers Price Index.

The CPI contract is, of course, the economist's dream contract. At last, people will be able to contract with each other in real terms exactly as they do in the price theory part of the textbooks. It is no accident that Milton Friedman, whose ideas helped to get the whole thing started in 1972, has also been among the most eloquent champions of this extension as well.

However brilliant its sponsorship, and however exciting the prospects of such a contract among professional economists, the CPI contract has not yet proven commercially viable. This failure reflects no lack of marketing skills on the part of the organizing entrepreneurs at the Coffee, Sugar, and Cocoa Exchange. The publicity surrounding the contract initiation and the subsequent efforts to pump up interest and trading volume have been ingenious. The campaign even included a contest whose prize was a free trip to the country with the highest rate of inflation. That was the second prize. The lucky first prize winner could settle for cash!

Nor has languishing of the inflation futures market been just a matter of the substantial drop in both the level and volatility of inflation in the last two years or so, though that's clearly a major part of the story. Two monetarist economists were overheard recently discussing the fate of the CPI index market. The optimist said: "The trouble with the inflation futures market was that it came too late." "No," replied the pessimist: "Too early." We shall see.

My own feeling is that it did come too early, but not because I am predicting that a new surge of hyperinflation lies ahead. The problem lies rather with the current technology of futures trading. The colorful open-outcry method of futures trading is not just a relic of the past as even some of the current CFTC commissioners seem to think. It is rather (as Sanford Grossman of Princeton University and I have come to appreciate in the course of a study we are currently undertaking on market liquidity) an extremely efficient way of supplying the service of "immediacy" in those markets, typically, inventory-propelled or arbitrage-driven futures market, where the demand for speedy executions of trades is high. In markets where immediacy is less crucial, however, there may be cost advantages in other forms of market microstructure— such as the once or twice per day batch call market of some European stock markets. In those markets, the need is not so much for speed as for making sure that as many transactors as possible on the other side have been informed of an impending desire to trade.

For the CPI index and for the even more abstract follow-on products that have been suggested (such as an industrial production index or the index of housing starts) there is not much demand for immediacy—not enough, at least, to justify a competitive industry of traders standing around all day in the pit waiting to handle urgent, incoming orders. If financial futures in these abstract products are to succeed, some way must be found to separate—or "unbundle"—the futures contract and its clearinghouse infrastructure from methods of trading that have their comparative advantage at higher ends of the volume and urgency scale. Devising such a method of efficient trading of low urgency contracts is not going to be easy. Important regulatory and competitive obstacles must be overcome. Perhaps the best way to overcome them at this point might be to start fresh by moving these markets for more generalized hazards out of the United States to Britain and Europe where there are already functioning models to draw on, such as the fabled Lloyds of London.

Financial Innovation: Is the Great Wave Subsiding?

That brings me to my final theme: is the great wave of financial innovation of the past twenty years likely soon to slow down? Or must we brace for further and possibly even more rapid bursts of innovation ahead?

The answer to these questions will certainly depend on what actually triggered the recent past surge. That the triggering had at least something to do with tax and regulatory changes is, I hope, clear enough from my admittedly somewhat impressionistic survey. But, of course, those triggers have always been with us. The process of adaptation and selective survival in response to tax and regulatory changes has been going on throughout recorded history, as has been called to our attention by the distinguished economic historian, Richard Sylla of the University of North Carolina. (See especially Sylla, 1980.) Apparently we owe even such fundamental financial instruments as paper money to the same basic process—the sand in the oyster in that case having been the British government's prohibition of the minting of coins by its then colonial subjects in North America. But something else seems to have happened about twenty years ago that shocked the system into a period of unprecedented rapid innovation.

I must confess that despite much pondering I have yet to come up with a completely satisfying first cause. There are certainly plenty of possibilities, both economic and technological, but, with the exception of the great oil shock of 1973-4, most had obvious counterparts at times (and often at several times) in recent past history. And, as for the oil shock, many of the key developments were under way well before it occurred.

Perhaps, then, there was no single, easily pinpointed cause, but just the coincidental coming together of a whole set of seemingly unrelated (to borrow still another term from statistics) events and circumstances. Most of the critical tax and regulatory frameworks that supplied the motives for the financial innovations I have been describing were put in place in the 1930s. In that depressed and war-scarred period, and even more so during the war and slow recovery years that followed, there were better outlets for innovative talents. We were just too poor and too distracted with other, more pressing concerns. The regulatory and tax constraints were not the most seriously binding ones.

By the middle and late 1960s, however, the recovery in world wealth (and trade) had proceeded so far that the taxes, interest rate ceilings, foreign exchange restrictions, security sales regulations, and other anticompetitive controls slapped on in the 1930s and 1940s were becoming increasingly onerous. It was not so much that new tax and regulatory burdens were being imposed (though that was happening too), but more that the existing burdens were increasingly binding, particularly so given the surges in the level and volatility of prices, interest rates, and exchange rates that were erupting in those years. The innovative wave then triggered was much like a snake bursting through its old skin.

If this view is correct, the prospect for the future is for a slowing down of the rate of financial innovation. Note that I said a slowing down of the rate of innovation, not an end to further progress. Clearly, much growth and improvement are still in prospect, especially in the important area of real estate and in market competition across countries and over the hours of the day. Nor should this slowing down in the rate of innovation in the coming twenty years be deplored. It will be good news, not bad, if it means that many of the inefficient tax and regulatory structures inherited from the 1930s and 1940s will have been driven at last from the scene along with so many of the obsolete economic and political doctrines that gave rise to them.

This chapter is based on a paper presented to the Distinguished Invited Speakers Series at the 1986 Meetings of the Western Finance Association, Colorado Springs, June 20, 1986, and later published in the Journal of Financial and Quantitative Analysis, *December 1986. An earlier version was presented at the Seminar on Financial Innovation in Leuven, Belgium, May 1986, and published in the September 1986 issue of* Revue de la Banque, *Brussels, Belgium. The author has benefited greatly from comments by John Stassen of Kirkland and Ellis, formerly Counsel of the Chicago Board of Trade, but retains responsibility for any remaining errors.*

References

Kane, E. J. "Technology and the Regulation of Financial Markets." In A. Saunders and L. J. White (eds), *Technology and the Regulation of Financial Markets: Securities, Futures and Banking.* Salomon Brothers Center Series, Lexington, MA: Lexington Books, 1986.

Landes, D. S. *Revolution in Time.* Cambridge, MA: Belknap Press of Harvard University Press, 1983.

Shaw, E. R. *The London Money Market,* 3rd edn. London: Heinemann, 1983.

Sylla, R. "Monetary Innovation in Economic History." Mimeo, North Carolina State University, 1980.

Telser, L. "Why There Are Organized Futures Markets." *Journal of Law and Economics*, 24, April, 1981.

2 Liquidity and Market Structure

with Sanford J. Grossman

Keynes once observed that while most of us could surely agree that Queen Victoria was a happier woman but a less successful monarch than Queen Elizabeth I, we would be hard put to restate that notion in precise mathematical terms. Keynes's observation could apply with equal force to the notion of market liquidity. The T-bond futures pit at the Chicago Board of Trade is surely more liquid than the local market for residential housing. But how much more? What is the decisive difference between them? Is the colorful open-outcry format of the T-bond futures market the source of its great liquidity? Or does the causation run the other way?

Those are some of the issues we propose to consider here. Our purpose is to present a simple model of market structure that captures the essence of market liquidity. A key feature of the model is its finer partitioning of time intervals and of roles for market participants than in standard treatments of the determination of market prices. Much economic theory, in the Walrasian tradition, still proceeds as if prices were set in a gigantic town meeting in which all potential buyers and sellers participate directly. Researchers in the rapidly growing specialty, sometimes dubbed market microstructure theory, have expanded the cast to include market makers in the sense of intermediaries who can fill gaps arising from imperfect synchronization between the arrivals of the buyers and the sellers. The focus of this literature has been on the inventory-management policies of market makers (see, for example,

Stoll, 1985) and on their responses to the threat of adverse information trading against them (see, for example, Glosten and Milgrom, 1985). Our intention here, however, is not to expand this important and interesting class of inventory models but to fit these intermediaries and their temporary inventory holdings into a larger framework that also encompasses the ultimate demanders and suppliers.

A Brief Overview of the Model:
the Supply and Demand for Immediacy

Our model of market structure has two participant groups, and we shall refer to them, for simplicity, as *market makers* and *outside customers*. For simplicity of exposition only, we shall take their basic tastes, including risk tolerances, as the same. Their roles are defined at this stage principally in terms of their initial endowments.

Within the group of outside customers are some who, for any of a variety of reasons, experience what we call a *liquidity event*, which leads them to perceive a gap at current prices between their desired holdings of a particular asset and their current holdings of that asset. Even if the gaps sum to zero across the whole group, as we assume, some customers might propose to remedy their portfolio imbalance immediately by undertaking a transaction in the asset; for concreteness in exposition, suppose these potential liquidity traders are net sellers. In our model the putative sellers can choose to offer the goods immediately to the market makers who happen to be in the market currently and who have no holdings of the asset, or at least no imbalance that they too are seeking to eliminate. Or, a seller can postpone the offer to sell for one stylized period until the potential buyer customers on the other side of the trade have learned of the offer and have had a chance to come to the market.

Clearly the seller faces a trade-off. By waiting until more potential buyers have been notified, the seller increases the chance of finding an eager buyer. But this delay carries risks; while the buyers are assembling, the ultimate equilibrium price may shift. The best selling price for a sale delayed to the second period may be substantially lower (or higher) than the price in a sale to a market maker in the first period. By selling immediately, that interim price risk is transferred to the market maker who then waits until the ultimate buyers have assembled. When we speak of *the demand for immediacy* by a seller, we mean the willingness to sell rather than wait. This demand depends on the volatility of the underlying price and the diversifiability of the risk of an adverse price move.

The market makers charge for bearing price risk by offering the immediate sellers a price that is not uncertain, but that is lower, on average, than the sellers could expect from delaying. The expected price rise between periods one and two is, of course, only the market maker's gross return before allowing for the costs of supplying the service. These costs include not only any direct costs of effecting and monitoring trades, but also the important, though often overlooked, cost of being available and open for business when the outside customers arrive to trade. These opportunity costs of maintaining a continuous presence in the market, which we model as fixed costs, play a key role in determining *the supply of immediacy* and market-making services.

The market makers, as emphasized earlier, must also assume the price risk that the immediacy demanders shed. That the aggregate price risk is merely shifted to the market makers does not, however, rule out efficiency gains from the arrangement. In our model, where all participants have the same risk tolerance, the gains arise essentially from diversification–the spreading of the transferred risks over the entire group of market makers. The larger that group, the lower, *ceteris paribus*, the risk and expected return per unit traded by each and hence also the lower the effective cost of immediacy to the customers. The number of market makers will adjust until, in equilibrium, the returns to each from assuming the risk of waiting to trade with the ultimate buyers just balance the costs of maintaining a continuous presence in the market. This adjustment determines the equilibrium amount of immediacy provided, that is, the amount by which price is temporarily depressed by a typical sell order.

Our model suggests looking to differences in the cost to market makers of maintaining a market presence and to differences in the demand by customers for immediacy for the keys to market structure and market liquidity. The greater the demand for immediacy and the lower the cost to market makers of maintaining a continuous presence, the larger the proportion of the transactions between ultimate customers effected initially through market makers, and hence the more liquid the market.

The Liquidity Spectrum in Real-World Market Structures

Successful futures markets are the leading examples of markets where the demand for immediacy is high. Futures markets are successful precisely for those commodities and in those time periods where price volatility, and hence the risks of delaying trading, are high. The price risks of volatility are further reinforced for potential hedger customers in those markets by the high leverage and extreme under-diversification of the underlying spot inventory positions that consti-tute their main line of business. Immediacy also becomes of particular concern where, as is frequently the case, the futures transaction is mere-ly one leg of an intercontract or intermarket hedge. Little or no risk may be incurred once all the components of the hedge have been put in place, but much risk is incurred when only some of the legs have been set. When the transactor is "naked," to use the colorful language of the trade, the delay of even a few seconds can become critical. (See, for example, Grossman and Miller, 1986a.)

The demand for immediacy in successful futures markets is not only urgent, but sustained. The regular seasonal build-up and build-down of inventories, as commodities move through the production chain, creates a continual desire to *trade*, not just to *hold* futures. In financial futures markets, dealers' inventories of the underlying securities build up and down in response to periodic auctions of US Treasury issues, to the flotation of stocks or bonds by corporations or to the restructuring of portfolios by large institutional investors.

The sustained demand for hedging and hence for trading futures quickly is often accommodated by designating a specific physical market place or exchange in which many competing market makers can offer their services simultaneously. Such arrangements help spread the fixed costs to market makers of maintaining a presence, as does the practice at most present-day futures exchanges of providing trading areas for many different contracts between which individual market makers can drift as trading interest changes. Many, but not all, futures exchanges also permit market makers to serve both as brokers for customers and as traders on personal account, though not, of course, on the same transaction. Most floor traders tend to specialize in one role or the other, but the freedom to switch roles can permit a quick adjustment in the number of market makers when the flow of orders changes abruptly.[1]

At the opposite extreme from the highly liquid futures markets, where intermediary market makers participate as principals in virtually all transactions, stand the highly illiquid markets, such as those for residential housing, where virtually none of the transactions pass through a dealer's temporary inventory.[2] Sellers of individual homes are typically less concerned with short-term price volatility, and hence with immediacy, than with making sure that the widest possible set of ultimate buyers can be informed of the house's availability. Potential market makers, moreover, face not only all the ordinary costs of maintaining a continuous presence in a thin market, but the additional moral hazards that arise from the owner's possibly adverse private information about the value of the property. The result is a market in which intermediaries, to the extent that they are involved at all, provide brokerage or search services, not immediacy.

---

[1] For a discussion of the benefits and the supposed abuses of dual trading on futures exchanges, see Grossman and Miller (1986b).

[2] Although the fraction of potential trades executed immediately by market makers rather than delayed for search is higher for futures exchanges than in virtually any other market setting, search plays a role even there. A case in point is so-called "sunshine trading" in which pending large and presumably informationless orders by portfolio insurers are publicized in advance throughout the investment community with a view to attracting a large inflow of counterparties prepared to take the other side. Whether such sunshine trading violates long-standing regulatory prohibitions against "prearranged trading" is a policy issue currently much in dispute.

The Structure of the Stock Market

Most real-world markets lie somewhere between these liquidity extremes and their structures will typically mix features from both the
search markets and the liquidity markets. US stock market institutions, for example, currently involve at least four distinct forms of market organization[3] operating simultaneously, but in different segments of
the market and with somewhat different immediacy clienteles:

1. For a few of the most widely held and heavily traded securities,
such as IBM or AT&T, the market at the New York Stock Exchange
(NYSE) often approximates the open-outcry pits at the commodity
exchanges. These are stocks in which the minute-to-minute order flow
is highly variable relative to the arrival of news about the underlying
value of the shares, and for which our model predicts a large number of
market makers in equilibrium. The "crowd" for those stocks, though
substantially smaller than in the T-bond futures market, is large
enough to offer a competitive discipline to the exchange's franchised
"specialist," who, in these particularly active markets, typically
plays more the role of an auctioneer (and a commission collector) than a
market maker on personal account.

2. The specialist's role as a market maker assumes greater prominence for the hundreds of smaller, less active stocks, some of which may
not even trade as frequently as once a day. In such stocks, our model
would not predict an equilibrium with many market makers. The des-
ignation of a specialist by the exchange, however, does at least

---

[3]In addition to these four, there may now be as many as six distinct stock markets if one counts the "after-hours" market (which now includes the trading of
big-name US stocks on foreign exchanges) and the so-called "fourth market" in
which large pension funds, especially those following "passive" or indexing
strategies, transfer baskets of stocks directly to and from each other in essentially informationless trades. The futures and options markets in stocks, of
course, constitute still another form of stock market, at least for the trading if
not the holding of stocks. Many European stock markets, where the volumes of
trading are still quite small by US standards, use "batch" or "periodic call"
systems rather than any of the continuous-trading systems we find in the USA.
See Whitcomb (1985) for a comprehensive survey of trading practices
internationally.

guarantee that someone will indeed be maintaining a physical presence in the market, ready to effect a transaction should an order happen to arrive. The potential for abuse of the specialist's monopoly position is mitigated by the same standard cross-subsidization approach long familiar in US public utility regulation. As a condition for keeping the franchise, specialists on the NYSE, for example, are encouraged by the exchange to limit price changes between successive transactions to no more than one tick (normally twelve and a half cents per share), using personal inventory to absorb any temporary imbalances along the way. This restriction, which is in fact monitored by the exchange, serves both to limit specialists' profit and to create the appearance of liquidity, though in practice only for very small transactions. Should a very large order arrive, however, and should it be larger than can be absorbed by the specialist or by any previously entered "limit orders" then resting on the specialist's "book," the market can switch to search mode. The specialist, with the permission of the exchange, can suspend trading in the stock and institute a search for counterparties to the imbalance, either elsewhere on the floor of the exchange or, more likely these days, off the floor at the block-trading desks of the investment bankers.

3. These desks are the third, and increasingly the dominant, form of market organization for trading common stocks in the USA, thanks to the concentration of so much corporate stock in a relatively small number of extremely large pension funds, mutual funds and other institutional holders. Because relatively small portfolio adjustments by these institutional holders would be far too large to be absorbed by any specialist firm, the large blocks of single stocks, or sometimes whole portfolios, are brought to the "upstairs market" maintained by the investment banking firms. Until recently at least, the upstairs desks functioned primarily as a search market. The upstairs traders essentially "shopped the block" among their customers, and when a suitable counterparty had been located and a deal struck, they reported the trade to the relevant specialists on the floor of the exchange. In the process, they picked up on behalf of the initiating side any limit orders

on the specialist's book that were transformed into market orders by the price change occasioned by the block trade.

Although search was the initial, and still remains the major function of the upstairs market, the amount of "positioning" and hence of market-making liquidity provided by the upstairs firms has increased substantially in recent years. The shift traces mainly to the highly liquid futures and options index markets which permit the upstairs firms to hedge their inventories while conducting the search for, or waiting for, the other side of the transaction.

4. Finally, at the other end of the spectrum from the upstairs wholesale broker-dealer market lies the retail dealer market in Over-the-Counter (OTC) stocks, for which, with a few well-known exceptions, the normal trading interest is typically too small to justify listing even on a regional exchange.[4] The market for such stocks is not a physical exchange floor but a set of computer terminals. When introduced in the 1970s, the computerized National Association of Securities Dealers (NASDAQ) market system for OTC stocks offered essentially only a "bulletin board" in which those market makers with access to the system could enter price quotes. The quotes, though deemed firm for some standard, minimum-size trade, were essentially advertisements, and the actual transactions were not executed automatically, but negotiated between the parties. The market makers in particular stocks, although they did position small inventories, assumed no obligation to maintain a continuous presence or to smooth price changes between successive transactions.

Later in this volume we will see that all four forms of market organization for trading common stocks, along with those of the index futures and options markets, were subjected in October 1987 to what seemed to be liquidity events, in our sense, of unprecedented magnitude.

---

[4]Some corporations of substantial size, however, may nevertheless choose to list in this market because there are fewer restrictions on size and capital structure (such as a one-share, one-vote rule) than on the NYSE or the American Stock Exchange (AMEX).

This chapter is a shortened version of a much longer, more technical paper of the same name presented (with the formal model alluded to) at the Annual Meetings of the American Finance Association, December 29, 1987, in Chicago, and published in The Journal of Finance, *43, 3, July 1988. Although published after the October 1987 crash, it is based on a study ("The Determinants of Market Liquidity") the authors undertook for the Chicago Board of Trade in 1986. Helpful comments on an earlier draft were received from Kenneth Cone, Kenneth French, T. Eric Kilcollin, Andrei Shleifer, Lester Telser, and Robert Vishny.*

References

Glosten, Lawrence R., and Paul R. Milgrom. "Bid, Ask and Transaction Prices in a Specialist Market with Heterogeneously Informed Traders." *Journal of Financial Economics* 14, March, 1985.

Grossman, Sanford J., and Merton H. Miller. "Economic Costs and Benefits of the Proposed One-Minute Time Bracketing Regulation." *Journal of Futures Markets* 6, Spring, 1986a.

_____. "The Determinants of Market Liquidity." Manuscript, University of Chicago, July, 1986b.

Stoll, Hans R. "Alternative Views of Market Making." In Y. Amihud, T. Ho, and R. Schwartz (eds), *Market Making and the Changing Structure of the Securities Industry*. Lexington, MA: Lexington Books, 1985.

Whitcomb, David. "An International Comparison of Stock Exchange Trading Structures." In Y. Amihud, T. Ho, and R. Schwartz (eds), *Market Making and the Changing Structure of the Securities Industry*. Lexington MA: Lexington Books, 1985.

3 Financial Innovations and Market Volatility

The past twenty years have witnessed an unprecedented explosion in the number and variety of financial instruments available routinely to the suppliers and demanders of investment capital. Some of the new instruments, like Ginnie Mae futures, have faded into insignificance, like once-trendy rock groups after a brief burst of intense popularity. But others, like US Treasury bond futures or Standard & Poors (S&P) 500 futures, have continued to grow rapidly in trading volume year after year, far outstripping even the most optimistic projections of their original sponsors. New, or at least seemingly new, strategies for exploiting the innovations are constantly being developed. Some strategies, most notably "program trading," have come virtually to dominate the financial pages. (In program trading an investor takes offsetting positions simultaneously, or as close to simultaneously as possible, in both the financial futures market and the stock market.)

Normally in economics such evidence of market acceptance would be taken as good news indeed. Since participation in these markets is voluntary, the users must clearly feel that they are benefiting from the activity. Since the users include pension funds, insurance companies, banks and many other kinds of business firms, the gains from trade inure indirectly via lower costs of service to the general body of consumers who do not themselves trade actively in these markets.

The monetary and regulatory authorities in the USA, to their very great credit, have recognized the vast direct and indirect benefits of financial futures and have resisted, to this point at least, the inevitable Congressional calls for more controls and restrictions. They have not always shown this forbearance to market sectors still so strongly associated with the evil word speculation. US stock markets, after all, are still saddled with restrictions (such as uptick rules on short sales, and the federally mandated margin requirements for purchases of common stock) which are intended to head off that most horrifying of regulatory nightmares, the "free fall" of stock prices of the kind that supposedly occurred in October 1929, and which in turn supposedly triggered the Great Depression of the 1930s.

But praiseworthy as has been their restraint up to now, the pressures on the regulatory authorities to "do something" about the new financial instruments are clearly building up. The feeling is widespread, fanned by almost daily horror stories in the financial press, that the recent financial innovations in general, and program trading in particular, are increasing market volatility and presaging a repeat of 1929. Congressional investigations are being threatened on the role of financial futures and options in recent hectic market sessions such as September 11, 1986, or January 23, 1987. Proposals are being floated calling for sharp restrictions on position limits in options and futures contracts, for increased margin requirements on both stocks and futures and even for a possible moratorium on further computerized program trading by financial institutions until its safety has been convincingly established.

It is this safety issue, for which the term volatility has become a code word, that I propose to address here. I will leave to others the study of price volatility in its technical statistical sense and the determination of whether in fact it has been increasing in recent years. (The studies of the issue to date suggest that day-to-day volatility has varied substantially over time and is currently well below its all-time high. The immediate political concerns, however, are more with within-the-day volatility, about which less is known.) I believe these fears that trading in index products may somehow precipitate a disaster along the lines of 1929 to be almost entirely misplaced. If there is a problem that the new products have created–and it is by no means obvious that there is a problem–it appears to be more a matter of inadequate peak-load trading capacity than of fundamental economic instability.

The best way to begin may be by reviewing why the index futures products were introduced in the first place and why the innovation they represented proved so successful. The reason is, I will argue, that index futures dramatically reduced the cost of an important class of transactions in the underlying securities, namely transactions motivated by near-term economy-wide rather than by company-specific events. Once these cost advantages of index products are understood, it becomes easier to see how the older and newer markets are linked together and what economic function the much maligned program trading actually performs. For concreteness, and for simplicity of exposition, I will take the key innovation to be the S&P 500 index futures contract traded on the Chicago Mercantile Exchange, but the argument would be essentially the same if I had taken the S&P 100 option contracts of the Chicago Board of Options Exchange.

The Key Innovation: an Index Futures Contract

Futures contracts are designed and introduced by exchanges with basically one consideration in mind: low-cost trading. As has often been noted, the exchanges achieve their economies relative to spot trading by standardizing the trading instrument, by offering centralized book-offset clearing rather than certificate shuffling, by monitoring the collateral posted and the contract performance of individual traders, by eliminating arbitrary restrictions on short selling, and especially by providing a centralized trading area to which buy and sell orders can be directed and executed. In this age of electronic marvels, the open-outcry trading pits of the futures exchanges often strike observers as quaint and anachronistic, but they are actually remarkably efficient trading structures in markets where the demand for immediacy is high, as is likely to be the case when inventory "hedging" is a major motive. The presence of many competing market makers reduces the risk that any one market maker must absorb when a large order hits the pit. Changes in the pit population of competing traders can also serve as an almost automatic device for adapting transaction-processing capacity to customer demand over a very wide (but, alas, not unlimited) range of transaction volume.

Although stock index futures share all the trading cost advantages of futures generally, they have other, and even more important advantages. The additional savings in transaction costs made possible by the S&P 500 futures contract can be traced to at least three different sources: (1) the index form of the contract, (2) the pricing of futures contracts relative to their underlying spot commodities and (3) the way the effective, tradeable supply of the contracts comes into existence. The first of these, the index feature, has received the most attention and has certainly been the major innovation. Before the index futures contract became available, the individual stock (some 2,000 or more on the NYSE alone) had always been the basic unit not only for organizing the market but for writing about and thinking about investing in equities. This viewpoint was capsulized in the old saying that the exchanges were not as much stock markets as markets of stocks. Suddenly, with the coming of index futures and index options it became possible to buy "stocks" and not just a stock. The possibility of buying and holding the individual stocks or investing in a mutual fund was always available so that no fundamentally new security is created by an index futures or option. But for the average investor (and even most above-average investors) the costs of buying and selling index futures or options are enormously lower than those of trading a do-it-yourself basket of the same stocks (or buying and selling index mutual fund shares). A recent staff study by the Federal Reserve System puts the estimated round-trip commission and spread costs incurred by a representative investor in an S&P 500 index futures contract at about $50. The comparable round-trip costs for an equivalent basket of all 500 stocks would come to $1,500, or some thirty times as much! (A round trip in index mutual-fund shares would currently be cheaper than the same trip in individual stocks, but only because so few investors actually try to take the trip via mutual funds.)

Although useful perhaps for its shock value, this estimate of cost savings by a factor of thirty in index futures almost certainly overstates the effective reductions in transaction costs. For one thing, the large institutional investors, who account for half or more of the ordinary trades in stocks, already pay substantially lower commission rates than those factored into the calculated comparison. As a practical matter, moreover, it may take many fewer than 500 separate stocks to replicate the performance of the S&P 500 index to an investor's desired degree of accuracy. Some index futures trades also are not so much substitutes for transactions in the stocks as temporary steps in accumulating or unwinding a portfolio. But even after making these allowances, the cost savings have clearly been substantial, as evidenced, if nothing else, by the almost explosive growth in the volume of transactions in the index futures contract.

Portfolio Balance and the Role of Index Futures

That these dramatic cost reductions should have uncovered so vast a new demand for transactions directly in index futures and options (over and beyond that of inventory hedging by underwriters and distributors) may well have been surprising to the investment community accustomed to thinking in terms of individual stocks and their stories, and for whom the movements in the S&P 500 or the Dow Jones Average are just summary statistics–quick and convenient ways of keeping score. But the latent demand exposed was less surprising to the academic finance community, for whom the notion of the "market portfolio" has long played the central role. In the academic view, achieving the appropriate risk position for an investor's wealth is less a matter of picking specific stocks with the right risk characteristics–since brute force diversification over a large enough universe of stocks can largely pool away individual company risks–as it is a matter of getting the right balance between debt and equity in the portfolio. Transactions in index futures and options are ideal for fine tuning that critical dimension of risk. *If you already hold a portfolio of the common stocks in the index*– and remember that the entire outstanding supply of stocks must always be in somebody's portfolio–*selling an index futures contract is functionally equivalent to selling off the stocks and investing the proceeds in Treasury bills or some equivalent, short-term fixed income instrument.* And in the other direction, buying a futures contract when you own the stocks is functionally equivalent to margining your portfolio, that is, selling short-term debt instruments and investing the proceeds in stocks.

The two separate debt and equity steps can be accomplished in a single transaction because of the way a futures contract is priced relative to its underlying spot commodity. Properly priced, the futures contract sells not at the spot price, but at a "premium" above it representing the so-called "cost of carry" net of any "convenience yield." In the case of stock index futures, where the storage costs in the ordinary sense are not at issue, the cost of carry is essentially the interest that would have to be paid on a loan whose proceeds were used to acquire the underlying stocks; and the convenience yield is just the offsetting flow of cash dividends on the hypothetical shares acquired. It is that difference–less transactions cost, of course (on which subject more later)– that you pick up when you sell your futures contract at its "warranted" spread, exactly as if you had done the underlying equity-for-debt switch directly. This insight, it may be worth noting, is basically the rationale of "portfolio insurance." The only difference is that a formal portfolio insurance program commits to a pre-specified rule for making the back and forth switches between debt and equity.

The differences in the cost of switching between debt and equity by index futures and by direct trading in the securities set up market forces that act in many respects like filters. Those transactions undertaken in response to anticipated (or feared) changes in the immediate macroeconomic environment–business cycle development, interest rate projections, and political changes of one kind or another–now tend to be directed first to the index futures market rather than the stock market. For this important class of transactions, the cost advantages of the index futures market has made it the dominant market. But the stock market remains the dominant market for the other class of transactions–those undertaken in response to company-specific events or as part of long-run, buy-and-hold programs. Because the two markets thus face a different flow of incoming buy and sell orders, their price levels follow separate paths and at any moment of time it is entirely possible–indeed, overwhelmingly probable–that the index futures premium over the spot index will deviate from its theoretically warranted value described earlier.

Program Trading and Market Linkage

The deviation cannot grow without bound, however. As soon as it exceeds the transaction costs of the lowest cost transactor in the combined markets, that transactor has an arbitrage opportunity. If the actual premium is greater, say, than the warranted premium by more than the transaction costs, and provided the transactor can put all the parts of the deal together quickly enough, the transactor can earn a sure profit, with no additional risk, by selling index futures and Treasury bills and buying the underlying basket of individual stocks. And that is one way, though not the only way, of seeing what the much-mooted computerized program trading is all about.

Looked at this way it is hard to see why program trading should ever have become the subject of so much concern and anxiety on the part of the regulators and the financial press. I suspect that the uneasiness traces in part to the price jumps that the programs often seem to set off when they cut in so suddenly and seemingly out of the blue. There is, of course, no presumption in economics that continuous price sample paths are socially superior to discontinuous ones. But, for a number of reasons, we have been conditioned to think of well-behaved stock prices as changing smoothly rather than abruptly. That, after all, is what the very notion of market "liquidity" seems to imply: the ability to absorb a large transaction with only a small change in price.

The expectation that stock prices would and should move smoothly seemed reasonable to investors and market observers in the light of the many years of past performance by the New York exchanges in transaction-to-transaction price stabilization. It has long been the proud boast of the NYSE that 90 percent or more of all transactions are executed within one-eighth of the previous quote. The NYSE could deliver on this boast because there was a specialist with that responsibility assigned to every stock and because the order flows and order imbalances were not large enough normally to threaten either his capabilities or his capital. And, if they happened to, on some particular day in one of his stocks, he could close down trading and run for help from other, less busy people standing around the floor.

But that was in the old days. Faced now with a sudden rush of large orders from program traders or other futures and options hedgers, any attempt to hold price changes to an eighth would simply blow away his capital. Nor can he look elsewhere on the floor for relief. The program trades are hitting all the booths at once. The specialist has little choice, then, but to stand aside and let the upstairs market find the clearing level–a task not always easy given the physical separation and communication lags between the traders. Sometimes, in fact, the market price not only jumps, but jumps so far as to kick off program trading in the other direction!

In principle, if communications were good enough and if all the legs of the arbitrage could be set in place together, the jumps would be small–just a hair or so plus the transaction costs of the lowest cost transactor. But the longer it takes to set the legs, the wider the spreads between the two markets must be to entice the low-cost arbitragers in (and the more and higher-cost arbitragers that will also be tempted to undertake the activity)–hence, the bigger the price jumps required to restore the futures/spot premium to a point within the range where arbitrage is no longer feasible. One would expect, therefore, that as techniques for performing the arbitrage are streamlined and improved, the price jumps needed to equilibrate the two markets will also become somewhat smaller and less likely to set off whipsawing. Indeed, there are already some signs that such is already taking place. February 17, 1987 was a day of spectacular market rise, nearly 2.5 percent, with program trading much in evidence throughout the day, but with no signs of the price whipsawing so conspicuous on January 23. The diminishing market impact of recent "triple witching" days points in the same direction.

But even if whipsawing and large price jumps never occurred, arbitrage-driven programs would still be under a cloud of suspicion in some influential sectors of public opinion. The reason lies in the emotional overtones of the very word arbitrage. To economists, the activity of arbitrage is clearly socially beneficial. Who can object to actions that help enforce the "law of one price" and thereby help avoid the wastes of committing resources on the basis of false or misleading price signals? The trouble is that the critical feature that defines the action as arbitrage in the economic sense–the ability to earn a sure profit with no investment–is precisely what makes it suspect particularly to those with strong populist leanings, like the influential Congressman John Dingell. It smacks to them of "free loading"–earning large sums of money not by merit or by patient research and investment but just by being big enough to be able to trade at low commission rates. Suggestions to the Congressman by the Securities and Exchange Commission (SEC) Chairman and others that even the fabled small investor could at least participate indirectly in the benefits flowing from low transaction costs by investing in mutual funds have been greeted with much the same scorn as if he had said: "Let them eat cake." The irony is that the small investor, thanks to arbitrage, is already trading at low institutional commission rates (or better) every time he trades in index futures. To see that it is necessary to step back and take a somewhat deeper look at the index futures contract and how it comes into existence.

Market Structure and Transaction Costs

An investor seeking to reduce the proportion of his portfolio in equities and increase the proportion in short-term debt securities is likely to find, for the reasons previously noted, that selling a futures contract is a far cheaper way of doing so than selling the stocks and reinvesting the proceeds in Treasury bills. Not perhaps thirty times cheaper, but surely cheaper by a factor of significant proportions. The standard academic finance reaction to any such tales of great bargains in security trading is not to deny that the bargains exist (as we are sometimes caricatured as doing), but to ask what is the source of such a great bargain. If the investor is selling at such good terms, who is the buyer?

In the case of an index futures contract, the selling is done by a floor broker and the buyer in the first instance is likely to be a floor trader who takes the contract into his own inventory. The floor trader's hope, of course, is to get that contract out of his inventory by reselling it later to a broker who is bringing in a buy order. The floor trader or market maker is thus really only an intermediary bridging the temporary order imbalances created by the lack of perfect synchronization between the arrival of buy and sell orders. The ultimate buyer of our hypothetical investor's sale of a futures contract in this case would be another investor who for any of a number of reasons happened to want to switch his portfolio balance in the opposite direction, from bills to equities. That their investment decisions happen to be just offsetting means that if the futures/spot premium were exactly at its warranted theoretical value, *both* sides to the trade would have avoided the commission costs of direct transactions in the underlying securities. Their trades have, for all practical purposes, been crossed at no charge on the floor of the stock exchange at the then ruling stock prices and the only direct expenses incurred are those for effecting the futures trades on the futures exchange.

There is no reason to expect, of course, that both sides of the inter-investor switch will always (or ever) be effected at a value of the premium exactly equal to its theoretical value. And to the extent that the premium departs from that value one (or perhaps both) may be paying (or receiving back) what amounts to an *implicit* transaction cost in the trades in the underlying securities.

There is a limit, however, to how high these implicit transaction costs (or implicit transaction cost rebates) can mount. If the flow of sell orders to the floor exceeds the flow of buy orders for more than just a temporary interval–which is to say that more ultimate portfolio holders want to shift out of equities than want to switch into equities– then the futures price will fall. If the average of the underlying stock prices is not falling or not falling as fast–remember that trades in the individual stocks are driven mainly by company-specific news–the premium will fall. Should it fall far enough, any cost-saving advantage of the futures route for debt/equity adjustment would be dissipated. It would become cheaper to make the switch directly via the stock and bill markets.

And here is where program trading comes back into the picture. Once a sustained order imbalance in the futures market has driven the premium far enough below its warranted value, the excess orders will be diverted to the now cheaper underlying securities markets and the transaction costs of those underlying markets now become ruling ones. But whose transaction costs? Costs vary widely in those markets. The answer, of course, is that thanks to program-trading arbitrage it is the costs of the large institutional investors who have the communication facilities and the trade execution capacities to carry out the arbitrage most efficiently. By selling the stock packages and buying the futures, their arbitrage activities are functionally equivalent to permitting small investors selling futures to sell stocks directly, but at low institutional rather than high individual commission rates.

The Recent Hectic Trading Days: Causes and Cures

Up to this point, the view presented both of index futures generally and of program-trading arbitrage in particular has been a benign one. Neither index futures nor program trading can be said, in any meaningful way, to be *causing* the underlying stock market to move in a direction or to an extent very different from what would have occurred in their absence. It may *look* that way to those on the floor of the stock exchanges, but only because the lower transactions cost of index futures now makes the futures market the one hit first on decisions to shift in or out of equities. (It is also the case that some index futures markets open earlier than the markets in New York.)

If this were all there were to it, the current agitation over volatility would probably best be regarded as a transitory reaction traceable more to the change in the way business is done than to any documented adverse consequences. The new instruments, after all, are only a few years old, and their very novelty can seem threatening. Education and experience can be relied on, in time, to allay the fears.

But apparently that is not all there is to it. There is concern, even among some who know how the new instruments work, that some kinds of index futures and options trading strategies are making things worse rather than better. These strategies are, as a heating engineer might put it, setting up positive feedbacks within the system that push the temperature further beyond the control bands once the temperature breaks through instead of returning it quickly to its thermostat setting, or at least so it seems on days like September 11, 1986, or January 23, 1987. The finger is pointed most often at a strategy known as portfolio insurance.

The Role of Portfolio Insurance

That purchases of portfolio insurance should have come to be suspected of exacerbating market volatility is ironic in that the term insurance, with all its positive associations, was deliberately invoked by the developers of the product to help conservative institutional investors overcome their fear and loathing of scary, speculative instruments such as the futures contracts or puts and calls that the strategies utilize. The term insurance as applied to these strategies is not to be taken in its usual sense of pooling of individual risks, but in its looser sense of investment policies designed to reduce or transfer the risk, especially the downside risk, of an entire portfolio of common stocks. One direct way, of course, for transferring this risk is by buying puts on an appropriate index or an index futures. But thanks to the way index option prices relate to index futures prices, the same transfer of downside risk can be accomplished even if puts of the desired maturity were not available. The investor can obtain the payoff equivalent of a put on his portfolio by selling an index futures contract and buying a call. But there is an equivalent though more roundabout method yet. A position tantamount to the put and the call can be generated by a *sequence* of transactions in futures alone. The sequence effectively replicates the same dynamic hedging strategy (that is, changing bond/stock portfolio mix) that defines the warranted or theoretical values of the desired options.

By themselves, of course, these synthetic or do-it-yourself options determine only who happens to be doing the dynamic hedging and associated trading, not how much. The trouble comes, however, or at least is supposed to come, from the timing of the transactions needed to deliver not just downside protection but the "guaranteed" minimum asset value promised under some of the plans sold as portfolio insurance. A sudden, sharp fall in stock prices dictates a protective increase in the portfolio share allocated to the lower-risk debt securities and hence a corresponding decrease in the equity proportion. A sharp, sudden run-up in stock prices will call for the opposite kind of adjustment, but in both cases the timing rule of the insurance program will trigger buying or selling transactions in real or synthetic options that appear to reinforce the direction of the initiating stock-market move.

This bias toward continuation or positive serial correlation of transactions, it should be noted, is a property by no means confined to formal portfolio insurance. The same reinforcing tendency has been found (and equally deplored) in such other well-known path-dependent trading strategies as "pyramiding" and computer-monitored, moving stop-loss programs. In fact, the current concern over portfolio insurance is reminiscent in many ways of the much longer-standing regulatory fears about the destabilizing properties of margin buying of stocks–a portfolio management strategy with more than a coincidental resemblance to some commercial portfolio insurance products.

Can portfolio insurance really be credited (or should it be debited) with the free fall of September 11 or the rapid whipsaws of January 23? Whatever the long-run consequences of portfolio insurance might be, it is certainly hard to believe that many of the purveyors of those products, given the diversity of their individual plans and their fears of being whipsawed, would have sought to transact in a market as frenzied as that of January 23, not once, but repeatedly and on opposite sides during the day as the market moved. But perhaps judgment about the participation of portfolio insurers should be withheld until historians have reconstructed the complete sequence of events on the two recent fateful days. The indications that the SEC staff has so far given seem, if anything, to be downplaying the roles of both arbitrage-related program trading and portfolio insurance. And, for what it is worth, the leading seller of portfolio insurance, Kidder Peabody Co., has denied even having been in the market on January 23!

But if program trading and portfolio insurance are not the real villains, who or what is? Why do markets usually so well-functioning and liquid sometimes become frenzied and illiquid? To see, we must look to the very notion of liquidity itself.

The Paradox of Liquidity

In some brilliant, but largely forgotten, passages on liquidity in his *General Theory*, John Maynard Keynes noted that the great advances in stock market trading technology in the 1920s had made it possible for any individual to withdraw his capital from the market or return it to the market on a moment's notice. Society as a whole, however, cannot withdraw its capital; and the attempt on the part of any sizeable portion of the community to try to do so must inevitably be frustrated. The stock market thus takes on some of the characteristics of a commercial bank in which each demand deposit account can be highly liquid even though most of the bank's loans and other assets very definitely are not. The individual accounts maintain their liquidity because the inflow of cash deposits roughly balances the outflow of cash withdrawals on most days. The balance is rarely exact, of course, so that buffer stocks of secondary reserves are maintained–reserves that can be mobilized quickly if a prolonged drain threatens to occur. But a large and unexpected series of withdrawals can drain even these; and if, for any reason, doubts begin to arise in depositors' minds about the bank's ability to continue to meet withdrawals, everyone rushes to be first in line to withdraw while there is still time. That can produce a run which closes the bank and lets no one withdraw. In a sense, it is the very belief that the deposits are still liquid that renders them effectively illiquid. And similarly with index futures.

As any market day opens, the first order of business for the market makers in the trading pit must be to absorb any net imbalance in the buy and sell orders that have accumulated overnight. Most of the time, the order imbalance is quickly taken into traders' inventories with little price movement. And most of the time, the initial inventory imbalance is quickly reduced by a flow of offsetting orders in the other direction, much in the same way as a stream of net withdrawals at a bank's opening might be offset by a inflow of deposits later during the day. But most of the time is not the same as all of the time. Every once in a while, the opening flow of orders happens to be both large, and not quickly offset by the usual flow of offsetting orders. Almost everyone seems to be withdrawing and almost no one seems to be depositing. Something very much like that appears to have happened in the index futures market at its opening on September 11.

The market makers on the floor, who are trying to be short-term temporary holders rather than long-term speculators, thereupon start to unwind their inventories and the price starts to adjust to a level better reflecting the change in sentiment represented by the initial imbalance. That, in turn, triggers the program trading (as earlier described), which communicates the news to the stock market proper. Again, most of the time this process of adjustment to the new price level would be unremarkable except, of course, to the market makers in both markets who may well have suffered substantial losses. But that's what they are there for, after all, and they can hope to offset those rare large bad days like September 11 with a string of smaller good days.

On a few of the already rare days with the large shocks, however, a second and even a third large shock can arrive in succession. The market makers' ability to absorb further orders into their inventory is quickly exhausted, in much the same way as the tellers' windows are drained of ready cash during a run. Momentarily, at least, the market is effectively deprived of its market makers. Orders cannot be executed or confirmed and some floor traders may not even know what they own or owe.

As word spreads of the chaotic conditions on the floor, the flow of additional orders may even accelerate. Nothing, after all, is more likely to encourage a bank run than the sight of a panicky mob of the bank's depositors all trying to fight their way to the withdrawal window. Potential traders off the floor do not, of course, actually see the mob scene, but they hear about it, and they do see the prices on their quote screens. The quotes at this point are likely to be far behind the real events, but for precisely that reason they can contribute to the illusion that it may still be possible to make a trade before things get worse. The result may be not only program-trading whipsawing, but a flood of small orders, further clogging and delaying the system's communications, and ultimately generating great resentment on the part of the politically potent mass of small traders over the profitable trading opportunities they feel they lost because of bad executions–opportunities, of course, that never actually existed, but were illusions based on unrealistic quotes in unreal markets. Something very much like this scenario appears to have occurred on January 23.

The Problem of Peak-Load Capacity

On that day, the net demand for index products surged beyond the effective transactions capacity of the market–both its order-handling and its market-making capacity and at both its Chicago and its New York ends. When a surge in the demand for trade executions meets an inelastic supply of those services, something has to give. The effective price of the service has to rise by enough to ration the limited supply among the most eager demanders. Since the "price" of transaction services is the price change required to elicit the other side of the order, the overload on the market shows up as price jumps, out trades, bad fills and no fills.

What is happening on the exchanges then is like a brown-out (or even a black-out) that can occur during a sudden hot spell when everyone turns on the air conditioning at once. To head off more such brown-outs, the transaction production capacity of the markets must somehow be expanded. No economically feasible amount of added capacity will guarantee against any recurrence of market brown-outs of course; but it can at least make them even rarer events.

What form this long-run capacity expansion should take I leave to others. It is mainly a problem in business organization and management, not economics. Some progress has clearly already been made. The spectacular price rise on heavy volume of February 17, 1987, as noted earlier, seems to have been taken in stride, though, admittedly, price "volatility" on the upside rarely attracts as much political attention as downside volatility. Also helping has been the recently instituted small-order automatic execution system of the Chicago Board Options Exchange–in which small trades are executed by computer at the last recorded pit price and assigned by lot to a participating market maker. This system is a particularly promising new direction, not because it is "electronic," but because it can attack the capacity problem on so many fronts at once. Shunting the small orders off to a separate track not only reduces congestion (and complaints!) but opens a new avenue for bringing additional market-making capital to the trading floors. Why restrict participation to the floor traders willing to sign up? Given the low moral hazards of the automatic executions and assignments, other out-side investors would surely be willing to take on the risks, leaving the floor traders free to concentrate their capital in the main arena where their comparative advantage is greatest.

Other exchanges are looking to automatic execution of small orders, and perhaps also to setting up separate pits for side-by-side trading in smaller contracts. Some big market users are pushing in the opposite direction to split off the really large trades to broker markets as in interbank foreign exchange. About all we can be sure of at the moment is that bringing in the new capacity in any of these forms will take time, particularly since there are vexing issues of competitive advantage, regulatory turf, free riding and information externalities to be resolved. That still leaves us vulnerable in the immediate short run, however. And here, I would suggest only that my economist colleagues give at least a few minutes of tolerant hearing to a proposal recently offered somewhat diffidently and defensively by the managers of the leading stock index futures exchange–a proposal to which most economists instinctively react with horror.

Are Trading Halts a Reasonable Short-Run Expedient?

I refer, of course, to the possibility (recently also raised by the SEC staff) of just *closing* all the relevant markets down for a brief period on days like January 23 when their capacity to process more transactions is clearly being exceeded or when the buy-sell order imbalance is substantially more than the floor population of an exchange can absorb. We sometimes forget how recently in economic time continuous trading in stocks (at least on weekdays and during the daytime hours) has displaced periodic batch trading. Such batch trading or, perhaps better, interrupted trading, is still found in many capital markets, including even the Tokyo Exchange in the land of electronic marvels. We do it frequently for individual stocks when a news item precipitates a major order imbalance. The "opening" for many stocks may be the first trade of the day for the stock by definition, but it doesn't always occur at the opening bell. Futures exchanges too will occasionally suspend trading, most notably in cases where daily price limit ranges are exceeded.

Continuous trading is undoubtedly better than interrupted trading, though in practice, most stock and futures trading tends to be heavily concentrated at specific times of the day, especially at the open and the close. But if continuous trading is better it is because the market makers on the floor are there to absorb the imbalance in orders. If they can't absorb it, then we simply have to find other ways of balancing the orders–which is to to say, we may have to switch, one hopes only briefly, to forms of market organization better adapted to the conditions of the moment, whatever may be the balance of advantages they may offer from a longer run perspective.

Unfortunately, it may well already be too late in the evolution of the US equity markets for these classical, run-stopping tactics to be effective. There are just too many alternatives now in time and space to carry off a complete trading holiday along the lines of the Roosevelt banking holiday of 1933. Closing down only some of the markets might actually increase the price distortions and intensify the system overloads when trading is finally resumed in the impacted markets.

And this brings us back again to the theme of capacity expansion in both the index futures markets and the stock markets. The managers and directors of those exchanges, I know, are currently and very actively studying a variety of ways to speed up and enlarge the flow of orders and trade information to and from their trading floors. Perhaps the best service I can render them as they approach this task, given the still rapid pace of financial innovation and given the accelerating regulatory concern with market volatility, is to remind them of some words of La Rochefoucauld. The old gentlemen went out on his estate one day with his young grandson to plant an acorn in a bare spot near the side of the road. "But it will be years before we get any shade from this tree," fretted the little boy. "Then we had best get started right away," said the old man. "We don't have a moment to spare."

This chapter is based on a paper presented at a roundtable sponsored by the Mid America Institute for Policy Research on May 28, 1987, in Chicago, and was later published as a pamphlet by that organization. An earlier version was presented at the Workshop in Investment Banking sponsored by the Institut für Entscheidungstheorie und Unternehmensforschung at the University of Karlsruhe, Federal Republic of Germany, March 26-27, 1987.

References

Federal Reserve System. *Financial Futures and Options in the US Economy.* Washington, DC, December 1986.

Keynes, J. M. *The General Theory of Employment, Interest and Money.* New York: Harcourt, Brace, 1936.

Part II

The Crash of 1987 and Its Aftermath

4 Index Futures During the Crash of 1987

Final Report of the Committee of Inquiry Appointed by
the Chicago Mercantile Exchange to Examine the Events
Surrounding October 19, 1987

*with Burton Malkiel, Myron Scholes,
and John D. Hawke Jr*

In our preliminary report we reached three tentative conclusions about
the role of index futures in the market fall of October 19-20, 1987:

First, the crash of October 19 did not originate in Chicago and flow
from there by means of index arbitrage, carried out by program trading,
to an otherwise calm and unsuspecting market in New York. Although
this charge was made at the time and has been repeated frequently
since then, the evidence shows clearly that the selling wave hit both
markets simultaneously. The perception that a price decline in the
futures market led the decline in the stock market was an illusion
traceable mainly to the different procedures followed in the two markets at their openings. At the NYSE the huge overnight imbalance of
sell orders had delayed the opening of many of the leading stocks in
the S&P 500 index. The prices for these stocks used in calculating the
publicly reported index value on Monday morning were, therefore, the
last available quotes from the previous Friday's close. By contrast, the
futures price at the CME reflected the Monday morning information.
Thus, while it may have appeared to some that a tidal wave was on
the way from Chicago, delayed openings at the NYSE showed that it
had already arrived there, even before the opening bell had sounded.

Second, on Monday, October 19, the futures market in Chicago appears actually to have absorbed selling pressure on balance. While some pressure from the selling of futures contracts by portfolio insurers and other institutional investors was indeed transmitted back to the NYSE by index arbitrage, the equivalent of 85 million shares–about 14 percent of the day's volume on the NYSE and 57 percent of CME S&P 500 volume–was absorbed by the market makers, day traders, anticipatory hedgers, institutional buyers, and speculative position holders in Chicago.

Third, the futures markets in Chicago were no more responsible for the turnaround in the market on Tuesday, October 20, than for the initial downturn on Monday, October 19. The dramatic recovery on Tuesday afternoon is more plausibly traced to the announcement of large corporate buyback programs and the promise of Federal Reserve support for bank liquidity than to any manipulations in the Major Market Index futures contract at the Chicago Board of Trade or to the rupture of the linkage between the stock market and the main futures market during the forty-minute period that the CME had suspended trading.

In the two months or so since our preliminary report presented these tentative conclusions at least five other investigative commissions and regulatory agencies have submitted reports on the crash and several academic studies of the trading record have been completed. These reports and studies have filled in many pieces of the puzzle that were still missing when we first wrote, and they have offered new insights and perspectives on the way the markets functioned. After examining these studies in detail, however, we find no compelling reason to retreat from or to alter the analysis or the conclusions presented in our preliminary report. In fact, some of the conclusions we put forth somewhat tentatively at the time can now be considered as having been strongly supported by the data that subsequently became available.[1]

---

[1]An example is the study, "Nonsynchronous Trading and the S&P 500 Stock-Futures Basis in October 1987," by Lawrence Harris, University of Southern California, manuscript, December 1987. Harris constructs a measure for the S&P 500 index that adjusts for delayed openings and trading halts on the NYSE. The revised series strongly confirms our view that the opening discount on

Later in this report we shall note some of the important new findings, particularly where they have a bearing on our policy recommendations.

Preliminary Policy Recommendations: Portfolio Insurance and Index Arbitrage Program Trading

Although our preliminary report sought mainly to establish what had happened, we tried also to give a preliminary assessment of some of the main proposals for change in market structure that had surfaced in the wake of the crash. For some of these proposals, we felt the evidence was already strong enough for us to take a clear stand. In particular, we recommended against any attempts to ban either portfolio insurance or index arbitrage carried out through program trading.

Portfolio insurance and the crash

Our recommendation against legislative or regulatory restrictions on portfolio insurance does not mean that we believe portfolio insurance selling played no role in the events of October 19. Certainly, as we showed, substantial portfolio insurance selling did occur. But it is important to keep the portfolio insurance sales in perspective. On October 19 portfolio insurance sales of futures represented somewhere between 20 and 30 percent of the share equivalent of total sales on the NYSE. The pressure of selling on the NYSE by other investors–mutual funds, security dealers and individual shareholders–was thus three to five times greater than that of the portfolio insurers. Price falls as large and market conditions as chaotic as those in the USA occurred in

---

October 19 was an illusion. An index adjustment by the Commodity and Futures Trading Commission (CFTC) similar to that of Harris also supports our interpretation of the seeming discount at the opening. See the CFTC's Divisions of Economic Analysis and Trading and Markets, " Final Report on Stock Index Futures and Cash Market Activity During October 1987" (CFTC report), pp. 15-18, January 1988. Although most severe at the openings, similar distortions in the normal relation between futures and cash market prices arose at several points during the critical two days in response to trading de-lays, reporting lags, and the efforts of some NYSE specialists to fill in any large gaps between prices on successive trades.

many countries on October 19–even in those with no portfolio insurance or index futures market.

Nor are we persuaded by the view expressed in both the Report of the Presidential Task Force on Market Mechanisms (Brady report) and the Report of the Securities and Exchange Commission's Division of Market Regulation (SEC report)[2] that the timing of the portfolio insurance sales magnified their impact. The SEC report notes that portfolio insurance and index arbitrage, though accounting for no more than 20 percent of S&P 500 volume during the entire day of October 19, and no more than 40 percent in the fateful 1:00-2:00 p.m. EST hour, did account for "more than 60 percent of S&P 500 stock volume in three ten-minute intervals within that hour" (SEC report, p. xiii). But since transactions are recorded sequentially there must surely have been shorter intervals in which the portfolio insurance trades approached 100 percent of total trades!

No reliable methods exist for relating observed price changes in active, competitive markets to the actions of particular sellers or buyers. Hence we chose not to attempt the detailed, almost tick-by-tick account of trading presented in the Brady and SEC reports. In our preliminary report we did provide (in Figures 12 through 15) a rough visual sketch of net trading activity by major groups for fifteen-minute intervals during the 19th and 20th, but we could find no consistent patterns of association with price changes. Because visual scanning can be deceptive, however, and because both the Brady and SEC reports claim they do see such patterns, we asked the CME staff to carry out a formal statistical analysis of the degree of association between the transactions by pension funds or broker/dealers and price changes on October 19 and 20. Their analysis finds no statistically reliable relation between price changes over fifteen-minute intervals on those days and trading activity during those intervals by pension funds and broker/dealers.

---

[2]The SEC report (1988) carries the caveat that although the Commission authorized publication of the report, it has expressed no view on the report's analysis, findings, or recommendations.

Some accounts of events on October 19 suggest that the fear of further portfolio insurance selling to come may have been as much or more responsible for frantic selling by the public, and especially by the large trading firms, as the actual portfolio insurance selling that did occur. Such perceptions, of course, are difficult to document, but to the extent they did arise on October 19 they point up the need, not for restrictions on portfolio insurance, but for better and quicker dissemination of information about the flow of insurance transactions waiting in the wings.[3]

Portfolio insurance and the pre-crash build-up

Concern has also been expressed that portfolio insurance may have contributed to the crash by pushing prices in the US stock market to higher pre-crash levels than might have been the case without the comfort that such insurance programs seemed to offer.[4] Once again, however, it is important to keep a sense of proportion about the relevant magnitudes. The US market rose between January and August 1987 by 30 percent, an increase in value of about $600 billion. The total value of pension fund assets under formal portfolio insurance plans at that point may have reached as much as $100 billion. Not all of this total was in equities, of course; pension funds typically also have substantial holdings of fixed income securities to reduce the downside vulnerability of the fund's assets. Believing that portfolio insurance could now play a similar risk reduction role for their equity component, some pension fund managers may well have decided to increase the equity portion relative to the fixed income proportion of their asset

---

[3]Some of these information-related problems of conducting portfolio insurance might have been avoided had the insurance been carried out with traded options, rather than with the synthetic options created by dynamic hedging with futures. See, for example, Grossman (1988). The much more restrictive position limits on options than on futures, however, have tended to discourage the use of options by the portfolio insurers.

[4]In testimony before the Senate Committee on Banking, Housing and Urban Affairs on February 2, 1988, Federal Reserve Board Chairman Alan Greenspan said: "To the degree that derivative instruments facilitate a better redistribution of price risk to those most willing and able to bear it, they can add to the appeal of cash equity investments to investors, encouraging them to hold larger permanent equity positions."

mix. But even if this shift in proportion away from debt and toward equity amounted to as much as $30 billion and even if it had all come in 1987, it would still have amounted to less than 5 percent of the increase in the value of US equities between January and the time of the crash.

Since the submission of our preliminary report the amount of portfolio insurance in force has, by all accounts, been dropping steadily and substantially. The programs have been modified to admit a wider and more flexible range of response by the managers when futures are selling at what appears to be a substantial discount to the cash market, as occurred often on October 19 and the days thereafter.[5] In short, the problems posed by portfolio insurance–if indeed they were problems– appear to have been largely self-correcting. Recognizing that fact, the calls for restricting portfolio insurance so frequently voiced in the aftermath of the crash (and again after the presentation of the Brady and SEC reports) have also largely subsided. Such has not proved to be the case, however, for index arbitrage program trading.

Index arbitrage program trading

In our preliminary report, we took the position, amply documented in extensive previous academic research on the subject (and apparently fully concurred in by the Brady Commission) that, given an index futures market, intermarket arbitrage was a benign rather than a malignant influence.[6] Index arbitrage carried out through trading is

---

[5]See, for example, Leland (1988). Leland is one of the inventors of portfolio insurance and a co-founder of Leland, O'Brien and Rubinstein, the leading purveyor firm.

[6]Among the many statistical studies of index arbitrage program trading, two recent ones are perhaps worth special notice. Stoll and Whaley (1988) can find no evidence that futures tend to "overshoot" their true values and hence to cause whipsawing of the kind pictured in the popular press. In a paper entitled "Report on Program Trading: An Analysis of Interday Relationships," and prepared for the Katzenbach study, Sanford Grossman could find no relation "between any measure of volatility or any measure of program trading. The days in which volatility was high were not, systematically, the days in which program trading intensity was high" (p. 2). The CFTC report also notes, aptly, that during the immediate post-crash period of October 21-23, volatility was extremely high but program trading had virtually ceased (CFTC report, pp. 107-136).

merely one among a large number of examples in economic life of how financial intermediaries, in this case the arbitrageurs, serve to lower the costs of transacting. Their presence links, and hence increases, the effective market-making capacity in both markets.

Nonetheless, while logic and the evidence of virtually every academic investigation of the subject suggest that index arbitrage program trading really affects only the route by which selling or buying orders reach the NYSE, such trading has come under increasing attack from legislators, as well as many in the investment community including some of the largest brokerage concerns. In part, this hostility may reflect a fear on the part of some mutual funds and other institutional investors of "front running" against them by the brokerage firms with which they do business–that is, trading in futures to profit on the knowledge of the customer's impending order in the stock market. In part, it may reflect a populist concern that sophisticated traders may be profiting by "locking in" profits without risk through techniques beyond the reach of the average investor. In part, it may also be a response to the strains that such trading sometimes imposes on the transaction processing capacities of the NYSE. Finally, some members of the brokerage community seem to believe (on the basis, however, of no foundation in evidence that we have been able to discover) that ending program trading will somehow reduce market volatility, increase investor confidence, and restore trading volume to pre-crash levels.

To deal in detail with each of these misconceptions about arbitrage program trading, some of very long standing, is a task best left to the educational arms of the futures and options exchanges themselves. The focus of our Committee is the narrower one of market performance in the crash and its immediate aftermath. Here perhaps we need only call attention once again to a key point emphasized throughout the Brady report: the markets performed most chaotically precisely when the arbitrage link between them was broken. Breaking the link knocked out market-making capacity on the floor at the futures markets at Chicago and at the upstairs, block-trading desks in New York. The specialists at the NYSE were then left to face the avalanche on their own.

The Critical Policy Issue: Who Should Set Futures Margins?

An issue that has dominated policy discussions since the crash has been that of index futures margins. Because percentage margins on futures are smaller than some margins required on purchases of stocks, the concern has been voiced that greater leverage can be achieved in the futures market than in the stock market, thus encouraging "speculation" and promoting greater volatility. Further, because stock margins are set by the Fed, while futures margins are set "privately" by the futures exchanges, it has been argued, in the wake of the crash, that not only equalization but governmental control of futures margins is necessary.

In our preliminary report we stated that we found no evidence that the level or method of setting futures margins had intensified the crash, and we cautioned that imposing fundamental changes in the setting of futures margins could easily have unintended and unpredictable consequences for the continued viability of the US futures markets. None of the studies of the crash published since our preliminary report has caused us to alter those views. None of the studies, in fact, attempted any detailed or quantitative appraisal of the role of futures margins. Absent such documentation, we fear that the frequent references to margins in the summaries and in the policy sections of those reports have only tended to reinforce widely held misconceptions about margins and crashes, past as well as present.

Sixty years of academic research, for example, plus a thorough study by the staff of the Federal Reserve Board, have not succeeded in dispelling the misconception that stock market margins on the eve of the Crash of 1929 were only 10 percent, or that the vast bulk of shares on the NYSE were held in these low-margined accounts, or that the forced liquidation of those accounts under the pressure of margin calls was mainly responsible for the severity of the crash. As noted, however, not in the text but only, alas, in an appendix to the Brady report:

> Beginning in the Summer of 1929, brokers began to increase margin requirements and by the time of the crash, actual margins were about 50 percent. Total outstanding margin debt at the time of the 1929 crash was equal to only about 10 percent of the value of outstanding stocks. It is difficult, therefore, to imagine that margin calls were sufficient to

account by themselves for any significant fraction of the secular decline in the stock market following the 1929 crash (Brady report, Appendix A, Analytical Study VIII, p. VIII-2).[7]

Similarly, while many may have come to believe that the level of margins on index futures was a cause of the 1987 crash, the facts are: that the entire open interest in margined index futures in October 1987 came to the share equivalent of only 2 percent of the value of shares listed on the NYSE; that far from contracting in a liquidation panic under the pressure of margin calls, the open interest in futures actually expanded slightly during October 19; and that futures traders whose margin accounts were classified as "speculative" were, as noted earlier, substantial net buyers of futures, not sellers, on October 19.

Misconceptions about the role of futures margins, if translated improvidently into legislative or governmental policy decisions, could have significant consequences for the efficiency of markets. It is crucial, therefore, that the margin issue be addressed with a clear understanding both of the facts and of the valid purposes and functions of margins.

Futures margins as guarantors of contract performance

Participants in futures markets buy and sell "contracts" that embody promises to make payments of a fixed sum at some future "delivery" date. The value of such a contract depends upon the relation between the fixed price and the value of some specified "spot" price at the maturity date of the contract. The credibility of such promises to pay in the future is maintained in part by requiring the parties, both the buyer and the seller of the obligation—and not just the buyer, as in stock market margins—to post collateral in the form of a cash margin with their brokers. Brokers in turn post margins with a clearinghouse member when they undertake a trade. For further protection, the margin account is marked to market daily. If the price movement during a day is favorable, and more margin is on deposit than needed, the excess is credited to the customer. But additional margin must be posted whenever prices move adversely and the value of the collateral on

---

[7]Essentially similar findings were in the FRB study.

deposit falls below a specified maintenance margin level. Thus, knowing that continually updated margins will be required–and knowing also that the members of the clearinghouse, and ultimately the membership of the entire exchange, are committed to make good any failures–a trader may take a position in futures with no concern about the other party's ability to perform as promised because the clearinghouse is, in effect, substituted for the other party.

How futures margins are set by the exchanges

Futures exchanges currently set their margins by economic standards comparable to those in any other private sector business. Exchanges have the institutional concern of protecting the financial integrity of their clearing system, and they are naturally aware of the basic economic importance of trading volume to their members' operations. They must therefore try to balance the gains to their members from a reduced risk of customer default against the higher costs that the extra degree of protection demanded might impose on the users of the system. Of course, individual members can and do elect on their own to increase customer margins on deposit with them to protect further their own obligations to meet exchange requirements.

The margins required to meet the exchange's goals are not set arbitrarily but depend, among other things, on the price volatility of the contract and the speed and assurance with which additional margin can be collected. Since the futures exchanges make their cash settlements daily, the margins they set have typically approximated the maximum price move likely in a single day, plus an added safety factor that can be further increased whenever the underlying price volatility suddenly increases. Margins are also lower for "hedgers" and spreaders than for speculators, since the hedger's position in the underlying commodity, or the spreader's in the offsetting contract, is itself an implicit guarantor of the resources to fulfill the promise in the futures contract.

Performance of the margin process during the October crash

That the US futures exchanges have in fact succeeded in finding an appropriate balance of costs and benefits in their margin policies–and that they have not short-sightedly sought to build up trading volume with margins set too low–is clear from their survival. On October 19, a day that saw the largest one-day price change ever recorded in the S&P 500 futures market, no trader suffered losses because of a contract default by a counterparty, no clearinghouse failed, and no futures clearing firm failed to meet its obligations to its customers, despite the unprecedented volume of margin-related cash flows and the intraday margin calls.

This is not to suggest, of course, that no problems or difficulties with the clearing and margining process were encountered on October 19 and 20. Serious strains occurred, particularly in the options markets, where the setting of margins for writers of options, or for combinations of option positions, is technically more difficult than setting margins for futures. Even in the more experienced futures markets, however, rumors of impending collapse of particular brokers and clearing firms appear to have circulated at various times during the two days, unquestionably intensifying a sense of panic. Such apprehension can become important because margin accounts at clearing firms and the retail futures commission merchants have some of the characteristics of demand deposits in banks–not including federal deposit insurance. If rumors start that a brokerage firm is failing or that holders of under-margined accounts are not posting more cash because their banks are refusing to transfer funds, every holder of a margined futures position has an incentive to withdraw any free cash balance as quickly as possible and to refrain from further transactions, even stabilizing ones.

Fortunately, the banking system, with the normal liquidity support to be expected from the Federal Reserve in a threatened crisis, was able to avert a financial collapse in October 1987. Steps for further strengthening the liquidity support system, based in part on the experience gained during the crash, are already being taken by clearing firms and their banking connections. Whether this strengthening should aim for a unified clearing system covering stocks, options and futures as recommended in the Brady report is far from clear, however. There are no obvious economies of scale or management that we can see in merging the many separate and highly specialized clearinghouses into a single giant firm. Competition in providing clearing services, like competition generally, can be a spur to innovation and improved efficiency. Some of the presumed gains from unified clearing, moreover, can be accomplished simply by better sharing of information between banks and clearinghouses along lines already being implemented. We believe that if the economic advantages of more integrated intermarket clearing are as large and as unambiguous as the Brady report suggests, the various exchanges will find ways in their mutual interest to bring about such a consolidation without mandating a national clearing monopoly.

The costs of changing the present system of setting futures margins

The demonstrated success of the margin policies of the private-sector futures exchanges carries with it a direct implication for public policy, albeit one that many who recognize that success seem reluctant to accept. If private-sector margin policies are currently being set on rational economic grounds, and if they are passing the survivorship test, not only routinely, but in the face of the most dramatic market collapse in our history, then, absent clear evidence that the futures markets are benefiting unjustly from costs that their margin policies impose on others, the adoption by a public-sector regulator of any different set of policies can be presumed to be socially inefficient.

In particular, the frequently heard call for 50 percent performance margins on index futures contracts–far higher than experience has shown necessary to protect the clearing process–would amount, in effect, to the imposition of a tax on futures transactions (although not a tax, of course, from which any government revenues would be collected). All the negative effects of an excise tax would be present, however, including in particular the reduction in sales volume. That higher margins, arbitrarily imposed, are effectively a tax on futures transactions must be emphasized. The tax is reduced, but not eliminated, by the interest paid on the account either directly by the broker or by the return on any US Treasury bills deposited in lieu of cash. Funds tied up in such low-yield uses usurp other, more productive, opportunities for employing the resources.

The argument is sometimes made indeed, we made the point in our preliminary report–that even a 50 percent margin requirement might not be onerous for true hedgers because they could, in principle, meet the margin requirement by depositing the assets against which they are selling the futures contract. Quite apart from the fact that 50 percent margins might leave no one in the market to take the other side of the hedgers' trades, the argument that high margins do not deter hedgers overlooks the small, perhaps, but still nontrivial risk of banking large sums without insurance coverage. Margin deposits, although segregated, are still ultimately at risk in the event of a catastrophic crash. Therefore, a pension fund hoping to hedge 25 percent of a $1 billion portfolio of equities would, if faced with a 50-percent margin requirement, surely and quite properly be reluctant to deposit as much as $125 million in cash or Treasury bills with an outside broker. Nor would it be likely to turn over custody of any substantial fraction of its $1 billion in shares merely to reduce the interest loss from pledging low-yield liquid assets. The most prudent strategy for such a fund for reducing its equity proportion would be to avoid exchange-traded futures altogether and turn to substitutes–either selling $250 million of stocks and investing the proceeds in Treasury bills directly, or perhaps undertaking an equivalent hedging transaction on an overseas exchange or in an off-exchange dealer market.

Driving major classes of users to seek alternatives to futures exchanges not only reduces the revenues of those exchanges but undermines the liquidity and market depth that is, after all, the very reason for their existence. Some of the calls for higher margins on futures appear, in fact, to have just such an undermining of the market's liquidity as an objective. The fear is that thanks in part to the development of index futures, the market for equities has become too sensitive to news and hence too volatile. Whatever the merits of those arguments–and we, at least, do not find them persuasive–they do not appear to recognize the alternatives to futures transaction that pension funds and other large institutional investors already have at their disposal, let alone the alternatives not yet on stream but that will surely be developed if the US index futures markets can no longer function efficiently.

One of the alternatives to an index futures transaction is, of course, a transaction directly in the stocks that make up the index. Some of the clamor for higher margins on index futures, notably that in the Brady report, appears to be less a call for killing the futures markets or reducing their liquidity than an appeal for restoring competitive equality between these two specific alternatives.

The point is made that whatever may be the original motivating differences between futures margins and stock market margins–good faith deposits in the case of futures, and down-payments on a purchase in the case of stocks–the margins are functionally equivalent for some classes of traders. As a means of establishing a leveraged position in equities, many speculators and even some longer-term investors have a choice between buying futures on the one hand and borrowing to buy stocks on the other. If they invest on the stock side they may be required to comply with the 50-percent initial cash margin requirement imposed under the Federal Reserve's margin regulations. That requirement is far higher than the margin currently required by the futures exchanges (about 15 percent) for initial speculative positions in index futures.

Futures margins and stock market margins: some misconceptions

In evaluating this competitive equality argument, however, it is important to avoid a number of widely held misconceptions about current stock market margin rules.

First, very few stock market margins are currently at 50 percent. Market professionals, such as specialists and member broker-dealers, are exempted from the regular margin rules. They must comply instead with certain minimum net capital requirements. The Brady report (p. 65) puts these requirements as the effective equivalent of initial margins of 20 to 25 percent.

Second, not all stock market margins, or their equivalents, are set by the Federal Reserve System. The Federal Reserve sets only the initial margins. The critical maintenance margins–the requirements that trigger margin calls and any intermarket spillovers–are set by the stock exchanges. The maintenance margin for stocks, currently 25 percent, is as much a private sector responsibility as the maintenance margin for futures. The same is true for bank or other loans against already existing, as opposed to newly opened, stock positions. Furthermore, it is not the Federal Reserve that sets the capital requirement for market professionals, a subject that was of concern to the Brady Commission. Those requirements are set by the exchanges and self-regulatory bodies such as the National Association of Securities Dealers.

Third, rules on extensions of credit as well as the risk exposure to exchange member firms are very different in the two markets. Futures contracts, unlike stock, are marked to market daily, and in times of rapid price change are subject to intraday margin calls. The objective of the futures margin system is to avoid the accumulation of credit obligations. An initial stock purchase, by contrast, need not be settled for five days, and if clearinghouse funds are used for payment, one additional business day may lapse. Maintenance margin calls, moreover, particularly for good customers, are much less peremptory for stocks than for futures. In other words, larger cash buffers are substituted by stock brokers for the quicker speed-of-collection approach adopted by the futures industry.

Finally, the 50-percent initial margin requirement applicable in the cash market applies to individual stocks, while index futures contracts relate to portfolios of stocks. It is a well accepted principle of finance that the price volatility of a portfolio of stocks is less than that of any of its particular components. Hence, if the function of margins is to protect the integrity of the clearing process, margins on baskets of stocks *should* be lower than on individual stocks–and if margins on stock baskets were to be set in the private sector, like those on futures, they presumably *would* be lower. The problem of competitive inequality would disappear.

Federal Reserve margin rules and speculative excesses: a skeptical view

That so simple a solution to making margins consistent as removing the Federal Reserve altogether has not so far been seriously proposed is testimony to the lingering power of the notion that control over stock market margins plays an important role in controlling excessive leverage and speculation. The conventional wisdom, echoed repeatedly in the Brady report, is that the control of leveraged investment in stocks through the Federal Reserve margin rules is necessary to curb speculative excesses. It is worth noting, however, that the Federal Reserve itself, in its 1984 staff study and evaluation of the margin rules, was far less confident than the Brady report about the role of stock market margins in this respect. The Fed's detailed historical review of market volatility turned up no discernible relation between stock margin levels or margin changes and market movements, either in the aggregate or for particular highly speculative stocks. In the words of the FRB study (p. 163), the evidence pointed up "the lack of any positive demonstration that margin regulation has served to dampen stock price fluctuation."

Certainly the Board's actual decisions on margins over the years suggest no great confidence in that agency's ability to affect stock market speculation. The current initial margin of 50 percent was set in 1974 and has been kept unchanged at that level ever since. Nor is the Federal Reserve justly to be censured for this passive policy. Neither economics nor legislation offers any clear guidelines to the Federal Reserve as to when speculative "excess" is in fact occurring. Absent any universally accepted indicator that the stock market is at or approaching a level that is unsustainably high, can the Federal Reserve Board reasonably be expected to take dramatic steps to curb stock market credit, and thus risk precipitating a panic that might, like the Crash of 1987, reduce national wealth by half a trillion dollars? Or if trading volume is languishing can the Federal Reserve reasonably be expected to lower appreciably a margin rate that has remained unchanged for almost fifteen years, particularly with a recent major crash still so vividly in memory?

The political setting in which the Fed necessarily operates will inevitably cause it to act with great caution–particularly against the backdrop of its own 1984 study, which reflects strong misgivings about the utility and effectiveness of margins as a tool for curbing "speculative" investment and market volatility. In short, public-sector controllers of margins—whether the Fed, the SEC or the CFTC, and whether directly responsible or merely exercising final review powers–bear only the political costs of being charged with setting margins too "low" should another crash occur. The natural tendency, therefore, will be to avoid setting margin levels that might subject the agency in the future to public criticism and political pressures. Margins set in the private sector, by contrast, can go up and down as economic circumstances change because the exchanges themselves both bear the costs and get the benefits of setting margins too high or too low.

Margin rules as a private-sector responsibility

We recommend, therefore, that the equalization of margins called for by the Brady report be undertaken in the most direct way possible, namely by turning over to the private sector those remaining parts of the stock margin process still administered by the Federal Reserve System. We recognize, of course, that in an important sense the issue of competitive equality of initial speculative margins may already have become academic, although some in New York may believe futures margins are still inadequate. The Board of Governors of the CME has made substantial concessions to this view. It has recently voted to raise initial speculative margins to 15 percent–a level three to five times that on even the most volatile physical commodity and higher than would have been set in the past for the day-to-day volatility currently being experienced. Margin levels higher than needed to protect the settlement process may perhaps serve to deflect political pressure from the futures markets in the short run, but if long maintained they are also likely to add impetus to the kind of search for cheaper methods of portfolio adjustment that led to the development of index futures in the first place.

Trading Halts and Circuit Breakers

The tidal wave of selling on October 19 had effects on both the New York and Chicago exchanges that were similar in all essential respects to those that afflict an electric power utility when all its customers turn on their air conditioners at once. The demand for service then exceeds the system's capacity to supply it at normal cost and a variety of formal and informal rationing and "peak-load pricing" mechanisms come into play. In the equity markets these peak-load pricing and rationing adjustments took the form of widened bid-ask spreads, large gaps between successive prices, over-loaded printer buffers, crossed markets, lost orders, unanswered telephones, bans on program trading, and so on, as described in great detail in the Brady and SEC reports, as well as in the report of the General Accounting Office (1988). Under such conditions of system overload, the Brady report's call for the installation of circuit breakers is certainly understandable, and the possible need for circuit breakers has also been a concern of the exchanges.

Shortly before our committee was formed, the CME had, in fact, instituted temporary 30-point per day price limits for its S&P 500 contract–a limit of approximately 15 percent. Daily price limits had, of course, long been a feature of commodity futures contracts and even financial futures contracts, notably Treasury bond futures, but had been dropped from stock index futures shortly after their introduction. We summarized in our preliminary report the main arguments for and against making those temporary limits a permanent feature of the contract and we need not repeat them here. Since a 15-percent limit would be reached only rarely, and since its very presence might be reassuring to some panic stricken investors, our inclination was to keeping the 15-percent limits in place on stock index contracts, particularly if the consequences of reaching the price limit were to trigger only a brief pause, rather than a halt, in trading activity until the next trading day.

In the period since submitting our preliminary report, however, the CME has reduced the daily price limits to 15 points–roughly 7 percent–and has instituted a smaller 5-point limit–about 2.5 percent–at the opening. We have no great concern with the new limit at the opening since the delay before trading may be resumed is only ten minutes. All of the studies of the crash have shown that congestion and confusion on October 19 and 20–and even later in the week–was greatest at the open and, as we suggested in our preliminary report, some rethinking of opening procedures in all of the markets was clearly needed. The new

15-point daily limit, however, is only half that of the initial margin and hence appears narrower than needed to protect the integrity of the clearing process. Limits that narrow are likely to slow the return to equilibrium. If so, they serve only to reduce the value of the market to hedgers, to exacerbate problems at the resumption of trading and, over the longer run, to weaken the case for maintaining futures exchanges–particularly US futures exchanges–as a primary medium for portfolio transactions by large institutional investors.

The same concerns apply with equal or greater force to the price limits recently proposed by the NYSE that would deny access to the Exchange's Designated Order Turnaround (DOT) system for program trading once a price movement of 50 points on the Dow Jones Industrial Average–about 3 percent–is experienced on any given trading day. Rationing access to the DOT system does not, of course, completely sever the link between the cash and futures markets. Theoretically, index arbitrage could still be carried out manually, as it was before DOT was available, but only at a slower pace and subject to more uncertainty.[8] The higher costs of program trading in New York widen the arbitrage bounds around the index and hence raise the effective costs of trading index futures in Chicago. Moreover, the higher cost of hedging positions in Chicago reduces the ability of the block-trading desks in New York to take positions, which in turn reduces the market-making capacity of the NYSE's specialists, thus raising the cost of trading for everyone.

Removing Regulatory Obstacles to Market Efficiency

The exchanges are privately owned business organizations. As outside observers with no investments at stake we are reluctant to offer advice

---

[8]Under a NYSE rule adopted in February member firms are prohibited from using the DOT system for index arbitrage program trading on any day during which the Dow Jones Industrial Average moves more than 50 points. The first such movement after adoption of the rule occurred on April 6, 1988. According to a press report, sophisticated traders who were prepared for a shutdown of DOT simply switched to manual execution to perform index arbitrage. One floor broker stated, "It made things slightly less efficient, but they could still do the trades." *The Wall Street Journal*, April 8, 1988, p. 3.

about specific methods for making or processing transactions or about other details of running those businesses. We understand that the NYSE is currently planning computer capacity for a one-billion share day. In fact, we suspect that if the orders were to come in large enough lots and at a steady enough pace, the NYSE could handle a load that size even with its present capacity.

The challenge, however, as we see it, is not one of meeting maximum processing targets for a few rare peak days, but of developing market mechanisms that can, over the longer run, better accommodate the trading needs of the public, and especially the portfolio-based trading of large institutional investors. We believe that none of the reports on the crash has faced up to this critical issue. The main preoccupation of the Brady Commission has not been with the needs of the users, but with the lack of a unified regulatory structure. This focus, we believe, is misdirected. The chaos and confusion of October 19 and 20 may well have been compounded by regulatory failure, but if so it was not so much a failure to coordinate policies across agency lines as a failure of the policies themselves.

We propose to call attention here to some of these long-standing regulatory policies that, we believe, served to weaken market structure and performance on October 19 and 20, and that will continue to inhibit the expansion of market capacity, at least in the USA, for institutional trading.

The "uptick" rule

The SEC's so-called "uptick" rule[9] governing short sales of registered stock on a securities exchange allows short sales to be executed only at a price higher than the price of the last different trade price preceding it. Hence when prices are falling, as they were through much of October 19 and 20, short sales by public traders are effectively ruled out. The rule was introduced originally, and is still defended by some today, as a

---

[9]Rule 10a-1(a) (1) of the SEC's General Rules and Regulations under the Securities Exchange Act of 1934.

way of preventing "bear raids" against the shares of thinly traded corporations.

An unintended consequence of the uptick rule, however, has been to keep selling pressures from being spread efficiently between the index futures market and the stock market. When selling pressures happen to hit the futures market first, the market makers on and around the floor absorb the initial shock into inventory, hoping this will be a temporary condition. Should still more selling orders arrive before these initial positions have been offset, increasingly large price concessions must be offered to the market makers to induce them to commit what may still remain of their available capital resources. Additional capacity can be made available from the stock market, however, if index arbitrageurs can take over some of the market makers' inventory of futures contracts and simultaneously sell shares to market makers and other buyers in the cash markets.

By blocking short sales the uptick rule limits index arbitrage to the smaller number of players who happen to be long in those of the underlying stocks that are not trading above previous trades at different prices. If the access of futures traders to the additional market-making capacity of the stock market is reduced, price concessions in the futures market, and hence the effective cost of transacting there, must increase. Some transactors who might otherwise have preferred to sell futures are then driven to sell stock directly, and some who might have preferred to buy stock are driven to buy futures. Distortions in normal trading patterns of precisely this kind, representing substantial increases in the effective costs of trading to all market participants, were a conspicuous feature of markets throughout the entire week of October 19.

The 30-percent or "short-short" rule

The pernicious effects of the SEC's uptick rule in weakening intermarket linkage have long been known both to academic researchers and to market professionals. However, the adverse consequences, particularly on October 19 and 20, of an important provision of the Internal Revenue Code, section 851(b) (3), have so far gone largely unremarked. Under this section, often dubbed the "30-percent" or "short-short" rule, a regulated investment company, such as a mutual fund, may derive no more than 30 percent of its gross income for any taxable year from the sale of securities held for less than three months. Profits from a futures or options transaction, even when resulting merely from the closing out of a successful futures or options hedge, fall under the rule. When the market falls as far as it did on October 19, even partial hedges can quickly exceed the rule's limits, with the result that the fund's entire earnings, not just its profit on the futures component of the hedge, become subject to full income taxation. It is not surprising, in view of this rule, that mutual funds in the USA have virtually shunned the futures markets.

The effects of the 30-percent rule in keeping mutual funds and the effects of many state insurance statutes in keeping insurance companies from employing futures or options are particularly significant in the light of the substantial and persistent discounts of futures under the cash index on October 19 and thereafter. Mutual funds and insurance companies seeking "yield enhancement" are natural buyers of under-priced futures; to the extent that they can anticipate regular inflows of cash subscriptions, they are, in effect, precisely the kind of potential institutional "sellers" of portfolio insurance whose absence has caused major concern over the possibly destabilizing effects of portfolio insurance.

Position limits and sunshine trading

Position limits raise issues that are similar in many respects to those discussed earlier in the setting of futures margins. When the position limits are set by the exchanges and their clearing firms they give little ground for concern. The incentives to balance costs and benefits are appropriate, exactly as with margins. But when the limits are set by outside regulators, the emphasis of the regulators is inevitably less on strict economic efficiency than on avoiding being seen as too soft on "manipulation" or "speculation." The position limits are thus likely to be set below those that the exchanges would consider reasonable on their own, and in the process to introduce unintended market distortions and imbalances.

We noted earlier, for example, the effect of the SEC-mandated position limits on exchange-traded options as a factor in keeping institutions out of the option market and, in particular, in inducing many portfolio insurers to turn to constructing synthetic puts with futures. At the same time, the CFTC's position limits on "speculative" holdings of futures were intensifying the seller-buyer imbalance in the futures market, because the limits on the speculator buyers are much smaller than those on the portfolio-insurer hedger sellers.

We recommend, therefore, that both the SEC and the CFTC undertake a thorough reexamination of their policies on position limits for index options and futures. Whether there is a rationale for traditional position limits in thinly traded markets, where there may be some threat of cornering, mandated position limits appear to be pointless, at best, in the index markets, and quite possibly destabilizing.

We believe also that the CFTC should give urgent priority to a review of what has come to be called "sunshine trading." Under sunshine trading, a pension fund or portfolio insurer intending to sell a large number of futures contracts announces that intention in advance. The possible buyers, having been notified of what is being put up for sale, can then develop purchase plans in the spirit of an announced public auction. Under current CFTC rules, however, such an announcement might be construed as "prearranged trading"–although even now it is far from clear how the CFTC would have responded to a selling announcement by a large portfolio insurer on October 19. In the face of that uncertainty no one, apparently, was willing to try. Instead, some big selling orders were sent directly to the pit where they strained the capacity of the locals.

Open-outcry futures markets are remarkably efficient trading facilities, but they cannot be expected to do everything. They tend to be most effective when the order flow is continual and heavy, but the typical order is small relative to the combined capital of the market makers in and around the pit. The agricultural futures pits, in their heyday, could offer deep and liquid markets because so many of the industry's largest traders were directly on the floor. The NYSE, by contrast, adopted the franchised specialist system long ago, not for any unique advantages that that system of market-making possesses, but simply because the order flow for the typical stock was too small and too irregular to support a pit of competing market makers. When the fixed commission was finally eliminated in the early 1970s, and block trading by institutional investors surged, the effective trading market for many big customers moved off the trading floor altogether and on to the trading desks and screens of the large broker-dealers.

The relation of institutional trading to financial futures markets has been subject to a quite different evolution. The first financial futures were in foreign exchange, where a huge, dealer-based "upstairs" forward market already existed–and along with the off-exchange "swap" market still, in fact, dominates the transaction flow. The upstairs dealer markets in US Treasury securities were also well-established long before futures trading was opened in those instruments. But for stock index futures there was, and still is, no functioning alternative dealer-based market in the baskets of stocks that are now the relevant trading unit for so many institutions. Institutional investors have become the main force in equity futures, but they are not on the floor and the rules governing their dealings off the floor are far from clear.

We do not mean to suggest, of course, that allowing upstairs block trading of futures or of stock baskets would be an unmixed blessing and that regulation should encourage it. There are important social benefits in centralized, competitive public markets, especially for "price discovery." Off-exchange trading also raises serious concerns about regulatory "free-riding." Clearly, many delicate trade-offs must be studied and appraised before a coherent regulatory policy can be developed. But we fear that by delaying taking a clear stand, the CFTC may be retarding the development of new ways of adapting futures markets to the needs of traders, particularly large institutional traders.

A Final Note

In the face of so many commissions and studies inspired by the October 1987 crash, we are reluctant to recommend the formation of still another study group. There is a clear need, however, to examine the capital markets and their regulation from a perspective broader than that of a single day or week and with a concern beyond that of the individual investor. In the wake of an event as dramatic as the Crash of 1987 there is a great tendency to look for easy or politically appealing remedies, "fixes" that can be put in place quickly. It is this spirit, we believe, that has caused so much clamor for changes in margin rules, despite the absence of evidence that margins had any relation to October's events, let alone evidence that variable margin requirements can be effectively administered by a public body to dampen "excessive" speculation or curb volatility. Any new study group should include–as principals, not merely as support staff–professional economists who are knowledgeable about futures markets and especially some who have contributed to the revolution in the economics profession's thinking about market regulation that has taken place over the last fifty years. The time for an in-depth study of market mechanisms–a study focusing on means for removing impediments and restrictions that inhibit the efficient functioning of the market–has indeed arrived.

On October 28, 1987, the Chicago Mercantile Exchange (CME) appointed an independent committee to study the role of CME's futures market during the Crash of 1987. The committee consisted of the above authors with myself as chairman. Each of the three academic committee members (myself, Burton Malkiel of Princeton University and Myron Scholes of Stanford University) had conducted research and written extensively on issues relating to the stock market, the futures and options markets, and the interrelations between the markets. The fourth member (John D. Hawke Jr of Arnold and Porter), a practicing attorney, had substantial experience in financial regulatory matters, including serving as General Counsel to the Board of Governors of the Federal Reserve Board. The committee submitted its preliminary report on December 22, 1987, and its final report about two months later.

References

Board of Governors of the Federal Reserve System. *A Review and Evaluation of Federal Margin Regulation*, December, 1984 (FRB study).

CFTC Division of Economic Analysis and Trading and Markets. "Final Report on Stock Index Futures and Cash Market Activity During October 1987," January, 1988 (CFTC report).

General Accounting Office. "Financial Markets: Preliminary Observations on the October 1987 Crash," GAO/GGD-88-38, January, 1988.

Grossman, Sanford J. "An Analysis of the Implications for Stock and Futures Price Volatility of Program Trading and Dynamic Hedging Strategies," *Journal of Business*, July, 1988.

Harris, Lawrence. "Nonsynchronous Trading and the S&P 500 Stock-Futures Basis in October, 1987," University of Southern California, manuscript, December, 1987.

Leland, Hayne. "Dynamic Asset Allocation: After the Crash," *Investment Management Review*, January/February, 1988.

Securities and Exchange Commission, Division of Market Regulation. "The October 1987 Market Break," February, 1988 (SEC report).

Stoll, Hans and Robert Whaley. "The Dynamics of Stock Index and Stock Futures Returns," Working Paper Series 88-101, Fuqua School of Business, Durham, NC, January, 1988.

5 The Crash of 1987 and the Crash of 1946

The many references to the Crash of 1987 and portfolio insurance must make Mark Rubinstein, as one of the co-inventors of that strategy, feel like Harriet Beecher Stowe, the author of *Uncle Tom's Cabin*, who was invited by President Lincoln to the White House, and introduced as "the little lady who brought on this great war."

Lincoln was surely exaggerating, and so are those who credit the liquidity illusion spawned by portfolio insurance with fueling the remarkable rise of 30 percent in US equity values between the end of December 1986 and the peak reached in August 1987. The added demand for equities by the insured was too small to account plausibly for a boom of that order, as Rubinstein points out (and, as was noted also in at least one of the post-crash reports, to wit, the *Report of the Chicago Mercantile Exchange's Committee of Inquiry* of which I served as chairman). In the period just before and surrounding the fateful day of October 19, portfolio insurers were indeed among the conspicuous sellers, but none of the many post-crash reports has successfully isolated their contribution either to specific price movements at given times or to the cumulative price change over the interval.

Far too much attention has been devoted, in my opinion, especially by the Brady Commission, to these painful and so far fruitless attempts to relate the sequence of price changes on October 19 and 20 to the activities of particular transactors. These well-intentioned post-mortems serve only to reinforce the delusion that once the "cause" of a crash has been found, appropriate regulatory remedies can prevent further recurrences.

The remarkable persistence in the USA's politics of this "accident reconstruction syndrome" struck me with great force when I had occasion to look into the contemporaneous accounts of an earlier crash. I refer to the Crash of September 3, 1946–not one of the more storied episodes in US financial history perhaps, but at -4.4 percent (equivalent currently to a drop of 120 points in Dow) a noteworthy enough event to call for an official investigation that had some striking parallels to the more recent one.

The study of the Crash of September 3, 1946, was undertaken not by a specially appointed task force, like the Brady Commission, but by the staff of the US Securities and Exchange Commission, then a regulatory agency at the height of its prestige–the jewel in the crown of the New Deal reforms. The report by the Commission's Trading and Exchange Division, published almost a year later, was shorter (only sixty-eight pages of text) than the 1987 crash report by the SEC Division of Market Regulation, and much duller (with over a hundred pages of detailed cross-classifications of transactions); but at least the authors of the August 1947 report were open-minded.

The staff approached the task with no preconceptions as to who or what the villains might be. As in 1929 and 1987, no major bad-news economic or political event could be singled out as the precipitating cause, though, as in 1987 after the August peak, a certain souring of the atmosphere seems to have accompanied the downward drift in prices in the weeks before the crash. To pinpoint cause or causes of the selling wave, therefore, the Commission staff supplemented its own voluminous records on the day's transactions with a detailed interview study of most large transactors and a sample of smaller public customers who bought or sold securities on September 3. (The Brady Commission, in similar circumstances, went–in Appendix V of its report–even further, sending a detailed questionnaire not just to market participants but to "other interested parties.")

In the staff interviews after the 1946 Crash, two specific reasons for selling on September 3 were given with great frequency. The second most frequently cited reason (accounting for about 28 percent of the shares sold by the largest largest sellers and about 17 percent of those by other sellers) involved a trading strategy in which the sell orders were triggered by a known mechanical rule or formula. Obviously that rule could not have been portfolio insurance; it hadn't been invented yet. A fairly primitive prototype of portfolio insurance had long been followed, of course, through stop-loss orders, and the commission staff was fully aware of their destabilizing potential. But stop-loss orders appeared to have been involved in only 9 to 10 percent of all transactions. In the crash of 1987, by comparison, portfolio insurance selling played a somewhat larger role on October 19, but still amounted to at most 20 to 25 percent of the total volume of the day, though the fact that selling by others was thus three to four times as large as that by the portfolio insurers may not be readily apparent from the many censorious references to portfolio insurance in the accounts of the 1987 Crash by both the Brady Commission and the SEC's Division of Market Regulation.

Nor was the destabilizing selling on September 3, 1946, induced by margin calls. The cascade-producing potential of such calls had been, and in many quarters still is, regarded as the major accelerant in the October 1929 Crash, though subsequent research has substantially downgraded their probable role. The folk view of speculative margin buying as the major culprit in the 1929 episode was strong enough, however, in the early 1930s to have led Congress to take margin-setting authority away from the private-sector securities exchanges in 1934 and assign it to the Federal Reserve Board. Although the Board had kept margin requirements between 40 and 75 percent through the 1930s and the war years, it had set the initial margin rate at 100 percent in January 1946 so that by September 3 there was no margin to be called. Nor could the selling frenzy be laid at the door of bear-raiders, hammering down prices with self-reinforcing waves of short-selling. That barn door, too, had been locked by the institution of the uptick rule in 1937.

With so many of the usual suspects eliminated, what then was the formula-based strategy cited by so many sellers on the fateful day? Amazingly enough, it was the Dow Theory! That theory, of course, has long since lost its vogue with investors, though we are daily reminded of its once prominent role by references, especially in *The Wall Street*

Journal (Dow Jones and Co. publishers) to the Dow Jones Industrial Average. That average and its companions, the Dow Jones Transportation Average and the Dow Jones Utility Average, were the key indicators in what Wall Street argot designates as a "technical" (and we might prefer to call an informationless) trading system. A "bear market," calling for immediate sales by followers of the rule, was signalled whenever all three Dow Jones averages had broken through their "resistance levels"–essentially their recent previous lows. Just such a conjunction of the averages apparently had occurred by the close on Friday, August 29, the last previous trading day; and the Dow Theory true believers (plus the nonbelievers who knew of the true believers) had the long Labor Day weekend to stew over their moves for the Tuesday open.

But if the Friday close led the Dow Theorists to produce the same kind of order imbalance on the next trading day's opening that the close on Friday, October 16, supposedly led the portfolio insurers to produce on October 19, what accounts for all the subsequent selling? The Dow Theory, it will be recalled, was only the second most cited reason. The reason for selling most frequently mentioned in the 1947 SEC tabulation was that prices were falling and other people were selling! That, of course, was precisely what Bob Shiller found years later in his now famous questionnaire on the 1946 Crash; and I suspect he would have found the same had he distributed his questionnaire in October 1929 or any other crash in market prices accompanied by heavy trading.

Nor is it really helpful to interpret as hopelessly irrational those frantic attempts by some sellers to get out before prices fall even further. As in a bank run, such efforts may make perfect sense even for those who know that much of the selling by others is informationless, if they have reason to believe, or even to suspect, that they can execute their own sale before the price drops to, or below, the level needed to accommodate the reduced demand to hold equities. Efforts by market makers to slow the fall in prices, combined with the inevitable stale bids on the limit order books, may serve only to intensify their belief that they can be among the fortunate early leavers. As markets go, the NYSE is particularly vulnerable to this perversity, precisely because it has so successfully sold its clientele on the price continuity that its vaunted "specialists" are supposed to provide. And, indeed they do, on any ordinary day when they face very minor asynchronizations between the random arrivals of buyers and sellers. But when faced with order imbalance of massive proportions, their attempts to lean against the storm may actually be counterproductive.

The sight of panicky sellers ritually acting out the fallacy of composition on live television is far from edifying, but hardly serious enough by itself to warrant major regulatory changes that might well impair the efficiency of the market on the vastly more numerous noncrash days. One minor restructuring, however, for which I believe a case can be made, is instituting the kind of coordinated, intermarket circuit breakers hammered out recently by the CME and the NYSE after long negotiation, which are extensions of procedures they had jointly developed earlier for expiration-day imbalances. The case for such arrangements rests not on any social worker-like concern for protecting panicky sellers from their own folly, but on the recognition that continuous double-auction market systems, and especially those like the NYSE with designated market stabilizers, are not the best possible market structures in all circumstances. Under conditions of large, known imbalances, particularly those induced by portfolio insurance, futures expirations or similar informationless trades, temporary call-auction procedures might be preferred–and with good reason–by most market participants.

My Japanese friends assure me that they understand better than we do this need to be able to switch between market types when extraordinary imbalances suddenly arise, and that is one reason why their capital markets are less susceptible to panicky runs than ours. I suspect we may soon have a chance to put that proposition to the test.

This chapter is based on a Comment to the paper "12 Months After: Comments on the Market Crash," by Mark Rubinstein, University of California, Berkeley, presented at the Conference on Crashes and Panics in Historical Perspective held at New York University, October 19, 1988.

6 The Crash of 1987: Bubble or Fundamental?

In the Chinese calendar, 1987 was the year of the rabbit; for finance specialists, however, it will always be known as the year of the Crash. The 508-point drop in the Dow Jones Average on October 19, 1987, was the largest one-day drop in US stock prices (about 22 percent) ever recorded. And unlike the previous record holder of October 1929, which could only be re-enacted later in the movies, the Crash of 1987 and the attendant chaos on the trading floors was seen in progress on live TV.

What made the spectacle even more compelling for US television audiences was not just the frantic activity, but the ominous parallels that the press and commentators were drawing to the events of October 1929. Remember that in American folklore the Crash of 1929 is seen as the "cause" of the Great Depression of the 1930s and the miseries of prolonged unemployment and political instability both at home and abroad that followed in its wake. Furthermore, the folklore sees the New Deal "reforms" of the 1930s, and especially the establishment of the Securities and Exchange Commission, as having been instituted precisely to prevent a repetition of the experience of the 1920s. The Crash of 1987 thus seemed to suggest that a major breakdown in essential regulatory controls must have occurred, leading to insistent calls in the US Congress for "modernizing" and strengthening government supervision of trading in stocks and financial futures.

As it turned out, none of the dreadful consequences so widely feared in the days after the Crash actually materialized. The US economy has remained buoyant, at least to the time of this writing in early 1989, despite the continued presence of parallels to the late 1920s and early

1930s such as the steep rise in the number and size of bank failures, the increasing debt-service problems of the major debtor nations (now including the USA) and the incipient signs of protectionism and related threats to the international division of labor. The calls for regulatory reform have also become less insistent, though concerns over regulatory restructuring could erupt again at any time in the course of struggles for jurisdiction between US Congressional oversight committees. The great Crash of 1987 has thus become a matter more of intellectual, and especially of academic, interest than of urgent practical concern. What could have caused such a massive destruction of wealth? Was it a unique event or merely one more episode in a long sequence of similar market breaks? Can anything be done to prevent such occurrences or at least to reduce their frequency and severity? Should we even try?

In the immediate aftermath of the Crash the conventional view in the press and in the US Congress was that the Crash must surely have been a preventable accident with an identifiable cause. Hence the setting up of numerous investigating commissions, both governmental and private, to sift through the wreckage and pinpoint the source of the failure. Despite the thousands of man-hours devoted to the search, no unmistakable evidence was found of the equivalent of a failing O-ring, as in the *Challenger* disaster, or of a planted bomb, as in the recent Pan Am explosion. Nor should this failure to find a major mechanical breakdown proportionate to the event itself really be surprising. Markets are enormously more complex systems than aircraft, if only because the millions of interacting parts in markets are thinking human beings, not inert components reacting according to well-understood physical principles. In fact everywhere, perhaps except for Congress, recognition has grown that the very term "crash" with its overtones of an identifiable major structural failure is an inappropriate metaphor for what happened on October 19.

A better analogy for the events of that day, some suggest, would be an avalanche in the sense of an increasingly unstable buildup of snow on a mountainside, triggered finally by some trivial and normally harmless event like the snapping of a twig. Certainly there had indeed been a long buildup in share prices in the USA, starting in 1982, accelerating a bit in the first half of 1987 and by August 1987 reaching levels, relative to current dividends and earnings, that were on the high side of the historical range. And there were certainly plenty of twigs lying about in October, ready to serve as triggers, including sharp runups in short-term interest rates, naval encounters in the Persian Gulf and especially the announcement, in the days before the slide, of proposals by the chairman of the major tax-writing committee of our Congress to place tax penalties on the arbitrage-holders of the active takeover stocks then dominating the economic news. But even these potential precipitating events have received more attention than they deserve in the opinion of many. The stock market in the autumn of 1987 was like an overinflated balloon that was doomed to burst of its own accord. It was, in the words of Chairman Greenspan of the Federal Reserve System, "an accident waiting to happen."

At the moment, the view of the Crash of 1987 as a bursting balloon is probably the dominant one not only among practical men of affairs, like Chairman Greenspan (and Leo Melamed, the guiding spirit of the Chicago Mercantile Exchange), but among academic observers as well. The academics, of course, can take a somewhat longer perspective and tend to see the events of 1987 as merely the latest manifestation of an underlying market process that they have dubbed "bubbles." In this chapter I propose to sketch out briefly the main distinctive features of the modern theory of price bubbles and to survey some of the empirical evidence that has led so many to believe that such bubbles and their inevitable bursting do, in fact, occur. I shall also direct attention to another, and currently somewhat neglected, way of looking at large, sudden price jumps, like those on October 19–a way that is consistent with the view of markets as efficient aggregators of information about the fundamentals.

The choice between these two conflicting interpretations of the Crash cannot now, and perhaps never will, be settled definitively. The issue is more than merely a matter of academic controversy, however. The bubble-theory in one or another of its manifestations serves as the main intellectual support for the measures taken recently in a number of countries, and threatened in more, for raising dramatically the cost of transacting in capital markets. I will conclude with some strictures on this class of what I regard as essentially pernicious and misguided policies.

Was the Crash a Bursting Price Bubble?

The notion of price bubbles is a long-standing one that traces back at least to the "tulip craze" in seventeenth century Holland where prices of particularly rare specimens were supposedly bid to absurdly high levels only to come crashing when the fad for fancy tulips had run its course.[1] The term price bubble is invoked precisely to contrast such episodes of frenzied, almost manic trading (at least according to the folk tales) with "rational" prices based on the "fundamentals." A period of sustained price growth for a stock or an index of stocks, however prolonged and substantial, need not be considered anomalous if it reflected the increased earning power of the companies in question. Even a sharp price break could be considered an entirely rational response by a market hit suddenly and unexpectedly by major bad news about future earnings prospects. A price bubble, on the other hand, is essentially a psychological phenomenon. It can swell and burst largely independently of any changes in the underlying economic realities. Once started, perhaps by some chance event, its growth becomes self-sustaining. Each price rise ratifies the wisdom of the previous buy decision; and the process may even accelerate as those outside the market are drawn in by the prospects of further price increases to come. Eventually the bubble bursts, perhaps in response to some purely chance event that disappoints the expectation of ever-higher prices.

No economist, even those most skeptical about the rationality of stock market valuations generally, would claim that stock price movements are governed entirely by psychological whims or fads. Too much evidence exists of sensible price responses to observed changes in the

---

[1] Actually, that's not what really happened. The oft-repeated tale of the tulip bubble appears to have been originally largely a fabrication by the Dutch establishment of that time with a view to throttling the then upstart futures and options markets in commercial tulip bulbs (see Garber, 1988).

fundamentals for that to be credible. Many have thus come to an inter mediate view in which the price changes we observe are taken to be neither purely rational nor purely bubbles, but a combination of both. The bubble component is superimposed, as it were, on the fundamentals.

Some have argued that the combined movements may even be "rational" in the specific sense that, over the long pull, and allowing for the downs as well as the ups, the real return to the typical investor from holding shares is exactly the same as it would have been in a world governed entirely by the fundamentals. The ups and downs of the bubble component would serve only to transfer wealth between investors. They need not by themselves either create or destroy lasting value. The combined process might be "rational" also in the sense that investors cannot be considered to be acting foolishly or irrationally if they choose to participate in the process even if aware that they may be riding a bubble doomed someday to burst. At any point in time, thanks to the inner dynamics of the bubble process, the prospect of loss on a sudden collapse would be balanced exactly by the prospect of continued supernormal returns before cashing in. Thus, looking back, everyone always seems to stay in too long, except, of course, for the annoying few who did manage luckily to get out in time and who never cease reminding us of their prescience.

The notion of rational bubbles is clearly an appealing one, combining ingeniously as it does two lines of explanation for price movements that seem at first sight to be antithetical. As noted earlier, a mountain of evidence has been amassed by researchers in recent years to document the presence of the rational elements in valuations. (For surveys, see Fischer and Merton, 1984, or Barro, 1988.) But what of bubbles? Do we really have persuasive evidence that bubbles, rational or irrational, really exist? Or are they, as some have suggested, merely the name we apply to that part of the observed price movements for which we have not so far found an explanation in terms of the fundamentals? It may be worthwhile, therefore, to survey briefly some recent academic work devoted to those more general questions before focusing on any specific, bubble-like features in the Crash of 1987.

The presence of bubbles cannot, alas, be established by any direct test. Economics is not like chemistry. Unable to conduct controlled experiments at an economy-wide level, the researcher must live with such experiments as nature and history have actually provided, hoping to extract the essence with elaborate and painstaking econometric analysis. Even to attempt to summarize the details of this research approach would be far too space-consuming for a paper of this kind, but the findings to date, and the limitations of two of the main strands in this research can be briefly sketched.

Do Stock Prices Fluctuate Too Much?

One strand, known as excess-volatility tests, seeks to establish whether observed stock prices fluctuate more than can plausibly be attributed to changes in the underlying fundamentals. If so, the excess volatility can be taken as indicating the presence of nonrational or at least non-fundamental forces influencing prices including, but by no means only, cumulative bubbles. The original pioneer of this class of tests, Robert Shiller, of Yale University, claimed (and still claims) to have found evidence of just such excess volatility in stock prices. (See especially Shiller, 1981).

Ingenious as the Shiller excess-volatility tests have been, they suffer from at least two drawbacks that have kept finance and econometric specialists from accepting his findings at face value. First are the problems of establishing the benchmark: how much observed volatility in stock prices would be just enough? Shiller identifies the rational fundamentals with the dividend stream, taking off from the well-known proposition that the price of a share can always, in principle, be expressed as the appropriately discounted sum of all future dividends anticipated on the share from now to eternity. Needless to say, we cannot actually wait until infinity to verify our predictions, but we do get each year another installment on the infinite stream. Shiller finds that the year-to-year percentage variation in this new piece of fundamental information about the future dividend stream is much smaller on average than the percentage variation year-to-year in stock prices. If stock prices were really rational forecasts of future dividends, stock prices should, if anything, fluctuate less than dividends.

Corporate finance specialists were quick to point out, however, that in the USA and many other countries, dividend streams are deliberately kept smoother than the underlying stream of corporate earnings as a matter of corporate policy. Dividends are often maintained in the face of disappointing earnings by selling off existing assets or by issuing new securities to outside investors. The market price of the shares can certainly be expected to react negatively to the unexpected shortfall in cash earnings and the consequent diminution of the owners' equity even though the dividend remains completely unchanged from the year before. A more meaningful test approach, though one still not completely free of difficulties, would be to focus on price response to changes in earnings or cash flow at the level of the firm. Reliable data on earnings cover a much shorter time span than do the series on dividends used by Shiller so that the tests are not always easily comparable. Still, for what it is worth, the tests using earnings for the years such data are available fail to show the substantial supposed excess volatility reported by Shiller in his dividend tests (see Kleidon, 1983).

A second drawback to the use of Shiller excess-volatility tests for detecting the presence of possible bubble-like elements in stock prices is of a more basic, and to academic researchers, of a more frustrating kind. For the particular statistical procedures used by Shiller to be applicable, the underlying time series–in Shiller's case dividends and stock prices–must have a technical property called "covariance stationarity." Precisely what this property entails need not detain us here. Suffice it to say that stock prices and dividends almost certainly do have substantial nonstationary components. Even though we go through the motions of applying the standard statistical tests and dutifully reading off the results, the numbers we seem to be getting are not really trustworthy answers to the questions we are asking. It's like trying to fit inch bolts with metric wrenches. The tools just can't get the job done.

The skill and patience shown by Shiller and others in attempting to devise ways around the obstacles imposed by nonstationarity have been amazing. But, as with a weakened inner tube, each patch applied to the standard technique has seemed only to shift the leak further down the tube. New and more reliable techniques for testing excess volatility and equivalent relations between nonstationary series may someday become available. Indeed, there are hints of some already in the offing. (See Durlauf and Phillips, 1988; especially page 1947.) But at the moment, at least, the case for the existence of bubbles based on the supposed excessive volatility of stock prices must be regarded as still unproved.

Do Stock Prices Tend to Overreact?

Additional support for the likely existence of price bubbles in stock prices is found by some in what they see as pervasive evidence that stock prices systematically overreact to news. The initial price response to a spectacular good-news announcement makes the company better known among investors and gives rise to a "bandwagon effect" as more and more investors seek a share of the action. The first burst of enthusiasm and rapid price gains cannot be maintained, however, and the price growth soon slows or even falls as investors turn their attention to the next news sensation.

Anecdotal evidence and folklore about such bubble-like price patterns exists in abundance, of course, but, in recent years, some serious statistical studies of stock prices by academic researchers have also seemed to point in the same direction. Two kinds of such studies are particularly worth notice. The first kind (see, for example, De Bondt and Thaler, 1985) claim to show that the high-flying stocks tend to be overbought, in the sense that stocks that have substantially outperformed the market in any one year will typically underperform it the next, and that stocks that have substantially underperformed the market are, on average, oversold and will tend to earn higher than normal returns in the period after the selloff. By contrast, standard rational-pricing models rule out any possibility of using past price changes for predicting future above-normal or below-normal returns.

Although the issue is still far from definitively closed, more recent research has not tended to confirm the De Bondt-Thaler finding of price reversals incompatible with the principles of rational valuations. Most, if not all, of the De Bondt-Thaler supposed abnormal returns in the follow-up period have been traced to their failure to adjust adequately for the change in perceived investment risk for a company that typically accompanies a major change in its price (see, for example, Chan, 1988). Suspicion that De Bondt and Thaler have not turned up valid evidence of systematic price overreactions is reinforced by the failure of other researchers to detect significant short or medium term price reversals following episodes of sharp runups in price (see, for example, Brown, Harlow and Tinic, 1989).

The second kind of study, and in some ways a more directly relevant kind of support for the presumed existence of price bubbles, lies in the time series behavior not only of individual stocks, but of the aggregate price indexes themselves. The recent new results are in a sense byproducts of long-continuing efforts within the profession to establish key statistical properties of stock prices and price changes (or returns), including the previously noted critical property of stationarity or nonstationarity. In a nonstationarity time series, changes in the level, when they occur, tend to be "permanent" changes. Permanent, in this statistical sense, does not mean that the series never reverses; clearly the market does fluctuate. But the likelihood of a reversal in direction at any time is essentially independent of the changes that have occurred to that point. The *trajectory* of the time series is forever altered by a permanent shock.

Permanent change in this sense is to be contrasted with a "transitory" change. Such a change is temporary and wears off, as it were, with the underlying series eventually reverting back to the point on the long-run path it would have reached had the original transitory disturbance never occurred. Bubbles, if they existed, would be transitory components in this sense. Or to put it the other way around, without convincing evidence of transitory, that is to say, stationary components in stock prices, it is hard to build a strong positive case for the existence of bubbles.

Until recently, virtually all research on stock prices had tended to support the nonstationary or permanent change view of stock prices.

The statistical tests being used, however, were under increasing critical attacks on grounds of "low power," that is to say, of being unable to discriminate adequately between series that are truly nonstationary and those that are stationary, but only just barely. Part of the concern with those early tests was their tendency to focus on price changes or returns over fairly short intervals such as days or months. It was not that returns over longer intervals such as a year, or five years or a decade, were uninteresting. But the statisticians need large numbers of price changes or returns as raw material for their tests, and there weren't enough separate ten-year or even five-year return intervals in the databases (the leading one of which starts only in 1926) to constitute the statistical equivalence of a quorum.

Technological innovation did occur in the early 1980s, however, in the form of procedures that would work with "overlapping" intervals, and thus greatly enlarge the usable sample of long-period returns. In the sixty years between 1926 and 1986 there are only six separate, non-overlapping ten-year returns. But even taken a full year apart, there are fifty overlapping ten-year returns (years one to ten, two to eleven, three to twelve, and so on) and more yet if taken a month apart.

The results obtained with the new procedures did seem to show, for the first time, strong indications of what could be interpreted as temporary or transitory components of returns particularly in the interesting, but hitherto neglected, three-to-five-year return interval. (See especially Fama and French, 1986, and Poterba and Summers, 1987; for similar results using related but somewhat different methods, see Lo and Mackinlay, 1987.) But the extent to which these findings can support the case for bubbles still remains very much in dispute. Some have argued that the seeming departures from nonstationarity detected by the new procedures, properly calibrated, may not really be larger than what might plausibly be expected from pure chance alone (see Richardson, 1988). Even more to the point, Fama and French (1986), themselves among the pioneers of the new methods, are careful to warn that other, nonbubble interpretations exist for the seemingly transitory components of returns that their research has uncovered. The patterns may reflect not so much drifts away from and then back to the fundamentals, as changes over time in the returns expected on stocks as the economy itself swings between prosperity and recession. A recent paper by Kim, Nelson and Startz (1988) suggests, in fact, that the transitory components may be reflecting nothing more than the huge up-and-down swings imposed on both stock prices and the US economy by the Great Depression of the 1930s. They find no substantial transitory components in the forty-year postwar period 1946-86.

Was the Pre-Crash Buildup a Bubble Driven by a Liquidity Illusion?

Whatever the outcome of the wide-ranging statistical search for bubbles in general, many observers remain convinced that the pre-crash buildup, particularly in the USA, was not driven by the fundamentals, but traces to the systematic misperception that equities were a more liquid and hence a lower-risk investment than they proved to be or could possibly be. A similar view had been advanced earlier about the pre-1929 buildup, notably by J. M. Keynes in a famous chapter of his *General Theory* (1936). Liquidity, according to Keynes, offers a classic example of the fallacy of composition: what is true for a part is not necessarily true for the whole. The ability to reverse positions and get out quickly vanishes when everyone tries to do it at once. That the US stock market was indeed being perceived as more liquid, at least in the small, is seen in the steady rise in turnover rates through the 1980s, approaching–though still remaining below–levels not seen since the 1920s. The rise reflects, in large part, the steadily increasing role played by institutional investors, particularly pension funds. Such investors can be expected to trade more actively than ordinary individual investors because their costs of doing so are substantially lower, especially so since the ending of fixed brokerage commissions in the early 1970s. Transaction costs were further reduced by an order of magnitude, at least for trades in "baskets" of stocks, by the introduction in 1982 of futures markets for stock indexes. These highly liquid futures, and especially their use in a portfolio management strategy known as portfolio insurance, have widely been held responsible for creating the liquidity illusion and the unstable price runup it fostered.

Putting a major share of the blame on portfolio insurance for creating and overinflating a liquidity bubble in 1987 is fashionable, but not easy to square with all the relevant facts. For one thing, the orders of magnitude seem out of line. The conventional estimates place the total value of pension fund assets under portfolio insurance at the time of the Crash at $90 to $100 billion. But not all of those assets were in equities. Pension funds typically keep the equity proportion between 40 and 60 percent of the total with the rest in bonds and real estate. It is entirely plausible that the seeming added protection of portfolio insurance might have led them to shift their equity proportions to the high side of the customary range. If so, we are talking about $10 to $20 billion of added demand for equities, spread out over a period of many months. Yet, between January 1987 and August 1987 the value of US equities increased by more than half a trillion dollars. No study of price-quantity responses of stock prices to date supports the notion that so large a price increase (about 30 percent) would be required to absorb so modest (1 to 2 percent) a net addition to the demand for shares.

Even more telling, we know that portfolio insurance, for all its notoriety, was almost entirely a US phenomenon in 1986 and 1987. Yet, virtually every equity market in the world rose over that interval, some by substantially more than the US market. Some of this world-wide rise may well have been just a reflection of the US rise. The equity markets of the world are surely linked, but the coupling is far from tight. In fact, as Roll (1988) points out, October 1987 is the only month in which all the world's stock markets moved in the same direction!

Does the Absence of Major Bad News Imply that a Bubble Must Have Burst?

Many who regard the 1987 episode as a bubble might still accept the view offered here that the positive evidence in the data suggestive of bubbles, rational or irrational, is far from compelling. They would state their case for their bubble interpretation, rather, in the form of a question: with no commensurate bad news being reported, what else but a bursting bubble could account for a one-day fall of more than 20 percent? And, indeed, it must be conceded that no such catastrophic news event did occur, nor is it even easy to imagine any single news item, short of the outbreak of nuclear war, that might have justified a fall of that magnitude. But–and it is important to keep this in mind–the relation between news and market valuations is far less simple and direct than that seemingly crushing rhetorical question tries to suggest.

The question seems so devastating partly because we have become so accustomed to thinking and talking about valuation in terms of short-hand expressions like price/earnings ratios or dividend yields relating prices to current, and sometimes even past, levels of the presumed cash-flow fundamentals. But the relevant fundamentals governing today's prices are the anticipated cash flows far into the distant and highly uncertain future. Given the natural and substantial momentum in any economy, the task of projecting dividends, say, with reasonable accuracy for one, two or in some industries perhaps even five years ahead may not seem beyond the econometrician's art. Remember, however, that in the summer of 1987, with dividend yields averaging 3 percent, even five years projected dividends for the typical stock would have represented less than half the value of the typical share. The remaining half would necessarily have rested on the much more problematic projections of long-term growth rates for dividends far out into the future.

Even those who work frequently with such projections sometimes seem to forget how sensitive our highly nonlinear valuation formulas can be to small changes in anticipated growth rates. Suppose, for example, that the appropriately risk-adjusted discount rate for a company's dividends were 10 percent and that the current dividend was expected to grow for the indefinite future at a rate of 7 percent per year. (Needless to say, these numbers are for illustrative purposes only.) Ignoring taxes and other real-world complications, the share would have a warranted value of thirty-three times the current dividend.

Suppose now that the market lowers that dividend growth projection merely by half a percentage point to 6.5 percent; and, at the same time, the market comes to see the stock as riskier and raises its appropriate discount rate again by a mere half percentage point to 10.5

percent. Then even without the bad news of an actual cut in the current dividend, the warranted price of the share would fall to twenty-five times the current dividend–a drop of 24 percent! Note, moreover, that a rise in the risk-adjusted discount rate from 10 to 11 percent could have produced the same price fall with no change whatever in the projected mean growth rate of dividends.

Revisions in risk allowances and/or in long-run growth projections can be triggered by what might well, in other circumstances, be considered only trivial changes in the immediate objective conditions. That point was made more than twenty years ago in a brilliant, but neglected, paper by the French mathematician and statistician, Benoit Mandelbrot, one of the early pioneers in the statistical analysis of "speculative prices" though now perhaps better known as the originator of "fractal geometry." (See Mandelbrot, 1966, and also his earlier and very influential paper, 1963.) The kind of scenario modeled by Mandelbrot in 1966 was dramatically recalled to our attention during the great drought of 1988 in the US Midwest. As the summer wore on and the drought persisted, the prices of corn and soybeans rose each day for many days in succession. Suddenly, one day a slight sprinkling of rain occurred, hardly enough to make up even one past day's lost rainfall. Yet the prices of corn and soybeans dropped dramatically.

Was this rapid readjustment a sign that the prices before the fall had been driven up by irrational buyers in bubble-like fashion to absurd and unsustainable levels? Or that panicky speculators had overreacted to events on both the way up and the way down? Not at all. The rapid readjustment signifies only that farmers and other knowledgeable participants in these markets recognize that weather patterns tend to be persistent. Each day, as the drought lasted, the market took account not just of that day's rainfall deficiency, but of the deficiencies likely to occur on the next day, and on the days after that as well if the weather pattern causing the drought continued. When the pattern of persistent drought was broken, however, even though only by a small amount, the market had to make a substantial revision in its estimate of the likely future supply of corn and soybeans to be available at harvest time: it had both to remove the influence of the continuing weather pattern of future drought it had been projecting, and also to allow for the possibility of making up some of the past deficiency should the current sprinkle be a harbinger of a new pattern of persistent rainy weather for the rest of the growing season.

Although the relevance for pricing of persistence (and interruption) in environmental patterns is most easily visualized in terms of weather and climate–which is surely why Mandelbrot used an agricultural example for his model–the political and economic climate can play an analogous role in the valuation of assets such as equities or real estate. That point, surely, hardly needs emphasis to those who have somehow managed, like me, to live through the Roaring Twenties, the Hungry Thirties, the Wartime Forties, the Eisenhower Fifties, the Vietnam Sixties, the Oil Shock Seventies and the Reagan Eighties. In virtually every one of those eras occasions arose when US equities were subject to major revaluations in response to perceived changes in the persistent economic and political climate (and not always on the downside by any means).

If the Mandelbrot climate-persistence model is the applicable one, the long-sought missing "fundamental" explanation for the Crash of 1987 may thus come down to nothing more than this: on October 19, after some weeks of external events, minor in themselves, but that cumulatively may have signalled a possible change in what had been up to then a very favorable political and economic climate for equities in the USA and other countries as well, many investors simultaneously, and based on the same information, came to believe that they were holding too large a share of their wealth in risky equities and too little in safer instruments such as government bonds. Alternatively, as my colleague Andrei Shleifer might prefer to put it, and as the sharp rise in volatility at the time of the Crash seems to confirm, they came to believe that equities had become a much riskier investment relative to bonds than they had hitherto been assuming. With aggregate supplies of each type of security largely fixed in the short run, that desired shift in portfolio proportions could come about only by changing the prices in the two markets.

In principle, instantaneous changes in price quotes of this kind in the two markets might actually have brought about the desired switch in portfolio proportions with little or no increase in turnover beyond the normal daily volume, as is often the case in markets, such as commercial real estate or farm land. In markets organized as centralized exchanges, however, with specialized market makers and with posted bids and offers for continuous trading, transactions typically play a more conspicuous role in establishing and confirming the new value level. In fact, even after most outsiders have become aware of the general change in sentiment that has taken place, the very presence of market makers supposedly, and sometimes actually, charged with stabilizing prices tends to give outsiders the impression, false for the group of outsiders as a whole, but not necessarily so for some as individuals, that they can still execute their own trades at prices better than they will obtain in the new equilibrium.

Since the stakes are high and since no one can be sure of not being one of the lucky winners, the result is often a frantic surge of attempted transactions–a "rational panic" as someone has so aptly dubbed it– strikingly similar, in many respects, to what seemed to have been occurring in so many stock exchanges and related centralized markets around the world on October 19 and 20.

Bubble or Fundamental: Does It Really Matter?

Mandelbrot's "climate-shift" model, working through either growth rates or risk-adjusted discount rates and acted out in the context of a centralized exchange market, can thus offer a coherent line of "fundamental" interpretation of the 1987 episode alternative to the psychological bubble or speculative-excess view of the Crash. There is no claim here, of course, that a strong positive case for this alternative interpretation has, in fact, been established; but, as should be clear from the discussion in the earlier sections, neither has such a case been established for the opposite, bubble view. Here, as all too often in economics–witness disputes over the US budget deficit–we are faced with competing theories that can seemingly account for the same facts and we have no way of conducting decisive experiments that can distinguish between them.

Since the Crash was a historical episode, already beginning to fade from memory, the general public may well wonder whether the choice between these contending views of it really matters much outside academia. But, as Keynes himself noted in the famous passage that closes the *General Theory*, the views of academic economists do have an impact on a nation's lawmakers, and through them on very practical matters indeed. Many very sweeping proposals for the further regulation– some might even say strangulation–of financial markets did in fact surface in the wake of the Crash, most tracing their intellectual origins back to some variant of the bubble theory. Nor has the "reform" movement run its course. It is important, therefore, to weigh carefully the real policy implications of the two contending views of the nature of the Crash.

Bubble and Fundamentals: the Policy Issues

For many who see the Crash of 1987 as merely the latest in a long series of bursting stock exchange speculative bubbles, the natural remedy seems to lie in curbing the public's speculative ardor by making it more costly for them to trade. As J. M. Keynes, the patron saint of the bubble theorists, put it: "It is usually agreed that casinos should, in the public interest, be inaccessible and expensive. And perhaps the same is true of Stock Exchanges." (See Keynes, 1935, p. 159.) Higher margin requirements for stock purchases (and for futures and options where they exist) are one way of raising the costs of trading; but for most governments taxes are an even better way since they also bring in revenue. Hence the turnover tax recently imposed in Sweden and the stiff capital gains taxes recently introduced in certain other countries.

Aside from the added revenues, what are the specific social benefits presumed to flow from these punitive levies on trading? Some, like Keynes himself, stress that the activities of the individual traders vastly complicate the already difficult task of guiding society's capital resources to their highest and best uses. Others, particularly legislators, tend to focus on the aftermath of the crash phase itself, pointing to the loss of confidence it engenders not only in the stock market but in the political and financial institutions of any society that tolerates such sudden and massive destruction of private wealth. Nor, bubble theorists would argue, can the damage always be limited to the wealth of the feckless stock market speculators whose greed and unrealistic expectations fueled the boom. Crash-related stock market losses that undermine the solvency of major investment banks and brokerage firms are quickly communicated to their commercial bank creditors and can cascade from there into a full-blown financial panic and economic contraction.

These presumed benefits from imposing heavy tax penalties on trading to restrain speculative buildups–and let it be noted here again that there is no scientific evidence that compels us to believe in psychological bubbles–do not come free, however. The taxes designed to drive out those trading on mere "noise" must also serve to slow the rate at which even valid new information gets incorporated into prices. How, after all, is the tax collector to know which is which? The reduced liquidity of the stock market under a heavy transactions tax, which is likely to be further reinforced these days, as the recent Swedish experience confirms, by the elimination of market makers and the partly consequent drying up of "hedge" instruments such as futures and options, materially decreases the attractiveness of equity capital as a portfolio investment for individuals, and hence, in turn, as a source of funds for corporations.

So damaging to an economy's long-term health and growth potential are these side effects of transactions taxes likely to be that by the end of his famous Chapter 12, even so convinced a bubble theorist as J. M. Keynes was led essentially to reject the very case for a transactions tax that he himself had tentatively proposed earlier in the chapter. Since the weighty name of Keynes is invoked so often these days by supporters of such taxes, it may be worthwhile to quote the relevant passage in its entirety:

> The spectacle of modern investment markets has sometimes moved me towards the conclusion that to make the purchase of investment per-

manent and indissoluble, like marriage, except by reason of death or other grave cause, might be a useful remedy for our contemporary evils. For this would force the investor to direct his mind to the long-term prospects and to those only. But a little consideration of this expedient brings us up against a dilemma and shows us how the liquidity of investment markets often facilitates, though it sometimes impedes, the course of new investment. For the fact that each individual investor flatters himself that his investment is "liquid" (though this cannot be true for all investors collectively) calms his nerves and makes him much more willing to run a risk. If individual purchases of investments were rendered illiquid, this might seriously impede new investments so long as *alternative ways* in which to hold his savings are available to the individual. This is the dilemma. So long as it is open to the individual to employ his wealth in hoarding or lending money the alternative of purchasing actual capital assets cannot be rendered sufficiently attractive (especially to the man who does not manage the capital assets and knows very little about them) except by organizing markets wherein these assets can be easily realized for money. (Keynes, 1935, pp. 160-1; italics in the original.)

Keynes's endorsement of liquid markets, grudging as it sometimes seems to be, has particular relevance for policymakers in the Pacific Basin countries. These are countries, after all, that cannot hope to raise living standards by exploiting vast mineral resources and that cannot offer domestic investors the prospects of huge and protected consumer markets. They must rely entirely on the industry and frugality of their citizens and especially on the ability of their entrepreneurs to channel the local labor and capital resources into productive enterprises serving worldwide markets and facing worldwide competition. Transactions taxes that undermine the liquidity of their local stock markets and that add thereby to the already high risks of domestic firms facing international competition encourage local investors to seek more liquid havens abroad. Local enterprises are put at a further disadvantage *vis-à-vis* their foreign competitors who can obtain the necessary risk capital for new ventures on more favorable terms in liquid capital markets overseas.

Some economists and policymakers in the Pacific Basin countries might nevertheless be prepared (like those who have imposed transactions taxes in Sweden, and are calling for them currently in the USA) to accept the adverse consequences of transactions taxes as the inevitable price of averting market catastrophes like those of October 1987.

They would destroy the markets to save the economy, as it were, to invoke a phrase reminiscent of some failed policies in another sphere. I would argue, however, that the wiser and ultimately more conservative policy, even for those who still believe in bubbles, is not to seek to prevent stock market crashes at all costs, but, if one does occur, to localize any damage and keep it from spreading to other sectors of the economy.

The Crash of 1987, despite its huge size and despite the dire predictions at the time, did not drag the economy down with it. That it did not is a tribute not to wise policy actions by US legislators and regulators (though the Federal Reserve System, to its great credit, did act quickly to maintain the liquidity of the banking system) but to the enormous capacity and resiliency of US financial institutions. They held, though in some cases just barely, despite the almost complete absence of prior contingency planning on the part of the exchanges, the banks or the regulatory authorities for so massive a price break and volume of orders. Much of this hitherto neglected contingency planning has since been undertaken by the major players and more pressure-release safety valves, such as coordinated "circuit breakers" and intermarket cross-margining are being put in place.

It would be ironic indeed, though by no means unprecedented in history, to impose new liquidity-destroying taxes and regulations on our capital markets even while the presumed case for them, never terribly strong, is growing weaker.

This chapter is based on a keynote address presented at the First Annual Pacific-Basin Finance Conference in Taipei, Taiwan, March 11-12, 1989. Thanks for helpful comments are owed to my colleagues George Constantinides and Andrei Shleifer.

References

Barro, Robert J. "The Stock Market and the Macroeconomy: Implications of the October 1987 Crash." In *Black Monday and the Future of Financial Markets*, R. W. Kamphuis, R. C. Kormendi, and J. W. H. Watson (eds), Chicago: Dow Jones Irwin, 1988.

Brown, Keith C., W. V. Harlow and Seha M. Tinic. "Risk Aversion, Uncertain Information and Market Efficiency." *Journal of Financial Economics*, 1989.

Chan, K. C. "On the Contrarian Investment Strategy." *Journal of Business*, 62, 2, April, 1988, 147-63.

De Bondt, Werner, and Richard Thaler. "Does the Stock Market Overreact." *Journal of Finance*, July, 1985.

Durlauf, Steven N., and Peter C. B. Phillips. "Trends versus Random Walks in Time Series Analysis." *Econometrica*, November, 1988.

Fama, Eugene, and Kenneth French. "Permanent and Transitory Components of Stock Prices." *Journal of Political Economy*, 96.

Fischer, Stanley, and Robert C. Merton. "Macroeconomics and Finance: The Role of the Stock Market" in *Essays on Macroeconomic Implications of Financial and Labor Markets and Political Processes*, K. Bruner and A. Meltzer (eds), Carnegie-Rochester Conference Series on Public Policy, Vol. 21, Autumn, 1984.

Garber, Peter M. "Who Put the Mania in Tulip Mania?" A paper presented at the Conference on Crashes and Panics in Historical Perspective, New York University, October 19, 1988.

Greenspan, Alan. "The Crash of October 1987 14 Months Later." Remarks before a Joint Meeting of the American Economic Association and the American Finance Association, mimeographed, New York, NY, December 28, 1988.

Keynes, John Maynard. *The General Theory of Employment, Interest and Money*. New York: Harcourt, Brace and Co., 1935.

Kim, Myung Jig, Charles R. Nelson and Richard Startz. "Mean Reversion in Stock Prices? A Reappraisal of the Empirical Evidence." University of Washington, November 21, 1988.

Kleidon, Allan W. "Stock Prices and Rational Forecasters of Future Cash Flows." Ph.D. Dissertation, University of Chicago, 1983.

Lo, Andrew, and Craig Mackinlay. "Stock Prices Do Not Follow Random Walks: Evidence from a Simple Specification." Wharton Business School, University of Pennsylvania, February, 1987.

Mandelbrot, Benoit. "Forecasts of Future Prices, Unbiased Markets and 'Martingale' Models." *Journal of Buisiness*, January, 1966.

_____ "The Variation of Certain Speculative Prices." *Journal of Business*, October, 1963.

Poterba, James, and Lawrence Summers. "Mean Reversion in Stock Prices: Evidence and Implications." NBER Working Paper, August, 1987.

Richardson, Matthew. "Temporary Components of Stock Prices: A Skeptic's View." Stanford University, Graduate School of Business, November, 1988.

Roll, Richard W. "The International Crash of October 1987" in *Black Monday and the Future of Financial Markets*, R. W. Kamphuis, R. C. Kormendi, and J. W. H. Watson (eds), Chicago: Dow Jones Irwin, 1988.

Shiller, Robert. "Do Stock Prices Move Too Much to be Justified by Subsequent Changes in Dividends?" *American Economic Review*, June, 1981.

7 Equilibrium Relations Between Cash Markets and Futures Markets

The organizers of this conference asked me to speak on "the determinants of equilibrium relations between cash, futures and options markets." They actually said "between cash and derivative markets," but derivative, in this context, is a term I cannot bring myself to use. The phrase derivative products, somewhat like the term "junk bonds," seems to carry a pejorative connotation as if contrasting the "real" stock market in New York with the parasitical options and futures "casinos" in Chicago.

Strictly speaking, of course, the valuation functions for futures and options do contain the spot stock prices as arguments; and to that purely definitional extent they can be said to be derivative. But, as a practical matter these days, thanks partly to their lower transaction costs, the true prices of equities are often set first–or, perhaps better, "discovered" first–in the index futures and options markets, and not in the stock market. Properly understood, this seeming lead of index futures and options prices over stock prices is no cause for concern. But when the lead appears to be large and growing, as was the case on the fateful Crash day of October 19, 1987, the futures and options markets will inevitably be blamed for the disaster. Potential users (and regulators) of the proposed new Deutsche Terminboerse must, therefore, understand both the normal price relations between the two types of markets and the real source of the intermarket anomalies that arose when the US markets faced extraordinary selling pressures as those on October 19, 1987.

One terminological note before proceeding: for ease of exposition, I will speak not of index futures and options markets, but simply of index futures markets. Much of my description of index futures arbitrage applies with equal force to index options, but the intermarket equilibrium that drives the arbitrage is more easily seen for futures.

The Cost-of-Carry Formula

The sometimes troublesome relations between stock indexes and index futures are best approached by first reviewing the essentially similar, but more familiar, connections between the spot prices for physical commodities, like soybeans or gold, and the prices for deferred or forward delivery of those commodities. The two sets of prices must be related, of course, because spot transactions and forward transactions are simply two alternative, and hence substitute, ways of accomplishing the same objective.

If you need soybeans for processing at the end of ninety days, you may enter an agreement today to purchase 5,000 bushels of soybeans for delivery at a price, say, of $7.40 a bushel. Or, you may buy 5,000 bushels of No. 1, yellow, Central Illinois soybeans now for a spot price, p, of $7.35 per bushel and store them on your premises or in a grain elevator for 90 days. The spot purchase at $7.35/bushel may look cheaper at first sight, but you will have storage bills and insurance to pay; and to come up with the $36,750 purchase price for the beans, you will either have to borrow $36,750 or reduce your earning assets by that amount. On the other hand, if you store the beans, you may avoid some costs of possibly running out of your regular inventory before the ninety days are up and having to pay extra for emergency deliveries.

Given these costs and benefits of the storage approach, we can always define a break-even forward price which will leave you as a potential soybean buyer just indifferent between purchasing spot or forward. In symbols, the break-even forward price, f^*, can be expressed in the simplest possible way as

$$f^* = p(1 + r + s - y) \tag{1}$$

where r = the cumulated interest bill over the ninety days, s = the cumulated ninety-day storage cost, and y = the cumulated value of any convenience yield on the inventory during the storage period. (Precisely how these elements are to be computed must be left for another occasion. The concern here is with general strategy, not precise tactics.)

Note that, in general, $f*$ will differ from p and that difference is known in the trade, for some reason, as the "basis." The basis is usually a positive number, but it need not be. It can become negative when the convenience yield is high, typically when the spot commodity is in very short supply.

Arbitrage and Transaction Costs

The cost-of-carry formula of equation (1) tells us only the break-even forward price for a presumptive soybean buyer. The actual forward price may differ from its break-even value, but not arbitrarily so. If the forward price were to rise substantially above $f*$, soybean buyers would find it profitable to become sellers of forward contracts in soybeans. In terms of our earlier illustrative numbers, suppose that the break-even forward price were $7.38 when the current spot price was $7.35, implying that $(1 + r + s - y) = 1.004$. If the forward price were $7.40 per bushel then, transaction costs aside, you could make a sure profit of $100 on each contract $[5,000 \times (7.40 - 7.38)]$ by selling it forward at $7.40, buying 5,000 bushels of spot beans at $7.35 per bushel and storing them for ninety days at a total net storage cost of $0.03 per bushel ($0.004 \times 7.35$). Such a transaction would involve no risk. Whatever the spot price may happen to be in ninety days you are committed only to the delivery of 5,000 bushels at $7.40; and your stored beans can always be used to satisfy that obligation.

Transaction costs, alas, can be set aside only in classroom illustrations or in brokers' advertisements. In the real world, they have to be paid and they force us to supplement simple equations like (1) with weak inequalities like

$$f_L = f* - c_L \le f \le f* + c_U = f_U \qquad (2)$$

where c_L is the present value of the commissions and other transaction costs incurred in simultaneously buying a forward contract and selling the spot commodity; c_U, which may in principle differ from c_L, is the present value of transaction costs for a simultaneous sale of forward contract and a purchase of spot commodity, and f_U and f_L are, respectively, the upper and lower "arbitrage bounds," in the sense that prices for forward contracts beyond those bounds would create sure profit opportunities for any trader whose transaction costs for simultaneous trades in the spot and forward markets were no than c_L or c_U.

Because the arbitrage transactions would tend to slow, and ultimately to reverse, any continued movements of f away from f^*, we can speak of f^* as the "equilibrium" price of forward contracts, though, strictly speaking, we can really say only that f^* lies within the equilibrium range. How important that qualification becomes will depend, of course, on how wide the range is and on how and why the markets are being used. It can become crucially important to anyone intending to use forward transactions for "hedging" the price risk on inventories of the spot commodity. Unless the forward price f closely tracks the break-even price f^*, the presumed hedge from a forward transaction may prove illusory. The contract is said to have too much "basis risk." Failure to track sufficiently closely–that is, arbitrage bounds too wide–has been a main cause of failure for futures contracts. (Futures contracts are basically just standardized and exchange-traded forward contracts, marked to market and settled daily.)

To put it another way, the notion of intermarket equilibrium is more than just a matter of equations. For futures exchanges it can be a matter of life or death. And that is important to keep in mind when you read calls in parts of our financial press for putting an end to index arbitrage program trading. These attacks are not really concerned with arbitrage, which, as we have seen, serves merely to maintain the equilibrium relation between two markets. Arbitrage and program trading are just code words in these attacks. The real targets are the futures exchanges.

Arbitrage and Equilibrium in Index Futures Markets

To show the determinants of intermarket equilibrium for stock index futures requires little more than some slight changes in the notation of previous formulas, plus a brief reference to one conspicuous institutional difference between the contracts for stock index futures and ordinary commodity futures (including most financial futures). Stock index futures must be settled in cash, rather than by physical delivery (subject only to the minor exception of negotiated off-exchange, after-hours exchange for physicals–called EFPs). The settlement or delivery-equivalent price of the S&P 500 contract, the leading index future, was taken originally as the closing index value on the third Friday in the last month of each successive quarter during the year. But fears–largely unfounded, but widely publicized–that the heavy concentration of settlements of futures and options at the close on those days–the so-called triple-witching days–might cause excessive volatility at the close on the NYSE led to moving the settlement from the close to the open, where prices are set by a process closer to a "call auction" than to a continuous market. Open or close, however, the import of cash settlement is the same. Arbitrage positions can be unwound at settlement with no slippage whatever. Both cash index and futures contract must have exactly the same value at that end point, no matter how far they may have diverged from each other before then.

As for the break-even value of an index future, equation (1) continues to apply with some straightforward reinterpretations. The storage cost term for stocks can safely be set to zero; and rather than a "convenience yield," the holder of the spot stocks would earn a dividend yield, d. Thus, taking all terms as known in advance, we can restate equation (1) as just

$$f^* = p(1+r-d) \tag{3}$$

Note that since interest rates normally exceed dividend yields, the basis in stock index futures is normally positive. For concreteness, suppose the S&P 500 index stands at 300; that ninety-day interest rates are at 8 percent on an annual basis; and that the dividend yield on the index stocks over the next ninety days can be taken as 3.5 percent, again, on an annual basis. Then the breakeven value of a ninety-day index futures contract would be

$$(300)\left(1+(0.08-0.035)\frac{90}{360}\right)=f^*=303.375 \qquad (4)$$

The basis would thus be 3.375 index points, or about 1 percent of the index value.

Equation (2), describing the arbitrage bounds around the cost-of-carry commodity futures price, will also apply to stock index futures; and, in fact, we can get some feel for the likely minimum size of the range from current average commission rates. Institutional customers might expect to pay commissions of 0.05 per share on an average share of $40 so that an arbitrage round trip would come to 0.25 percent. Commissions on the futures, plus the opportunity and handling costs of futures margins, might come to perhaps $25 on a contract with a face value of $150,000, or about 0.02 percent. (Note how much lower the commissions are for futures than for trading the stocks separately.) Combining these costs, we would expect to find no profitable arbitrage opportunities until futures prices had drifted at least 0.252 percent away from their warranted prices in either direction. In terms of the specific numbers for r, d and p used in (4), the range would thus be about 0.81 index points on either side of the break-even price 303.375 or from 304.185 on the upside to 302.565 on the downside.

Let me emphasize again that these are minimum ranges. They make no allowance for the bid-ask spread, for possible market impact costs of the orders or for any additional slippage that might arise from the lack of perfect simultaneity in the execution of the orders. At the time of the Crash, these added market-impact costs were conventionally reckoned at about 0.2 index points, making the range about 1.0 index point on each side. Because the current, post-Crash markets are less liquid, the conventional arbitrage limits now are somewhat higher, perhaps 1.15 to 1.2 index points each way.

Arbitrage and Intermarket Equilibrium During the Crash

So much for the simple mechanics of intermarket equilibrium between index futures and the underlying cash market. With that as background let me turn now to the unfortunate episode of October 19, 1987, when the equilibration mechanism seemed to have broken down completely.

As a benchmark of success against which to calibrate the failures on October 19, I have selected the performance of the markets on October 14, 1987, five days before the Crash. I chose that Wednesday not because it was a normal or uneventful day; it was, in fact, a highly stressful day with the index falling by 3 percent (equivalent then to a fall of about 75 points in the Dow Jones metric). Yet intermarket equilibrium was for the most part successfully maintained. Index arbitrage is not something that needs calm waters to work successfully.

Figure 7.1 shows the path during the day of both the S&P 500 index (solid line) and the S&P 500 December futures contract. Note that the futures series tracked the spot index closely and that the basis maintained its normal positive value through the entire day, except for two brief intervals, one at the open and one at the close.

To focus more directly on those episodes, figure 7.2 shows the deviation of the actual futures price during the day from its break-even or cost-of-carry price, represented by the horizontal line through zero. The width of the arbitrage band has been set at its then common rule-of-thumb value of ±1 S&P points and that range, as can be seen, appears a reasonably accurate approximation. The futures price lies within the band most of the day, though, on several occasions in midsession, selling pressure appears to have driven the price through the lower bound.

The sharp price reversals subsequent to these break-through points are a sign of arbitrage buying of futures (with an offsetting selling leg taking place in the spot market). There may even perhaps have been some upside arbitrage in the 2:00-2:30 p.m. CST interval, though it would probably require a special research study to establish that fact. Despite all the hue and cry about program trading, the NYSE has only relatively recently been compiling regular data on program trading activity.

Even without detailed scrutiny of the trading records, however, we can be reasonably sure that nobody made great profits by "arbitraging" out the seemingly huge three-point (1 percent) discount of the futures price below its lower arbitrage bound at the open. Gaps of that size or even larger can occur at the opens and are partly responsible for the widespread folk belief in the USA that the "derivative" market often acts as the Judas-goat that leads the "true" market to disaster. And who can blame them for so concluding? After all, the futures price did open substantially below the index; and prices in both markets did fall substantially by the end of the day. *Post hoc, ergo propter hoc.*

But the gap at the open, large as it may loom, was almost entirely illusory. The seeming discount traces mainly to the differences in the procedures for conducting the daily opens in the two markets. When the opening bell rings in the futures market, trading begins immediately and the prices reported out of the trading pit are the actual current transaction prices. If a large flow of sell orders has accumulated overnight, as was the case on October 14 in both markets, then the first transactions in futures just after the bell are likely to be at prices substantially below the previous day's close. On the NYSE, however, the franchised broker-dealers known as "specialists" have an "affirmative obligation" to avoid large gaps in the sequence of successive prices.

When such a gap threatens to appear at the opening of trading the specialist can delay the start of trading while he spreads word of the order imbalance to other market makers on the floor and in the upstairs trading rooms. During this interval of delayed opening, normally just a matter of a few minutes, the prices used by the information purveyors for computing the value of the S&P and similar indexes will be the most recent transaction price of each share. For stocks with delayed opening, that will be the closing price from the previous day. Thus, when widespread overnight selling pressure appears, as it did on October 14, many stocks in the index will have delayed openings simultaneously, and the computed index, based in large part on the previous day's close, will inevitably lag behind the more up-to-date quotes in the futures market.

The previous closing price on the NYSE, moreover, may itself be lagging, when the specialist, to create the appearance of gapless price continuity, makes offsetting adjustments in his own inventory in the face of a sudden and unexpected imbalance of orders as the trading day is drawing to a close. Something very much like that seems to have been happening at the close on October 14 and, also–though less dramatically, at several other points during the day.

Intense as the intermarket stresses were on October 14, they paled in comparison to what happened on October 19. Figure 7.3 shows the path of futures and spot prices during the day. Note first the opening discount–not a mere four points this time, but a huge twenty-two points, or close to 8 percent of the spot price. Once again, delayed openings of shares on the NYSE were primarily responsible for the appearance of a gap. The delays on October 19 were unusually large both in number and duration. One hour after the opening bell, in fact, fully one-third of the shares in the Dow Jones Index had yet to begin trading, including such bellwether stocks as IBM, Exxon and Sears. By 10:30 a.m. CST, an hour and a half after the opening, some semblance of order had been restored and the two markets were close to their equilibrium relations to one another, though clearly at a level substantially below that of the previous day.

Had the day ended at that point, it would still have been remembered as one of the worst ever recorded. But even worse was yet to come. Somewhere around 11:00 a.m. CST the bottom seemed to fall out and both series dropped steadily thereafter for the rest of that very trying day.

Unlike the down-drift on October 14, however, the futures price on October 19 remained at a substantial and steadily widening discount to the cash market for the remainder of the day. The two markets had become essentially disconnected as can be seen from the arbitrage bounds shown in figure 7.4.

Precisely why the normal arbitrage mechanisms broke down on that day is still a matter of dispute, sometimes acrimonious, between the various exchanges; and between them, their regulators and the many investigating commissions appointed in the wake of the crash. I do not propose here, however, to review these controversies in detail. I want to look forward, not back. I leave it to future historians to sift through and evaluate the possible explanations. But I am not confident that the job will be done soon. We still do not have a fully coherent account of the Crash of October 1929, after all. And historians are only just now beginning to understand the so-called "tulip bubble" in seventeenth century Holland!

Intermarket Equilibrium in the Future

Of more immediate concern than what may have shattered the inter-market equilibrium of October 19 is whether the episode is likely to be repeated in the near future; and, if so, what can or should be done to prevent it. My own view is that the markets are unlikely to de-couple again in the reasonably near future if only because the communication and processing capacity of the NYSE has been so much enhanced over the past two years. The threshold for a brown-out or black-out has been substantially raised at a time when the daily transaction volume still remains well below levels reached in the months before the crash.

For other countries, such as Germany, significant de-coupling of the spot and futures markets, like that on October 19, 1987, in the USA, is unlikely to occur even without a large protective buffer of overcapacity. The de-coupling pressure in the USA comes mainly from the differences in market structure in the spot and futures markets and especially from the previously noted policy of the NYSE and its franchised specialists of minimizing gaps and discontinuities in the price series. Whatever the presumed benefits of such a policy–and I, for one, see no overwhelm-ing *social* benefits, though there may well be substantial *private* benefits to the retail brokerage industry and to the NYSE specialists– these efforts to maintain continuity mean that when big news becomes public, the prices on the NYSE will inevitably be lagging behind "reality" in the more freely moving futures market. In a universe as parochial as Wall Street, of course, that sequence of events will be seen not as stocks lagging the news, but as program trading from the "derivatives" leading the stocks!

More is involved here, however, than just a misperception of the true direction of causality. The valiant intervention efforts by NYSE specialists to preserve price continuity can actually intensify transaction flows including arbitrage-driven orders. When major bad news strikes suddenly–including news that many others are planning to sell–everyone knows the currently quoted prices are stale. Many will thus rush to get their sales executed while the specialist is still walking the price down to its new equilibrium tick by tick, and before any slower moving potential buyers have pulled their resting limit orders from the specialist's book. Note that these periodic sudden transaction surges are endemic to the NYSE system–indeed, to any system that seeks to "stabilize" prices–and not to the relatively recent presence of index futures markets or arbitrage activities.

The seeming increased frequency of such surges in recent years stems from the substantial drop in commissions on stock transactions since the early 1970s. At current commission rates, it takes a lot less "news" than it once did to make resting prices stale. Even so, the quantitative importance of program trading should not be exaggerated. During the great bull market of 1987, program trading accounted for only an average of about 4 percent of the appropriately computed daily volume and never more than 20 percent on any day.

Because the market structures in Germany are so different from those in the USA, transaction surges, whether specifically from arbitrage program trading or of a more general origin, are likely to be much smaller and less frequent. With order-matching, screen-trading systems in both the spot and futures markets, prices can move more directly to a new equilibrium when news becomes public without having to be propelled there by a flow of essentially unnecessary arbitrage or other transactions.

Thus, while arbitrage program trading in the USA has come to be called by its detractors the Great White Shark of Wall Street, the appropriate metaphor for Germany must invoke a different and much less frightening imaginary creature. Perhaps, a Small Pink Rheinlachs.

This chapter is based on a paper presented at the Symposium on Financial Futures and Options, Frankfurt, Federal Republic of Germany, June 12, 1989. Thanks for helpful comments are owed my colleague Krishna Ramaswamy.

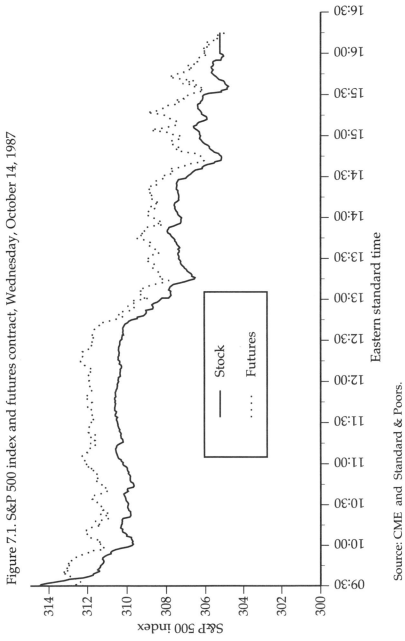

Figure 7.1. S&P 500 index and futures contract, Wednesday, October 14, 1987

Source: CME and Standard & Poors.

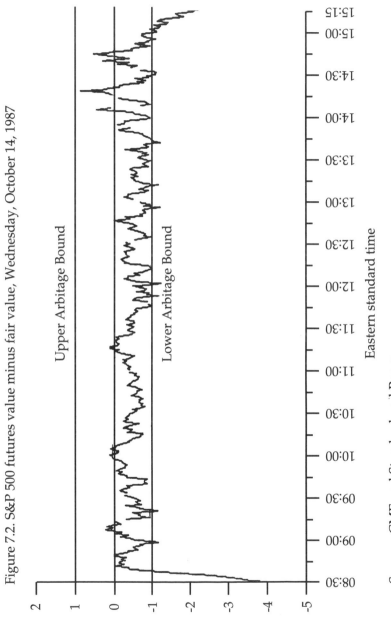

Figure 7.2. S&P 500 futures value minus fair value, Wednesday, October 14, 1987

Source: CME and Standard and Poors.

Figure 7.3. S&P 500 index and futures contract, Monday, October 19, 1987

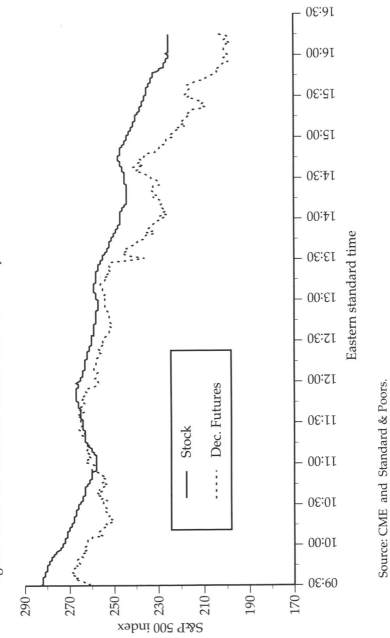

Source: CME and Standard & Poors.

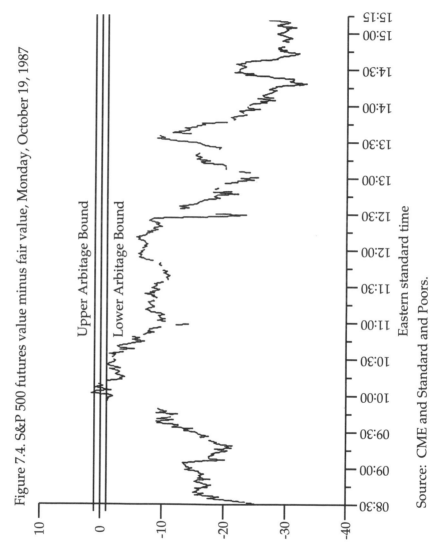

Figure 7.4. S&P 500 futures value minus fair value, Monday, October 19, 1987

Source: CME and Standard and Poors.

Part III

Markets and Volatility: Policy Issues

8 Strategies for Capital Market Structure and Regulation

with Charles W. Upton

In 1988 the Swedish government formed a special commission, with members representing the Swedish securities exchanges, the brokerage industry, investor groups and various governmental regulatory bodies, to review the structure and performance of the Swedish securities markets. Although the Report of the Securities Market Commission had not been presented at the time of this writing, the official terms of reference for the Commission, as well as discussions with Commission members and staff in December 1988, suggested that the Commission would inevitably and understandably focus on the specific issues that have been the subject of particular controversy in Sweden in recent years, such as the governance of the Stockholm Stock Exchange.

While it may well be true, as the great architect Mies Van der Rohe once put it, that "God is in the details," the concentration on the narrow subjects of immediate concern can sometimes lead to neglect of the broader matrix in which they are imbedded. It is all too easy to lose sight of the forest for the trees when the public is presented, as it surely will be, with a long list of controversial policy recommendations on a wide variety of separate topics.

To help bring a broader perspective to the issues and controversies under study by the Securities Market Commission, the Center for Business and Policy Studies asked us to prepare a background paper on the structure and regulation of securities markets, emphasizing matters of strategy rather than tactics, and taking account wherever possible of current international developments and the most recent research findings in finance and economics. Specific Swedish concerns and institutions are not to be neglected, of course; but they are to be treated rather as illustrations of more general propositions about market structure and regulatory policy.

One such general proposition is that securities markets, for all their glamorous history and their crucial role in the savings/investment process, are still just business organizations providing services for a fee. The service they offer is "liquidity," the ability to exchange specific assets such as shares in Volvo Corp. for generalized purchasing power. Like any other valuable service, the provision of liquidity requires the input of considerable labor, capital and other real resources. Unless the owners are adequately compensated for the use of their resources, they will withdraw them from the securities markets and transfer them to other uses. If, on the other hand, the compensation demanded by the providers of liquidity becomes too high, or if the quality of the service is allowed to deteriorate, then the clients will seek alternative arrangements (including, these days, arrangements abroad).

Given these equilibrating mechanisms for the supply of liquidity services by the private sector, what is the point in having additional regulation of the securities markets by the public sector? Regulation, after all, is not free; and even when great care is taken, additional waste is inevitably incurred in attempts to outflank the regulators. The expenditure of these regulatory resources by the state can be justified on economic grounds, in Sweden as elsewhere, only by showing that the private-sector security markets, left to their own devices, are not supplying the socially optimal amount of liquidity. Changing the supply of liquidity services by the private sector is what securities market regulation actually does, though its role is usually described more euphemistically as maintaining "fair and orderly" markets.

Some of the recommendations of the Securities Market Commission may well be liquidity enhancing, reflecting the view that unaided markets provide too little liquidity. Current Swedish regulatory policy, by contrast, clearly rests on the opposite presumption–that unregulated securities markets would supply too much liquidity. The

Swedish transactions tax, for example, which is, of course, a direct tax on liquidity, is the highest in the world by far. That tax, among other things, makes domestic futures markets uneconomic. It has already driven much of the trading in the stocks of large Swedish companies to foreign markets and, if continued now that exchange controls have been lifted, it will eventually do the same for trading in debt instruments. Trading in the stocks of smaller and less widely known Swedish companies is less likely to move abroad, of course, but that does not mean that small companies are unaffected by the displacement of trading. The shrinkage of the Swedish brokerage industry and the drying up of trading volume on all Swedish exchanges means higher transaction costs on all Swedish company shares. Continued imposition of the transactions tax at its present levels thus not only imposes substantial cost penalties on Swedish firms, particularly small firms, in the raising of equity capital, but also sacrifices any chance for Sweden to succeed in the international financial services industry–an industry where its highly educated labor force and its great strengths in electronic communications might have given it some comparative advantage.

The transactions tax is a major, but by no means the only, manifestation in Swedish regulatory policy of the belief that unregulated securities markets lead to too much liquidity. If that belief were to remain the guiding principle of regulatory policy in Sweden, and especially if the transactions tax were to be maintained at anything close to present levels, any technological, liquidity-enhancing proposals of the Securities Market Commission would have only academic significance. They would amount to little more than elaborate seating arrangements for a dinner party that nobody would eventually be attending. We propose, therefore, to begin by re-examining the intellectual basis for the view, widely held in Sweden and many other countries, that unfettered securities markets generate too many transactions that serve no valid social purpose. Our goal is not to establish whether that view is true or false; that issue, like most philosophic disputes in economics, is far too complex to permit so decisive a resolution. Our intention, rather, is to show that the traditional case for what we dub the "casino" view of the stock market, as opposed to the

"information" view, is far less compelling than the economics establishment, including such influential writers as James Tobin (1984),
appears willing to concede. When that task has been accomplished we
turn to issues of market structure and, in particular, to the kinds of externalities, positive and negative, that might justify regulatory intervention. We conclude with some brief observations on alternative
strategies for capital market regulation.

The Social Value of Stock Market Trading: Two Contrasting Views

That at least some of the transactions we observe in the securities
markets produce net social benefits, few would deny. Firms regularly
finance their investments in plant and in working capital by selling
securities to outside investors. Households that directly, or through
savings institutions, hold a substantial portion of their wealth in the
form of corporate securities will sometimes commit additional personal
savings to their investment portfolios and at other times withdraw
their accumulated capital for consumption. Households and financial
institutions may also sometimes rebalance their portfolios in response
to changes in their perceptions of and tastes for risk. Such "life-cycle"
and portfolio-balancing transactions by households and such "primary"
fund-raising transactions by firms represent, however, only a part of
the typical day's volume of trading on the stock exchange. That volume
also includes profit-seeking trades by investors either of shares in individual companies, or–increasingly in recent years, thanks to improvements in the technology of trading–of large assembled blocks of stock.
What, if any, are the presumed social benefits of profit-seeking transactions of this kind?

Two quite different answers to this question have been advanced and
we can refer to them, admittedly with some risk of oversimplification,
as the "casino" view and the "information" view.

The casino view and the information view

The casino view sees the stock market largely as a place where investors place bets on the near future prices of stocks rather than on the
numbers on a roulette wheel or the spots on a pack of cards. The casino

interpretation seems even more apt for futures and options exchanges where the very structure of the contracts traded emphasizes the "zero-sum" nature of the market. Casinos, of course, as suppliers of artificial risks to those with a taste for them, may well have their place in society, though presumably only a small place in a world already amply supplied with naturally occurring hazards. The danger some economists see is that, as socially acceptable casinos, stock markets may actually be too attractive. They may mislead the unsophisticated into believing that stock market speculation offers a better, and certainly a quicker, way to wealth than working or saving.

That short-term trading of stocks (or futures or options) is a risky activity can hardly be denied. Indeed, much of the research thrust of the academic discipline of finance has been precisely to specify the probability distributions of returns from investments in different assets and over various horizons. But those distributions arise in a way fundamentally different from those of a casino. The distributions of returns on risky stock market investments are driven not by the random fall of dice or the spin of a wheel (although it is sometimes convenient in exposition to pretend that such is the case), but by the revelation or disclosure of new information about the underlying value of the security.

The information needed to value securities is not, however, just a mass of computer printout stored in a vault somewhere. Rather than a single objective entity, information, as Hayek (1945) has stressed, consists of millions of subjective bits and pieces scattered over the whole set of economic actors. One key function of secondary trading in the stock market is to aggregate these separate fragments of information. The prospect of speculative profits is the "bribe," so to speak, that society offers investors to speed the incorporation of the dispersed bits of information into prices. Once the information is incorporated, of course, *everyone*, including the uninformed, and not just the successful speculators, benefits from having more accurate prices on which to base decisions.

The size of some of the bribes, however, strikes those holding the casino view as being vastly disproportionate to the values of the resources expended in research. They note that young people in the securities industry sometimes receive compensation that dwarfs not just that of college professors and civil servants, but even that of tennis players! Nor, they argue, is it easy to see what valuable insights about the prospects for IBM or Volvo are being contributed by an army of small retail investors responding to "tips" or to prepackaged advisory services. Still, reply those holding the information view, even the fabled "dentist from Peoria," often taken as the prototypical unsophisticated retail investor, knows at least whether his clients are paying their bills on time; and, while the bulk of the serious information research is provided by professionals, the retail customers, by the fees and commissions they generate, do at least help maintain the critical infrastructure of the industry. The securities exchanges, as noted before and as will be stressed again later, are business organizations. If they cannot support themselves from revenues, then any valuable liquidity and price discovery services they now offer to primary issuers of securities and to life-cycle or risk-management traders would have to be provided in some other way.

This relatively benign view of speculative trading under the information view might have been more easily accepted by some economists brought up in the casino tradition if they had been convinced that the vagaries of individual investor/speculators were just small amounts of random "noise" that would cancel out, leaving the true "signal" to be revealed in the price. Their fear, however, is that the errors are not small and definitely not independent. They may well be correlated across traders, for example, because of transitory "fads"–from whose influences not even sophisticated institutional investors are wholly immune. Errors may also be correlated over time in self-justifying bubbles of ever-rising prices, doomed eventually to collapse. Because of these correlated errors, the casino view fears that the market prices we actually observe may be far from those that would be justified by the "fundamentals." Rather than valid information, the stock market may really be sending out misinformation.

The frenzied stock-market boom of the 1920s, followed by the great Crash of 1929, lent seemingly irrefutable support to those seeing the stock market as a glorified casino with little redeeming social value.

That view left its mark on regulatory reform legislation in the 1930s in the USA, and was enshrined in the canon of economics by some brilliantly written and much-quoted passages in Keynes's *General Theory*. In fact, not until more than thirty years after the publication of Keynes's highly influential book was the casino view even seriously challenged by what we have here dubbed the information view.

The efficient markets doctrine

The challenge to the orthodox economic view, when it came, was partly a matter of new theories, but perhaps even more, a matter of new research technology. The electronic computer burst on the scene in the 1950s and by the middle 1960s large files of computerized stock-market data became available. Rather than simply guessing or conjecturing about how a stock market behaved, it now became possible, thanks in part also to some improvements in statistical methods, to look at the data and see. To those long accustomed to thinking of stock prices as dominated by unsophisticated, if not actually irrational investor/ speculators, the first statistical results must have come as a substantial shock. They showed, among other things, that stock prices reacted quickly to new information such as dividend changes, earnings announcements, merger proposals and any other economically relevant news that was specific enough to be identified. So quickly, in fact, did the market seem to react to specific "events" as to offer strong support to what finance specialists in the early 1970s had dubbed the "efficient markets doctrine"–the view that market prices at any time actually incorporated all publicly known information (See, for example, the classic 1970 study by Fama.) Clearly such a position cannot be "proved" correct; but in none of the many events studied was evidence ever turned up of specific information that the market had consistently failed to incorporate. Investors, in sum, appeared to be much less whimsical in their behavior than pictured by Keynes.

A further and potentially very testable implication of the efficient markets doctrine–an implication derived independently by Paul Samuelson (1965) and by the mathematical statistician Benoit Mandelbrot (1966)–concerned the evolution of stock prices over time. Recall that the traditional economics view sees prices as driven, at least some of the time, by fads or bubbles. If so, prices should display clear evidence of "trends" and possibly of long sequences of runs in the same direction. If, however, prices properly incorporate all currently available information, including any information about the likely persistence of the fundamentals, then price changes can reflect only the arrival of entirely new information. And that can come only as a complete surprise. If it could have been forecasted, it would have been. Prices, in an efficient market, will thus seem to fluctuate randomly. There will be no trends or runs in the data.

Tests of what came to be called, though somewhat inaccurately, the "random walk hypothesis" were conducted by the hundreds in the 1970s and early 1980s. As with the event studies, few, if any, rejections turned up in the earliest and most straightforward tests of randomness. The two sets of findings and their theoretical underpinnings led to a major restructuring not only of the academic field of finance, but of some very practical problems of macroeconomic regulation as well. In particular, much of standard central-bank lore about using margin requirements or other monetary controls to deal with speculative stock-market bubbles went by the board. No one could find any convincing enough statistical evidence of bubbles in progress for the authorities to control!

Every revolution gives rise to counter-revolutions, of course, and the efficient markets revolution has been no exception. Typically, each counter thrust starts by claiming that newly developed and more powerful statistical tests have turned up gross violations of the efficient markets model. The overthrow of the efficient markets regime is confidently announced. Subsequent research, however, steadily whittles down the grossness of the violation until ultimately the supposed anomaly cannot reliably be distinguished from normal sampling variations in the data.

Are stock prices too volatile? Good cases-in-point are the "variance bounds" or "excess volatility" tests of Robert Shiller of Yale University that were heralded, when they first appeared in 1981, as marking the end of efficient-markets theory. Shiller started from the common-sense observation that a time series plot of past stock prices appears choppy whereas the time series graph of dividends, which presumably represents the "fundamentals" that investors in stock are buying, is quite smooth. But if stock prices really met the rationality conditions set down by Samuelson and Mandelbrot, Shiller shows they should have fluctuated less than the fundamentals, not more. Shiller's critics, however, pointed out a number of critical biases and flaws in his statistical measures of "excess" volatility. They noted also that dividends, while certainly part of, are not the whole of the fundamentals. Over any finite sample period, account must be taken not only of the flow of dividends during the period, but of the value of the firm at the end of the period. When that account is properly taken (and that is no easy task), the seeming discrepancy in volatility between the price and the fundamentals largely vanishes. Shiller, to his great credit, has recognized these and related statistical problems with his original variance-bounds tests and has gone on to newer and ever more elaborate test designs. But citations to the earlier tests and their supposed decisive refutation of the efficient markets heresy still abound.

Thanks to recent improvements in econometric technology, the current focus of contention has shifted from the very short-term returns that constituted the battleground of the original "random walk" tests to returns on investment computed over horizons of two or three years, or even longer periods. Contrary to the presumed predictions of the efficient markets model, some researchers (notably Poterba and Summers, 1987) report strong evidence of "predictability" in long-period returns. In particular, they claim to find clear signs in returns of "reversion to the mean" in the sense that periods in which long-run returns have been below their historical averages tend to be followed by periods in which long-run returns are above their averages, and vice versa. A closer look at the data for the USA (by Kim, Nelson and Startz, 1988), however, reveals a subtle form of "survivorship bias," which perhaps wasn't sensed in the 1980s by the predominantly young economists and econometricians processing the numbers. The appearance of mean reversion traces almost entirely to the recovery of US stock prices from their lows in the mid-1930s. Looking solely at the forty or so years since the end of

the Second World War, no convincing signs of mean reversion appear.
Nor should this be surprising. We did, as things turned out, survive the
1930s and their associated horrors. But it was far from obvious at the
time that we would.

The failure of so many successive attempts to reject the efficient
markets hypothesis in a simple and decisive test has led some to
believe that perhaps it can't be done. The hypothesis is simply too
broad and too flexible (and has too much of the truth in it) to fall at a
single blow. It is closer to being a "paradigm" than a mere hypothesis,
bringing a common and coherent explanatory framework to a wide variety of seemingly unrelated phenomena. Like all scientific paradigms,
it will survive until displaced by a better one. At the moment, at least,
no such better paradigm is in sight.

This is not to suggest, of course, that for policy purposes we must
always proceed on the supposition that the efficient markets view is
necessarily the correct one. The presumption that the market is acting
sensibly is just that–a presumption subject to rebuttal by specific evidence. But to justify state intervention, the public has a right to demand
not just general sermonizing about stock market excesses, but real grounds
for believing that the intervention, like a prescribed medicine, is both
safe and effective. The case of margin requirements, noted earlier, is a
good example of what is likely to happen when these standards are
applied. Recognition in the USA that reliable evidence did not exist to
justify an activist policy of deliberately dampening stock market fluctuations has led, among other things, to its virtual abandonment as an
instrument of active central bank policy. The transfer of control over
margin requirements from the private sector to the Federal Reserve
System was a conspicuous element in the so-called New Deal reforms
introduced by the Roosevelt administration after the 1929 Crash. In the
first forty years after the authority was granted, margin requirements
were, in fact, changed by the Federal Reserve frequently and vigorous-
ly. By the early 1970s, however, the combination of general, efficient
markets research and specific empirical studies showing the ineffec-
tiveness of changes in margins had undermined the credibility of the

tool. Since 1974 no changes whatever have been made in margin requirements.

Though a positive case for frequent "fine-tuning" interventions in the stock market by the central bank is hard to establish, crisis intervention is another matter. The periodic crashes and "meltdowns" might still be of concern to the regulatory authorities because of both the massive shifts in wealth they entail and the threat they pose to the country's banking system.

The Crash of 1987

Crashes and market panics we have always had, but the Crash of October 19, 1987, was unique in that its progress could be observed on television by millions. Like many equally spectacular natural disasters such as earthquakes, the Crash was immediately seen by moralists and economic pundits as justly merited divine retribution for the investing public's sins of pride, greed and covetousness. The Jeremiahs pointed to the ominous parallels with 1929, and many newspapers routinely showed graphs of stock prices with 1987 values superimposed on those of 1929. For several weeks after October 19 the resemblance was indeed uncanny.

In the nearly two years since then, few of the dire predictions have come to pass and, partly in consequence, a more balanced perspective about that Crash, and crashes generally, has begun to emerge. Many observers at the time, for example, saw the Crash as just the bursting of a bubble that had been built up on the illusion of US pension funds that dynamic "stop-loss" strategies such as portfolio insurance could eliminate the risks in equity investments. The USA, however, was the only country in which these strategies were used on any significant scale. Yet, booms as large or larger (and crashes as large or larger) were found in many other countries. This is not to suggest, of course, that portfolio insurance played no role in the events of the day. Many observers believe, with some justification, that massive liquidations by portfolio insurers overwhelmed the normal market-making capacities of both the New York Stock Exchange and the Chicago index futures and options exchanges. The selling pressure was further intensified, some believe, by the public's inability at the time to distinguish adequately between "informationless" trades by portfolio insurers and those of informed investors. These views on the role of portfolio insurance in the Crash, if correct, are actually a hopeful sign for the future. Market structures have been strengthened since the Crash by expansions in order-processing capacity and by the provision of coordinated trading pauses to provide time for bringing in counterparties. The substantial growth in the number of investors following strategies like "tactical asset allocation" that, in effect, take the opposite side of portfolio insurance trades, also makes it unlikely that portfolio insurance, even if it recovers from its present moribund state, will ever again pose a major destabilizing threat.

Fears have also subsided that the Crash portended an indefinitely long era of high stock market volatility, and with it high costs of equity capital. Volatility did rise steeply after the Crash, as it always does, but it has since returned to its pre-Crash levels–levels, incidentally, that were not remarkably large by historical standards, despite the view so popular in hindsight that the market in the first three quarters of 1987 was in a furious speculative frenzy. The retail brokerage trade in stocks, of course, has not recovered, at least in the USA, but some likely reasons for that will be noted in due course.

Nor should the mere fact of a crash be taken as automatic evidence of irrationalities in valuation either before or after the Crash (or during the way down). Specific changes in the "fundamentals" that might produce a fall of 20 percent or more are admittedly hard to imagine, short of an outbreak of nuclear war, but there is much more to the "fundamentals," properly understood, than just short-horizon cash flows. Most of the value in common stocks represents cash flows projected far into the distant and highly uncertain future and then discounted back with appropriate adjustment for risk. Because the relevant valuation formulas are so highly nonlinear, even small revisions in risk-adjusted discount rates or estimated growth rates for future cash flows can sometimes produce large changes in what seem to be warranted values for shares.

Certainly there were many events in the days immediately preced
ing the Crash that might well have made investors more fearful of the
future for stocks, including new signs of weakness in the Reagan Administration, surges in interest rates, proposed tax penalties in the USA on
takeovers, and even shooting incidents in the Persian Gulf. The market
in New York had been down substantially in the previous week of
October 12-16, particularly sharply so on the afternoon of Friday,
October 16. Under the circumstances, it is hardly to be wondered at that
many investors, both in the USA and elsewhere, might have come–
more or less simultaneously–to the view that they were holding too
large a share of their wealth in risky equities and too little in the form
of bonds and other safer instruments.

Since the supplies of both kinds of securities are fixed in the short
run, the desired change in portfolio proportions can come about only by
changing the prices of the two assets, down for stocks and up for bonds.
Because the required equilibrating price adjustments in those circumstances are so abrupt relative to those on ordinary days, they have
come to be called crashes, though they hardly merit all the negative
connotations of that word. Many individuals, it is true, find themselves
less wealthy than they had previously believed. But for society as a
whole the deeper significance of a crash lies in the lessened attractiveness of equities as a way of holding wealth that the downward revaluation represents. The reduced participation by small retail investors
suggests that their shift away from US equities may still not have run
its course.

That stock market crashes should have acquired so sinister, if unde-
served, a reputation traces in large part to a misreading of the events
surrounding some past financial crises, particularly the Crash of 1929.
The popular perception in the USA is that the Crash of 1929 was the
cause of the Great Depression of the 1930s and all the miseries, political as well as economic, that the depression brought in its wake. We
know now, however, that unmistakable signs of a recession began to appear several months before the New York market reached its peak in
the summer of 1929. We know also that what might have been only a
moderate contraction by past standards was turned into a disaster by

the collapse of the US banking system and the, partly causal and partly consequent, collapse of the international payments system. That collapse led in turn to falls in stock prices in 1931 and 1932 that in aggregate far exceeded those of October 1929.

Very little of these troubles of the US banking system in the fateful years of 1931 and 1932 can be laid at the door of the credits extended either to individual stock market investors or to the brokerage industry. Those credits had dried up well before bank failures began to accelerate. The key problem was the unwillingness–some apologists have said inability–of the Federal Reserve to play a more vigorous role in maintaining the liquidity of the economy in the face of massive increases in the public's demand for money. There is little likelihood, needless to say, that the Federal Reserve System will make that mistake again.

More than pure faith, however, can now be invoked to allay concerns that the monetary authorities might not act to mitigate shocks to the banking system coming from a major stock market revaluation, up or down. Such shocks to the banking system did in fact occur on October 19 and 20, as the Brady Commission noted, and rumors of possible collapse of brokerage firms, clearinghouses and investment banks did circulate. A terse, but effective, statement of reassurance, however, from the Chairman of the Federal Reserve Board, Alan Greenspan, on the morning of October 20, forestalled panic and permitted the banks to carry on their normal financing of dealer securities inventories–inventories that had ballooned up under the immense waves of selling by their customers. Thanks to the Fed's timely intervention, the normal capital requirements of banks and brokerage firms could be effective in keeping failures from arising and snowballing. The only really distressing part of the whole episode is the realization that such crash-related shocks to the payment system as did arise could have been prevented by even a modest amount of prior contingency planning by the banking systems, public and private.

In sum, even today the stock market still suffers from the perception that it is a ticking time bomb, always threatening to shatter the economy unless kept thoroughly soaked in buckets of regulatory cold water.

Such views have found little support in serious academic research, particularly since the efficient markets revolution; and they have been belied by the almost complete absence of adverse macroeconomic consequences since 1987, despite the largest one-day price break in history. It is time then to turn from those negative views of the stock market to the more promising subject of the valuable services that securities markets do provide.

The Demand, Supply, and Regulation of Liquidity

Securities markets provide firms and investors not just with "price discovery" of the kind noted in our discussion of the information view, but also with "liquidity." Liquidity is a term that everyone understands, but few can define precisely. Rather than trying to do so at this point, it may be wiser to begin by asking what is the social problem that makes liquidity a matter of concern. That problem, in its most general sense, is how best to arrange the voluntary transfer of economic goods from those who value them least to those who value them most. The presumption, of course, is that such voluntary reallocations of resources leave one or both parties to the transfer better off and neither worse off so that on balance social welfare must rise. The sum total of the legal and economic arrangements for carrying out these welfare-increasing voluntary transfers is subsumed under the generic term "markets."

Market makers and the supply of immediacy

Markets can be classified in many ways. A particularly useful distinction for present purposes is that between "search" markets and "market maker" markets. Residential housing is the classic example of a search market. The seller of a house typically hires a "broker" to search for possible buyers. When a suitable buyer has been found and his or her offer accepted, the seller pays the broker a "commission" for having served as the seller's "agent" in the transaction. The retail used-car market, by contrast, is usually a market maker market. The seller turns the car over for cash to a "dealer" who holds it in inventory until such time as an interested buyer arrives and takes it out of the dealer's inventory. The dealer's compensation for his services to the two customers is not a commission but a "spread," that is, the difference between the dealer's buying price and his selling price. The relative size of the "bid-ask" spread quoted by dealers at any point in time is a widely used conventional measure of the market's liquidity.

By this or any other measure, the real world markets we observe vary substantially in the degree of liquidity they offer. The spreads on US Treasury Bond futures, for example, are typically three hundredths of one percent for transactions sometimes of $1 million or even more, while spreads for some smaller capitalization common stocks may be a hundred times that for trades of only a few thousand dollars. Such disparities in spreads, however, are in principle no more remarkable than the differences in price between a Volvo station wagon and a Citroën 2CV. The differences in the spreads between markets reflect mainly the differences in the market makers' cost of supplying immediacy to the users.

The average spreads in any market must at the very least be large enough on average to cover the direct costs of market making, which costs are mainly those of carrying inventory during the interval between the arrival of the seller and that of the eventual buyer. This carrying cost is partly a matter of interest on the capital committed to the inventory, but, even more, a matter of the risk of adverse price changes during the period of exposure. The market maker's main service, in fact, is precisely to bear this price risk during the interval between the arrival of customers. The customer selling to the market maker accepts a lower price than he might expect to get after searching on his own or through a broker for eager buyers. But it is a sure price that by its immediacy compensates the seller for the possibility that his search process might prove longer and less successful than anticipated.

The greater the price volatility of the seller's commodity, the more sellers are likely to opt for immediacy rather than search. Hence the prevalence of market maker markets in commodity futures trading where price volatility is extremely high. In the most active futures markets, like those of the Treasury bonds noted above, the price risk on large customer orders might be spread among several hundred market makers on the floor of the exchange plus an even larger number of "day traders" not directly on the floor but monitoring prices and volume closely via computer screens.

The spreads must compensate each market maker not just for his share of the price risk, but also for the opportunity costs of his being available (and being known to be available) when customers want to trade. The practice, once common on stock exchanges, of handling trades not continuously but in one or more scheduled "calls" during the day, arose in part as a way of permitting more competing members to participate in the periodic auctions. When not actually on the floor, they could be earning income and thereby defraying their overhead expenses of market making by carrying on other activities. Futures exchanges lower the costs of maintaining a presence by permitting "dual trading," that is, allowing their market makers also to serve as floor brokers executing customer orders (but only with other market makers). The exchanges also maintain several concurrently active trading "pits" to which market makers can flow as customer interests shift. Without such opportunities to spread the overhead costs of maintaining a market presence, the number of market makers would have to shrink and bid-ask spreads would have to be higher.

While market makers typically worry whether their earnings from the bid-ask spreads will be high enough on balance to cover the costs of staying in business, their critics and their customers (sometimes, but by no means always, the same group) often seem more concerned that the incomes of market makers, particularly on an age-adjusted basis, are too high. Keep in mind, however, that a natural corrective is always at work in such cases. If the average returns from market making persistently exceed the opportunity costs of maintaining a market presence, new market makers will ultimately enter the industry and compete away the excess returns. This mechanism of entry, so familiar and well understood in other industrial settings, is often overlooked in the securities markets, perhaps because the exchanges in which so much of the formal trading takes place are often seen not as businesses but as "guilds" to which entry is in fact severely restricted. There is certainly enough truth in this analogy to warrant our returning later to the subject of market maker competition. At this point, however, what needs emphasizing is that direct or head-to-head competition between market makers in the same product is by no means the only, or even necessarily the most effective, way that competition in the provision of liquidity services can take place. In recent years especially, competition of a very strenuous kind has taken the conspicuous form of introducing new products and new market structures.

Some examples of intermarket competition and innovation

Of the many examples that might be chosen, three perhaps are of particular interest. First, and in some respects the most substantial break from past arrangements, was the introduction in the USA in 1982 of cash-settled, stock-index futures contracts. The growth of the common stock holdings of US pension funds and other large institutional investors had created by the late 1970s a large demand for liquid trading in whole portfolios of stocks at once. The NYSE, though certainly aware of this demand for trading "baskets" of stocks by institutions, was structured historically to provide liquidity and price continuity in individual stocks for an essentially retail clientele. The unwillingness or inability of the NYSE to undertake the changes in its standard procedures that might permit significantly lower costs for trading whole baskets of shares encouraged entry by the commodity futures markets, in much the same way as they had previously entered the trading of foreign exchange contracts and of US Treasury securities. The results in terms of added liquidity were striking. For institutions, transaction costs for dealing in baskets dropped by at least 90 percent. The share equivalent of the index futures trades on a typical day is roughly equivalent, and sometimes even larger, than that of the NYSE itself.

A second and quite different example of new substitutes for old market arrangements is the *Instinet* computer network. Markets, as noted earlier, serve to bring buyers and sellers together either directly as in search markets with brokers or indirectly through the intermediation of market-making dealers. The market maker structure is designed to offer more immediacy and hence more liquidity than the search-market structure, but if the full complement of relevant buyers and sellers is not too large, a market that captures the main advantages of both market types can sometimes be constructed. Thanks to the wonders of electronics, the ultimate buyers and sellers can be put into continuous and direct contact with each other without recourse to intermediaries, except possibly voluntarily to preserve anonymity. Such "network" markets have long been standard worldwide in the case of interbank foreign exchange. The *Instinet* program, or "fourth market" as it is sometimes called, seeks to do much the same for the relatively small set of very large institutional holders of common shares. At the moment, the volume of trading on *Instinet* is quite modest, but all competing suppliers of liquidity to institutional investors are very much aware of its presence and they recognize that its volume could expand very quickly should the need ever arise.

Nor need one look always to the USA for examples of ingenious ways in which new entrants have responded to incentives to increase the effective supply of liquidity. The Swedish option market, OM, is an ideal case in point. Rather than waiting until an existing exchange can be persuaded to offer a new product (as the Chicago Board of Trade did when it initiated the exchange trading of options in 1973), or until a totally new exchange along traditional lines can be brought into being (like SOFE in Sweden), the organizers of OM relied on what might be called the industrial model of new product development. They simply set up an ordinary commercial firm and then marketed their product, in this case option trading, with a view to earning a profit. Had they overestimated the demand for liquidity in options, or had they not convinced their customers that their services as a market place were worth the fees being charged, then the venture would have failed, exactly as happens so often with new products generally. Whether this too will eventually be the fate of OM remains to be seen. But even if it were to close its doors tomorrow, its novel approach to expanding the supply of liquidity is likely to be much imitated in the years to come.

Do unregulated securities markets supply too little or too much liquidity?

The view presented here that market-making is "just another industry" has only recently begun to leave its mark on the academic literature (especially Grossman and Miller, 1988). There are, however, important advantages in looking at markets in this new and rather cold-blooded way, not the least of which is the reconsideration it suggests of the purpose of government regulation of securities markets. Securities markets have always been among the most conspicuously regulated sectors of the economy and especially so since the 1930s. The casino view of stock markets noted earlier undoubtedly accounts for some of the special restrictions that have almost everywhere been imposed on this industry. But the regulations in most countries typically go far beyond anything required for keeping naive investors from dissipating their life savings. Regulations in many countries prescribe, among other things, the rules governing the exchanges, the requirements for the disclosure of transactions and of information, the products that can and cannot be traded, the kinds of transactions that are prohibited (like short sales in Sweden) or that can be undertaken only under specified conditions (like the "uptick" rules on short sales in the USA). In some cases, like the USA until 1974 or Great Britain until 1986, the government prescribed even the commissions to be charged for executing trades. What principles can justify interventions of these kinds in an industry already exposed, as we have seen, to the powerful disciplining forces of supply and demand?

The principle to which economists look to validate the use of scarce, ultimately tax-financed government resources in regulating competitive markets is that of correcting for "externalities." The classic "negative" externality, of course, is found in the costs that a smoking factory chimney imposes on the rest of the community; a "positive" externality would be the benefits in pollenization that a bee-keeping farmer conveys to the owners of nearby orchards. Negative externalities mean that an industry's output is too large and should be cut back; positive externalities mean that the industry should be helped to expand its output.

In the particular case of securities, a substantial wing of opinion has always believed, in effect, that unfettered markets, especially stock markets, would supply far too much liquidity for the economy's good. Some of the presumed social costs of excessive liquidity, such as the overinvestment in information production and the possible repercussions of crashes, have already been considered. Recently, however, particularly in the USA, critical discussion of the stock market has focused on two new charges. One is that the dramatic reductions in commissions and transactions costs of recent years have led to a substantial increase in stock market turnover and a consequent rise in stock market volatility. The other charge is that the more liquid the market becomes, the more myopic are firms and investors forced to be, sacrificing thereby patient long-run returns for immediate short-term payoffs. Of these two charges the former is clearly somewhat easier to come to grips with. The data do show a steady and substantial rise in stock-market transactions, particularly since the ending of fixed commissions in 1974. That more transactions imply higher volatility is far from clear on theoretical grounds, however, and is certainly not strongly supported by the data. Volatility in the months before the Crash of 1987, for example, was not notably high by past historical standards despite the high transactions volume. The primary factor in the surge of volatility that did occur during and after the Crash traces not to high trading volume but to the Crash itself. The one solid and accepted fact in recent research about volatility is that it tends to rise in crashes and fall in booms.

The second main charge, that liquidity induces myopia, is–by its nature–less easily settled by reference to specific data. But despite this, or perhaps because of it, the concerns over induced myopia have been receiving much attention both in the press and in the academic economics literature. It may be worthwhile, therefore, to review these charges briefly before turning to possible positive externalities of liquidity.

Do liquid markets discourage long-term investment? The currently fashionable charge that liquid stock markets make investors too obsessed with short-term performance is actually a longstanding one. It was, for example, a major theme in Keynes's critique of the stock market in Chapter 12 of his *General Theory* and led him at one point there to propose half seriously that investments in stocks be made indissoluble, like marriage. (Keynes, of course, was writing at a time, 1936, and in a country, Great Britain, where divorce was still unusual). By the end of the chapter, however, he put aside his teasing of the orthodox, and in a passage all too rarely quoted, he made a strong case for stock market liquidity. Given the possibility of holding money or short-term, interest-bearing instruments, he argued that investors would be unwilling to take the huge, long-term risks of entrusting their capital for others to manage unless they felt they could retrieve those funds quickly when a need arose. This "liquidity preference," in fact, was one of the major new elements that Keynes saw himself as bringing to economics.

The liquidity preference envisioned by Keynes is most easily documented in the context of the term structure of interest rates. Holders of highly liquid, short-term debt securities do pay higher prices and hence receive lower yields than on less liquid, long-term securities of equivalent risk. Recent research on common stocks, where the context makes it much harder to hold other risks constant, also tend to show substantial price premiums for liquidity (see, for example, Amihud and Mendelsohn, 1986). Some of the most striking results have been those found in the USA for so-called "letter stock," that is, stocks usually in small companies that have been issued subject to SEC restrictions that limit their sale to the general public for a specified period of years. Such transfers as are permitted typically take place at prices running 20 to 30 percent, or even more, under those of unrestricted shares in the same company.

Evidence this strong for the value of liquidity in common stocks might well have carried the day had it not been for the great success of Japanese firms in the late 1970s and early 1980s in capturing markets for autos, steel and consumer electronics where US firms had long maintained a technological edge. So sweeping a reversal of roles seemed to demand an explanation and one of the popular lines offered was that of the supposed superior ability of Japanese firms to commit resources to high-risk ventures with great long-run prospects but no payoff during the long initial gestation period. American firms, by contrast, were held to be constrained by the need to meet quarterly earnings targets.

Even one bad quarter, so the story goes, and the stock price will fall; the institutional investors then become upset and the management becomes vulnerable to the threat of a hostile takeover. If investors only were more patient and less concerned with short-term trading profits and losses, US firms, like the Japanese, could undertake risky strategies with high, but long-deferred, returns.

Arguments at this level of generality, of course, based as they are on anecdotal or journalistic impressions, can never actually be refuted. The best one can hope to do is point to other considerations that put a quite different, but equally or more plausible, interpretation on the same supposedly supporting facts. In the matter of the market's response to reports of quarterly earnings, for example, much academic research in both finance and accounting has shown that for many firms, the time series of corporate earnings is well approximated as a "random walk." The best predictor of the future level of such a series is its current value. Hence, when a random walk series of earnings shows a drop or a rise, corresponding changes in price are only to be expected. True, the change covers only a single quarter, but, given the past history of earnings, the market reads the change as likely to be permanent rather than transitory.

The belief that US firms are systematically passing up profitable but long-deferred payoffs may perhaps have arisen simply because capital costs in the USA have been high by historical standards in recent years. When real, long-term interest rates were low in the 1950s, planning horizons of twenty to thirty years made perfect sense. But at the higher rates so common since the mid-1970s, the discounted present value of long-deferred sums drops dramatically. A shortening of investment horizons in response to higher costs of capital is thus not to be deplored, but applauded. Capital in short supply—and that, after all, is what an unusually high cost of capital signifies—is more effectively employed from society's point of view in projects that yield their returns quickly and thus help relieve the shortage. When capital becomes more plentiful, as seems to be the case in Japan, the pressure to economize its use is correspondingly diminished.

Finally, the crescendo of complaints about the excessively short-term emphasis of investors and firms may perhaps trace to the surge in highly publicized takeovers and buyouts of recent years. Many of these restructurings, including some of the largest and most reported on, have involved the breakup of well-known conglomerates. Yet these multi-industry and multinational conglomerates had been put together orig-inally—or at least so their very prominent managements assured us—so that those running the individual component units could be relieved of the pressures of having to meet short-term stock price targets. They would face instead only the conglomerate's internal capital market which would be more receptive to high-risk, long-term strategic in-vestments. Clearly, however, in the USA and perhaps also in Great Britain, investors in large numbers appear to have concluded that these presumed benefits of the internal capital market (at least for compa-nies that are mature and no longer growing rapidly) are overweighed by the waste and mismanagement that a lack of public accountability so often entails.

Whether investors were more correct in the 1960s when they sup-ported conglomeration or in the 1980s when "deconglomeration" became the order of the day cannot yet be settled conclusively. To urge trans-actions taxes, capital gains taxes, or related restrictions on market liquidity with a view to slowing takeovers and buyouts is, therefore, to prejudge the issue and, by insulating incumbent management from challenges to their corporate control, to do so in a possibly irreversible way. The verdicts of the public market may sometimes be too harsh, but the costs in wasted resources of being too lenient can be even greater.

Liquidity and the concentration of transactions. In turning from possible negative externalities of liquidity to positive externalities, we can begin with the well-known paradox that the best stimulus to liquidity is liquidity itself. Once buyers and sellers come to believe that a market is liquid, they direct more of their transaction orders to it. The expanded order flow reduces the average time lag between the arrival of buy and sell orders, thus reducing market makers' inventory risk and permitting them to lower their spreads. The lower spreads, in turn, attract still more customers, leading to further reductions until the demand and supply of immediacy is once again brought into balance.

So powerful and so well recognized has been this market-concentration externality that many governments have sought, in the public interest, to mandate the concentration of trading into a single market place. Examples include the Swedish grant of a monopoly in stock trading to the Stockholm Stock Exchange to prevent the fragmentation of the order flow among competing regional exchanges. Similar in effect have been the requirements in the USA that futures contracts may be traded only on approved exchanges.

The policy of forcing the concentration of transactions, however, is not without offsetting drawbacks. Gaining the economies of scale may well be a socially acceptable motive for creating a monopoly, but once monopoly power has been achieved, temptations inevitably arise to deploy that power in ways that enhance the interests of those who control the franchise. The problem is more than just the rigging of commission rates or restricting entry to market-making. The even more serious cost of enforced monopoly in these turbulent times may well be the resistance to major innovation that organizations protected from competition are all too prone to display.

The further irony is that these risks of state-enforced monopoly need not always be incurred to achieve the desired economies of scale. The order flow will tend to concentrate in a single market entirely on its own. In the USA, for example, new futures contracts of a closely similar kind are often introduced close to simultaneously by several independent futures exchanges. Without exception, trading quickly gravitates to one of the exchanges, with trading at the others first languishing and then ultimately being abandoned. Similar histories have been observed for so-called dual-listed options and in the experiments the NYSE has conducted in past years with multiple specialists for particular stocks. Had they not found other specialties and niches, the same fate would surely have befallen the many regional exchanges in the USA despite the electronic Intermarket Trading System (which routes orders to any regional exchanges that can better the NYSE price).

The tendency of trade to concentrate need not mean, of course, either that competition ceases or that such competition among market makers that survives is necessarily wasteful. Much of the most effective competition in any economy is "potential competition"–the threat that new market makers can enter if the prices charged by the incumbents are far out of line. One of the most encouraging propositions in post-Second World War economics, in fact, was the demonstration that under certain far from implausible conditions, the mere threat of entry by large firms, already well established in related industries, could serve to keep prices at or close to competitive levels even in industries very highly concentrated.

The economies-of-scale case for compulsory monopolization, moreover, whatever might be its strength at the level of whole exchanges, does not automatically extend down to individual market makers, such as NYSE specialists. Multiple market makers, it is true, will split the order flow, but they also split the risk. The fragmentation costs may well outweigh the risk-sharing benefits when volumes of trade are extremely small, as was the case when the specialist system was first introduced. But at higher volumes, studies have found no clear advantage in single-specialist markets over multi-dealer markets such as NASDAQ. At very high levels of volume, like those in some financial futures, the liquidity offered by the large population of competing floor traders is clearly unsurpassed.

Externalities in information: the case for transparency

Externalities that may create a case for government intervention can also arise from information, or more precisely, from the uncertainty about the true value of what is being bought and sold. Two kinds of such uncertainty must be distinguished. One shows itself whenever we ask "What is the market price today? If I want to sell, what price can I actually expect to get?" Resolving this "transaction price uncertainty," of course, need not dispel all doubts about the desirability of transacting. The question still remains: "Am I better off selling now or waiting until the future?" Future price uncertainty and current or transaction price uncertainty are often lumped together in discussions of "market transparency." Their implications for policy are substantially different, however; and to emphasize the differences we shall begin by first considering issues of market structure in a world where no uncertainties about future values existed, or at least, one where all market participants shared, and knew they shared, a common degree of ignorance about future values.

A simple setting such as this makes the strongest possible case for state intervention to assure complete market transparency–in the sense of assuring that anyone, and everyone, proposing to transact would have to identify himself and announce publicly the prices and quantities at which he is prepared to trade. The actual matching of the bids and offers as well as the clearing of trades might be implemented in any number of different ways. But the entire sequence of past trades–prices, quantities and traders–as well as current, standing limit orders would be a matter of public record.

Rules mandating such full market transparency under our information assumptions are socially optimal in much the same way as are the traffic rules governing stop signs. Each driver wants every other driver to obey the rules. While he might well like the personal freedom to ignore the rules himself from time to time, he knows that if any substantial number of drivers were to act that way, they would soon all be worse off. Thus, paradoxically, the state compulsion that may seem to reduce individual freedom actually serves to increase it.

Note that maintaining transparency in this sense need not require that all orders be executed on a public exchange. In principle, brokerage firms could cross their customer trades in house, provided the prices, quantities and counterparties were disclosed at the time of the transaction. The case for ruling out such off-exchange crosses, as is done for US futures contracts, is more a matter of preventing "free riding" on the exchanges' services (and possibly also of preventing frauds and defaults) than of maintaining market transparency.

Nor, needless to say, does the maintenance of market transparency preclude the presence of market makers acting as intermediaries. Market makers, as described earlier, would still supply immediacy by bridging the time gaps between the arrivals of buyers and sellers. But they require no special information advantages or privileges to play that role effectively. Hence the rules found on many exchanges that prevent market makers from trading ahead of their own customers' orders–orders that, in the nature of the case, are known to them but not to other market participants. Enforcing compliance with such rules and detecting violations is by no means easy or costless, however. Here as elsewhere, therefore, the best protection in the long run against abuse by market makers of their monopoly of information about their own customer orders is likely to be the competition for those orders among the market makers themselves.

Disclosure requirements and the incentive to produce information. A policy of enforcing transparency on all market participants is easy to justify under our provisional assumption that they face only a common, transaction-price uncertainty. No arrangement other than mutual full disclosure could command the unanimous support of all transactors. The picture becomes much less clear, however, when we allow for the very real possibility that some market participants may have important private information about the likely future price of the commodity or the security–information that may well have been acquired only after the investment of substantial resources in research. Unanimous support of universal full disclosure rules can then no longer be presumed. The policy issue now becomes the much harder one of making trade-offs between competing social goals.

The complexities of the policy issues can perhaps best be introduced by a retelling of the story, possibly apocryphal, of the Rothschilds after the battle of Waterloo. According to the legend, the Rothschilds had invested in a network of carrier pigeons and messengers to carry news of the outcome of the battle across the Channel to their London branch. A British victory would have led them to buy British government bonds, which were selling, of course, at a substantial discount because of the uncertainties about the outcome of the war. A British defeat, on the other hand, would have pushed prices even lower.

Clearly, any regulation that required disclosure before trading of any "material nonpublic information," such as who won the battle, would destroy the trading value of that information. And so it should, many may feel. But the full-disclosure policy also weakens the incentive to invest in news gathering. Hence the emphasis in much of the disclosure laws on information that is produced as a by-product of running the business, like accounting statements, or that is in the stockholders' best interest to disclose voluntarily, like much of the data in prospectuses for new issues of securities. Hence also the thrust of much recent insider trading legislation and litigation in the USA and elsewhere focusing on cases where the valuable trading information was obtained not by research but by "misappropriation" of confidential company data.

Forcing the disclosure of all nonpublic information before trading is merely the most direct way of destroying the private value of the information, and hence of the incentives to produce it. The same effect can result indirectly from the seemingly milder requirement of market transparency. Although only the Rothschilds may have had the resources and the enterprise to set up a carrier-pigeon network, most of the other traders must surely have known or strongly suspected that such a network did in fact exist. When, therefore, any broker known to be representing the Rothschilds entered the trading floor and offered to buy, all traders would realize immediately the British had won the battle. Prices would instantly jump up and the private information would lose its value as surely as if it had been disclosed. Unless the Rothschilds could somehow hide their identity in trading, their pigeon network would be a waste of money.

The ability of informed traders to make markets less transparent by somehow masking their true identities is thus essential for sustaining incentives both to produce information and to speed its incorporation into prices. The Rothschilds and their present-day counterparts do, of course, have many ways of avoiding the unintended disclosure of their trading intentions. Rather than relying on a single, easily identified broker, they may spread parts of the family business among many smaller independent brokers, sometimes even mixing in a few orders on the opposite side to throw watchers off the scent. In fact, one version of the Rothschilds's carrier-pigeon story has the Rothschilds using a broker, widely believed to be one of their agents, to *sell* conspicuously, driving prices down while many smaller brokers, hired by the Rothschilds for the occasion, were quietly buying. Much the same effect can sometimes be achieved by a skilled broker by breaking up a single large order into a sequence of smaller pieces, thereby sacrificing some immediacy for the advantage of better execution.

The opaqueness that benefits the informed serves also to impose costs on the other participants. These costs are not those of having sold to the Rothschilds too cheaply, as so much of the popular discussion of the evils of insider trading seems to suggest. Those sales may have created disappointments and regrets, but not social costs. They constitute mere "wealth transfers" or "distributional effects," as economists so quaintly put it. The true social costs imposed by the informed traders arise in a more subtle and indirect way. The social damage occurs because the immediate "victim" of a trader with information is likely to be a market maker. Market makers, as individuals, of course, are entitled to no more than the sympathy accorded other investors. But there is a difference: the market makers are suppliers of liquidity to the rest of the market. Their expected losses on information trades are a cost of doing business and must ultimately be reflected in wider average bid-ask spreads. The costs of information trading are thus shifted forward to the liquidity-demanders, much as if an excise tax had been imposed. In extreme cases, a market might even undergo a "death spiral"; the wider spreads drive away the liquidity traders, causing spreads to widen further, eventually leaving only the information traders and no way for the market makers to make a living. That unfortunate possibility is ultimately what justifies the position, advanced earlier, that even so-called unsophisticated "noise traders" may actually be serving a useful social purpose. Their trades give market makers a chance to offset part of their likely losses to the information traders, and thereby to remain available for supplying liquidity services to the rest of the community.

The possibility of incurring losses from traders with adverse information is of particular concern to market makers in networks of electronic screen trading where they must post bids and offers and must stand ready to trade certain minimum quantities at those posted prices. The public posting of such bids and offers amounts, in effect, to the grant of a free option to other traders, including other market makers. If the guaranteed minimum size is large, the damage to a market maker whose stale quotes have been "picked off" can be substantial. Cutting the size of the guaranteed minimum protects the market maker and decreases the pressure to widen spreads on small trades, but encourages larger traders to deal off the network, thus fragmenting the order flow. Some network markets have tried recently to meet these difficulties by restricting the large size guarantees to "public" orders only, hoping to prevent market professionals and other market makers from exploiting the inevitable lags in revising all posted quotes when the market maker trades in many different individual stocks.

The free-option burdens on market makers in an electronic screen network also help explain why the seemingly primitive "open outcry" markets can continue to survive in markets such as commodity and financial futures where the demand for immediacy is particularly high. That immediacy is supplied, as noted earlier, by the large pool of competing market makers bidding on the buy or sell orders that the customers' brokers have brought to the trading pit. Unlike screen traders, the market makers in the pit need not post bids that last until hit or withdrawn. The market makers' bids in the pit are made mainly in response to the offers of the customers or their brokers and the market makers' bids are valid, as the saying goes, only for as long as the sound of the voice lasts. With less vulnerability to the picking off of stale quotes, spreads can thus be narrower and hence effective transaction costs can be lower than in markets with seemingly more advanced technology.

Market institutions for informationless trading. Our concern so far has been with those who do have information but want to pretend that they don't. That coin has another side, however. Even had a hawk actually captured the Rothschilds' pigeon before it delivered its message, the market would have no way of knowing of that capture and certainly no reason to accept as true any statement the Rothschilds

might make to that effect. Hence any buy or sell order identified as a
Rothschild order would have moved the market against them in much
the same way as if the pigeon had actually gotten through.

This somewhat perverse property of market expectations creates the
need for market institutions permitting those traders, particularly
large traders who really do not have private information, to convey
that fact credibly to the rest of the trading public. Absence of such institutions in US index-futures markets added greatly and unnecessarily
to the sense of panic in the market during the Crash of October 19, 1987.
Heavy selling was undertaken on that day by portfolio insurers, acting
not on the basis of private information but entirely in response to
mechanical rules. The announcement in advance by the portfolio insurers of their intentions to sell specified quantities at a specified time
would have prevented any misinterpretation of those sales by other
market participants and might have encouraged the earlier entrance of
buy-side counterparties. But such "sunshine trading" announcements by
the insurers would have violated regulations requiring all futures
trades to be executed publicly on an exchange with no prearrangement.
The unwillingness of US futures markets, unlike US stock markets, to
accommodate these and other forms of "block trading," especially informationless block trading, has led to some dissatisfaction with
futures markets in recent years on the part of large, institutional
investors.

Block trades, even if informationless themselves, inevitably raise
issues of transparency because, under some conditions, the very knowledge that a particular market maker has acquired a large block of
stock from a customer can itself be a piece of valuable trading
information to other market makers. If the block is large relative to the
market maker's capital, he will seek to reduce his exposure to adverse
price moves by shifting some of his inventory and its attendant risks to
other market makers. But, if the number of such alternative market
makers is so small that they can act strategically rather than
competitively, the original market maker may find the terms of trade
turning against him once his predicament becomes known. Hence the
arrangements in some markets, like those in interbank foreign exchange

trading, for discreet "blind brokers" who offer to handle with complete anonymity a major trader's deals with other major traders. Hence also the rules in some stock markets, including the Stockholm Stock Exchange, that permit the announcement of the terms of block trades to be delayed until after the close of the day's trading. On the New York Stock Exchange, by contrast, block trades must be reported promptly, but as a practical matter, the upstairs market makers in New York will usually have enough time to hedge their inventory positions in the options or futures markets before the block trade is officially disclosed.

The presence of valuable nonpublic information thus poses some delicate and difficult problems of social choice. Unlike many problems of social policy, where the best interests of the "consumer" can often be taken as a clear standard for judging alternatives, the market structure issues involve several different groups of consumers, each with a valid claim to the liquidity services the market offers. That no single best way of balancing these interests exists is clear from the great variety of market structures that continue to thrive. Perhaps the best general advice that economics can offer market designers at this stage of our knowledge is to strive for sufficient flexibility in market structure to accommodate users with different needs. One such structure that has been receiving some attention recently is that of "mixed-mode markets" in which potential users have the choice of entering orders either in the regular, continuous double-auction market or in periodic, intraday single-price call auctions much along lines of the opening call. Those traders most anxious to shed future price uncertainty will presumably opt for the immediacy that the continuous auction offers. Those less anxious can enter limit orders. Those without special private information, but seeking to trade larger than average quantities, might well prefer to sacrifice immediacy in the interests of reaching the largest possible set of counterparties. They could choose to enter the closed-bid, single-price auctions. These auctions could accept both limit orders and market orders; and both sides of any block trades negotiated outside the market could be entered for crossing at the single clearing price. The number of such single-price call auctions to be scheduled would depend on the market's demand for transactions in that mode.

Beyond this, perhaps the only other overriding lesson to be drawn from the mass of recent academic research on market structures is the simple and obvious one: the securities industry must be free to adapt quickly to new trading technology, new products, and new customer clienteles. The pace of financial innovation shows no signs of slowing down. The need for flexibility becomes more urgent as "globalization" of capital markets moves closer to reality, and especially so for a relatively small, open country like Sweden.

Strategies for Capital Market Regulation

That Sweden has recently abandoned its long-standing controls over foreign exchange and international capital movements need not mean that its own internal capital markets are inevitably destined to wither and disappear.

True, small countries can no longer take much comfort from the once widely held view that each country had an unassailable comparative advantage in the trading of its own domestic securities. That myth has been destroyed by the emergence (or perhaps re-emergence) of London as the major center for trading many non-British securities, including not merely the common stocks of Volvo and other large Swedish firms, but even the government bonds of Germany, an economy whose wealth substantially surpasses that of Britain.

The concentration of the trading of the internationally known securities in London, New York and Tokyo is now substantial. In fact, thanks to the strategic placement of these centers in the world's time zones, some of the best known international securities can now be traded at literally any time during the course of the 24-hour day. Niches will continue to exist, especially for local options and futures markets, since those instruments (and hence also "synthetic stock"–which is just options or futures plus bills) are less costly than stocks to trade, and far less costly to settle. Survival is possible also for some local stock markets, and even for some markets for fixed-income securities of particular interest to local savers and financial institutions. To fill these niches successfully, however, the local markets must clearly be seen by their potential users as efficient and as cost effective in executing orders. On this score, at least, the prospects for Sweden seem reasonably encouraging. The recent revamping of the procedures on the Stockholm Stock Exchange puts its clearing and settlement processes among the best in the world and certainly among the very few to have achieved the key goal of eliminating all shuffling of paper certificates. The Swedish OM procedures for automatically adjusting limit orders in complex option positions as underlying prices change is still another example of unusual efficiency.

For the local markets to continue to thrive they must also be seen to be honest and "reliable" as well as liquid and efficient. If a customer sells a security, the price should be consistent with those reported for other trades, and the proceeds from the sale should be turned over as promised, without undue delay. Merely mentioning words like honesty and reliability in this context will inevitably seem to some a call for government regulation of the markets; and indeed the presumed need to "maintain public confidence" in the stock market is always invoked first in any defense of public regulation. Yet direct supervision by the state is by no means the only viable model of regulation to assure reliability.

Clearly, the biggest stake in maintaining the integrity of the market is that of the market makers and market professionals themselves. Hence the elaborate "self-regulatory" structures that every formal market system develops for governing relations between market makers and between them and their outside customers. Self-regulatory structures have the very great advantage that the detailed rules are made by those with both the greatest long-run interest in maintaining reliability and the greatest store of specialized technical knowledge about the market and its real vulnerabilities. But no set of rules, however sound conceptually, can be absolutely fool-proof. Conspicuous examples of rules being flouted are bound to arise, therefore, and when they do, the country's legislators are put under great pressure to increase the role of the state in both rule making and rule enforcement. Sometimes, unhappily, this pressure to intervene can become overwhelming, even where failure of the rules or the rule-making process was not really the cause of the scandal.

One such case, and a very influential one, has been US security regulation under the SEC Acts of the early 1930s. These regulatory structures were based on the view that the Crash of 1929 traced in considerable part to various "manipulative" abuses by brokers, banks, issuing corporations, individual investors and exchange officials (some of whom, including the president of the New York Stock Exchange, actually wound up in jail). That stock prices and trading volume fell to such low levels in the early 1930s was taken as evidence of the public's loss of confidence in the market because of those abuses. So widespread, in fact, was (and still is) this view of the stock market as steeped in corruption that the securities industry actually welcomed the institution of a tax-supported watchdog like the SEC. What better way to reassure a public still reeling from the Crash than to announce that a tough new government agency with police-like powers and responsibilities would henceforth be pursuing the cheaters?

We know now, of course, with the benefit of hindsight and much academic research, that failure of the self-regulatory structures had little if anything to do with the Crash of 1929. And, even more tellingly, we know that the mountains of detailed regulations introduced by the SEC in the fifty years since its creation failed to prevent the even bigger Crash of October 1987. But the problem is more than just one of wasted effort and the deadweight costs of bureaucracy and hidden subsidies to the industry. Replacing private rule making with public rule making also affects the nature of the rules that emerge, and not always in a way that benefits the wider public. The danger is well known that public regulators may, despite the best of intentions, use the power of the state to reinforce the existing tendencies toward cartelism in industries like the securities industry, even when the regulators have not actually been "captured" by influential segments of the securities industry (or, in the case of anti-takeover rules, captured by incumbent corporate managers). The subtler and less readily visualized effects, however, that have been stressed in recent academic research on regulation are those arising from the special motivational or incentive structure of regulators.

A good example of such incentive effects can again be found in the regulation of margin requirements on purchases of common stock on credit. As noted earlier, these requirements were set before 1934 by the exchanges themselves with a view, as in any other business, of finding the best balance of costs against benefits. Setting margins high would have the benefit of reducing the risks and costs to the exchange and its members of customer defaults; but it would make margin credit more expensive to the customers and thus reduce the exchange's volume of business and its members' commission income. Finding the right tradeoff is far from easy, but in their trial and error efforts the exchanges and their members at least have the powerful guidance of their own profit positions to check whether they are moving in the right direction.

What, however, can the public regulators take as their criterion for appraising the tradeoffs? Experience in the USA suggests that when the power to set margins was transferred from the exchanges to the Federal Reserve System in 1934, the monetary authorities did at first try conscientiously to find socially optimal margin levels. They came eventually to realize, however, that they had no sound basis for making or evaluating any of their margin decisions on general economic grounds. They opted eventually instead for the only margins policy that makes sense from a regulator's point of view: set the margin requirement high and leave it there. Keeping it high means that the regulator can never be blamed by his ultimate bosses in the legislature for having encouraged speculative excesses. True, the high margins cause the exchanges to lose business; but the loss is theirs, not the regulator's.

Direct regulation of securities markets may thus have an inherent bias towards over-strictness as is suggested also in the USA by the sight of supposed insider-traders being led away in handcuffs or by the businesses and careers destroyed in highly publicized prosecutions for offenses as trivial as stock "parking" (the disguising of the true ownership of the shares, for example, to avoid alerting a target firm of an imminent takeover). Some fear, however, that markets entirely self-regulated are likely to suffer from the opposite bias. The recent scandals at the Chicago futures exchanges are offered as a case in point. The exchanges have been accused of laxity in enforcing their own rules against influential trader-members and of blocking the introduction of new technological improvements like computerized screen trading that might make violations easier to detect. Some of this criticism, of course, reflects merely how unaccustomed the general public and the press are to thinking of the securities industry as "just another business." As businesses, the exchanges must balance the costs of increased surveillance against the increased patronage that the added confidence on the part of the public might bring in. There is no reason to believe that the optimal cost/benefit balance will always imply 100 percent elimination of all opportunities for abuse, any more than there is to believe that surveillance that yields zero-percent pilferage is the optimal policy for a supermarket or a department store. Nor, even if the frequency of abuses were believed to be too high, does it follow that vigorous surveillance is the only or the best way to reduce it. Raising the amount of visible monitoring of market activities can certainly deter some rule violations but will also require substantial additional investment of resources. The same degree of effective deterrence can sometimes be achieved far more cheaply merely by raising the penalties for those who do get caught.

Although private-sector self-regulation and intermarket competition can substitute for public-sector regulation, the conspicuous position of capital markets in the economy makes complete security market deregulation politically impossible. Deregulation, after all, has no obvious and effective political constituency. The firms already established in the industry will often, understandably, prefer the protective blanket of regulation to the rigors of competition. Consumer advocates welcome regulation because they think it comes free. Only the taxpayers who must finance the regulators are directly disadvantaged, and they, of course, are notoriously hard to organize. Under the circumstances, the best that the taxpayers can hope for is a compromise strategy of dividing the regulatory tasks between the public and private sectors, assigning to each those functions in which it is likely to have the least comparative disadvantage.

The exchanges, clearinghouses and related fee-financed self-regulatory organizations are better positioned than outside regulators to draw up the detailed operating rules for trading, clearing and settlement, including the appropriate penalties and sanctions for violating those rules. As emphasized earlier, public regulators, quite apart from how their activities are financed, do not have the right incentives for making business tradeoffs. For the same reason, the exchanges can best be charged as well with setting the disclosure requirements for their listed firms; and the firms themselves can best define the particular set of their officials and employees who must agree, as a condition of employment and subject to redress, to disclose all trading in the company shares and generally to maintain the confidentiality of company data. In principle, the exchanges could also set the conditions governing bidder auctions in takeover cases, though it must be emphasized once again that the current takeover issue is less a securities matter, strictly speaking, than a power struggle between contending managements and between incumbent managers and the firm's outside stockholders. The clearinghouses can best set the minimum capital requirements for their clearing firms and the clearinghouses and the clearing firms in turn can best set the margin requirements and the fee structure for their customers. The exchanges, broadly construed to include proprietary exchanges and market-making firms, are also best positioned to assess the risks and rewards of their investments in new product development.

The tax-financed public sector can then usefully focus on those traditional areas where private sector incentives to adhere to acceptable social norms of behavior may warrant further reinforcement. Placing major reliance on self-regulation, for example, need not imply any suspension of the normal civil and criminal remedies for theft or fraud. Some additional specialization within the criminal justice system may well be necessary to deal with securities cases, but the temptation to create special new securities felonies, like stock parking, should be resisted. The public sector should also maintain its regular rules against monopolization and price fixing, perhaps even strengthening them if necessary to assure that new market makers (and new markets) have full freedom of entry. But on matters of industry-specific detail such as trading procedures, the role of the public regulators should be limited to performing the true audit function of verifying that the exchanges and self-regulatory organizations are indeed conscientiously following the rules, including the customer protection rules that they have announced to the trading public. In the critical matters of new product and new market development, the role of the public regulators should be smaller yet.

The courtiers of the English king Canute—or Knut, as he was known to his Viking followers in Scandinavia—were unable to invoke his royal powers for controlling the tides. Regulators who seek to use the power of the state to control the tide of financial innovation will be no more successful. The securities markets of the world are now in intense competition. Capital market overseers in any country, whether it be Sweden or the USA, who cannot accept a limited role and whose regulatory interventions discourage innovation and drive up the cost of trading in their domestic markets, will soon learn the hard way how far the world's capital markets have already come along the road to globalization.

This chapter is based on a report prepared for the Center for Business and Policy Studies, Stockholm, Sweden, September 1989.

References

Amihud, Yakov, and Haim Mendelsohn. "Liquidity and Stock Returns." *Financial Analyst Journal*, May/June, 1986.

Fama, E. F. "Efficient Capital Markets: a Review of Theory and Empirical Evidence." *Journal of Finance*, May, 1970.

Grossman, Sanford, and Merton H. Miller. "Liquidity and Market Structure." *Journal of Finance*, July, 1988.

Hayek, F. A. "The Use of Knowledge in Society." *American Economic Review*, September, 1945.

Keynes, J. M. *The General Theory of Employment, Interest and Money*. New York: Harcourt, Brace, 1936.

Kim, M. J., Charles R. Nelson and Richard Startz. "Mean Reversion in Stock Prices? A Reappraisal of the Empirical Evidence." Department of Economics Working Paper, University of Washington, Seattle, November, 1988.

Mandelbrot, Benoit F. "Forecasts of Future Prices, Unbiased Markets, and Martingale Models." *Journal of Business*, January, 1966.

Poterba, James M., and Lawrence Summers. "Mean Reversion in Stock Prices: Evidence and Implications." NBER Working Paper, Cambridge, MA, 1987.

Samuelson, Paul A. "Proof That Properly Anticipated Prices Fluctuate Randomly." *Industrial Management Review*, Spring, 1965.

Shiller, Robert. "Do Stock Prices Move Too Much to Be Justified by Subsequent Changes in Dividends?" *American Economic Review*, June, 1981.

Tobin, James. "On the Efficiency of the Financial System." *Lloyds Bank Review*, July, 1984.

9   Margin Regulation and Stock Market Volatility

In the United States, common stocks are said to have been bought on "margin" if less than 100 percent of the purchase price was put up in cash by the buyer at the settlement date. The remainder of the cash flowing to the seller would come from a loan, typically supplied by the buyer's broker, and for which the purchased security serves as collateral. Prior to 1934, the minimum cash margin required for the purchase of stocks was determined in the private sector by the stock exchanges, who used essentially the same principles as creditors do generally for setting "capital requirements." Individual brokers or other creditors, of course, were always free to set requirements to particular customers higher than the minimums stipulated by the exchanges if they thought it necessary to protect themselves further against the risks of customer default.

In 1934, however, the US Congress transferred the power to set minimum margins from the private-sector exchanges to the public-sector Federal Reserve System. The move reflected the view, widely held at the time, that the exchanges, in their attempt to increase their commission revenues, had set margins too low in the 1920s, thereby precipitating the speculative stock market boom whose collapse in October 1929 was seen as ushering in the Great Depression of the 1930s. The Congress hoped that the Federal Reserve System would employ its new powers over margins to dampen speculative excesses; or, as we might put it in today's vocabulary, to reduce "market volatility."

What the Federal Reserve has done since then with its margin setting authority can be seen from figure 9.1, which shows the time paths of both margins and one measure of market volatility from October 1934 to December 1987. Margin requirements were set initially at 45 percent, raised to 55 percent during the boomlet of 1936 and then cut back to a low of 40 percent after the sharp stock market break in the late summer of 1937. The requirement stayed at that level for the remainder of the 1930s and throughout most of the war years, but was stepped up sharply as the war drew to a close, reaching 100 percent (that is, all cash, no borrowing) for most of 1946. Changes were frequent over the next two and a half decades, averaging once every eighteen months or so until January 1974 when margins were set at 50 percent. Since that time there have been no changes whatever.

It is difficult, under the best of circumstances, to know why the Federal Reserve System makes the decisions we observe; it is harder yet to account for the decisions it doesn't make! Part of the explanation for the Fed's neglect of its margin authority after 1974 may well have been the recognition that its past vigorous efforts in the 1950s and 1960s to use the tool to control volatility had largely been futile. Volatility had indeed dropped substantially since the granting of the margin authority in 1934, as can be seen from figure 9.1.[1] But academic studies, notably one by Robert Officer (1973) had shown that the drop was less a matter of policy than a return of volatility back to its normal longer-run levels following the severe banking crises of the early 1930s. Certainly no strong systematic relation between margin levels and volatility emerges from inspection of the two time series in figure 9.1. The scatter of margin requirements against average volatility shown in figure 9.2 does perhaps suggest a slight negative relation between the two, but that appearance traces mainly to the single point representing the period just after the Crash of 1937 when volatility was still near its post-1929 highs. Nor do the deliberate policy changes in the margin requirements appear to have altered volatility substantially, as is clear from the scatter in figure 9.3. Note, in particular, the absence of any clear indication that raising margin requirements had helped

---

[1] The volatility measure shown in figure 9.1 is a twelve-month moving average of monthly volatility used in a study of margins and volatility that is discussed further later in the chapter.

materially to reduce stock market volatility. If anything, the slope is slightly positive.

That margin requirements appear to have had so little impact on stock market volatility is not really surprising. Shares held on margin, even in the Roaring Twenties, never accounted for more than 10 percent or so of the value of equities and nowadays amount to less than 1 percent. Pension funds and other large institutional traders, who have played a steadily increasing role in the market, typically do not buy on margin. Investment banks, specialists, and other market professionals are not directly subject to the margin requirements (but rather to a separate set of business capital requirements). And even the individual investors who remain subject to the margin rules often have access to competing alternative sources of credit for carrying securities.

So uninteresting, in fact, had the Federal Reserve's margin requirements become after 1974 that many observers were predicting that they might be swept back to the private sector in the wave of financial deregulation running through Washington in the 1980s. Two events in the late 1980s, however, served to prolong the life of the margin requirements and to subject the whole seemingly dead issue of their efficacy to further intense scrutiny. One event, of course, was the Crash of 1987, which raised again the specter of speculative excess in the stock market. The other event was the publication of an academic study (Hardouvelis, 1988a) purporting to show that, contrary to previous research (and contrary also to what seems to be the story in figures 9.2 and 9.3), margin requirements really were effective, if somewhat neglected, tools for controlling stock market volatility. The study received more than the normal attention accorded academic studies because it appeared in a publication of the Federal Reserve Bank of New York, long the major regional bank in the Federal Reserve System thanks to its location at the heart of the nation's banking and financial center. To call further attention to the important new findings by Hardouvelis the New York Federal Reserve Bank even scheduled a press conference.

In this chapter I propose to reexamine the results reported by Hardouvelis and to explain why they appear to differ so strikingly from previous research. The problem, it turns out, lies in Hardouvelis's use of statistical procedures that were inappropriate for the data under study. When the necessary corrections are made, the Hardouvelis effect vanishes. The broader moral of the study, of relevance even in Germany and other countries without margin requirements, is simply this: important as it always is to base policy decisions on empirical grounds rather than on vague general impressions, it is particularly important that the empirical foundation be laid correctly.

Margins and Volatility: the Problem of Spurious Correlation

Given the results already seen in figures 9.2 and 9.3, one cannot but admire Hardouvelis for his ingenuity in constructing a "statistically significant" relation between margins and volatility from such unpromising material. The secret of his success turns out to be in his treating the sample not as the 23 points in figure 9.2 (one for each margin period) or the 22 points in figure 9.3 (one for each change in margins), but as the 627 separate points in figure 9.1 (one for each *month* from October 1934 to December 1987). When he regresses each month's volatility on the value of the margin requirement ruling in that month he obtains the results shown in table 9.1. Note that the coefficient on the margin variable (M_t) is negative, implying that raising margins reduces volatility. And it clearly appears reliably different from zero, since the reported t-ratio has the impressively high value of 10.8.

T-ratios that high are so impressive and so rare in applied econometrics that one instinctively becomes suspicious. Such suspicions are immediately confirmed by a glance at the diagnostic statistics presented elsewhere in table 9.1, which show how well or how poorly the computed regression meets the conditions for reliable inferences in least-squares estimation. Note, for example, the amazingly low value of 0.19 for the Durbin-Watson diagnostic coefficient (D.W.), very far from the value of 2.0 one would expect if the first-order serial correlation of the residuals really were zero as the standard tests for significance assume. Note also that the higher-order correlations of the residuals are also high and decay only slowly.

Table 9.1
Level regression of volatility on margin
October 1935 to December 1987

Independent variables	Dependent variable: $\sigma_{y,t}$
Constant	0.0713
	(0.0028)
M_t	-0.0487
	(0.0045)
R^2	0.15
$D.W.$	0.19

Autocorrelation coefficients of residuals:

Lag	
1	0.9450
2	0.8879
3	0.8274
4	0.7736
5	0.7210
6	0.6685
7	0.6114
8	0.5565
9	0.4952
10	0.4335
11	0.3702
12	0.3080

Some idea of the dangers in attempting to draw conclusions from regressions that are so far from meeting the required condition of uncorrelated residuals can be gleaned from table 9.2 which reports the results of some simulation experiments in which an entirely imaginary and artificially constructed series of pseudo-volatility is regressed on the real series of margin requirements. The random series of pseudo-volatility is constructed as a simple first-order autoregression with values of the autoregression coefficient ranging from 0 up to 1.0. Table 9.2 shows how frequently "significant" nonzero slope coefficients will be reported in samples of 500 simulated months of pseudo-volatility regressed on real margins. Note that when the serial correlation parameter for pseudo-volatility (*e*) equals zero, a 5 percent test will report a significant negative value for the margin coefficient roughly 5 percent of the time, as it should. But as the serial correlation rises to 0.5, the rejection rate rises to 17 percent; and when $\rho = 1.0$, a significant negative coefficient will be found some 40 percent of the time, even though one of the two series is completely artificial. In fact, if the replication sample had been larger than 500, the rejection rate would have been higher yet, approaching 100 percent in the limit.

Table 9.2
Simulation experiment involving spurious regression

Percent of replication rejecting the null hypothesis that $\beta = 0$.

	Nominal size left tail			Nominal size right tail		
ρ	1%	2.5%	5%	5%	2.5%	1%
Least squares with usual covariance						
0.00	1.07	2.58	5.03	5.38	2.58	1.12
0.50	8.73	12.54	16.64	17.35	13.23	9.16
0.95	32.47	34.82	37.25	38.32	36.02	33.42
1.00	38.93	40.74	42.37	41.32	39.82	37.88

Regression: $y_t = \alpha + \beta \overline{M}_t + u_t$,

where $\alpha = 0$, $\beta = 0$, and $y_t = \rho\, y_{t-1} + e_t$.

500 observations per replication.

10,000 replications.

The term "spurious regression" is used by statisticians to describe the seemingly "significant" coefficients that are found when two unrelated but highly autocorrelated series are regressed on each other. The conditions that produce spurious regressions are met by the variables used in the Hardouvelis study, namely the twelve-month moving average volatility and the continuous step function of the margin requirements. The seemingly significant negative relation between the two series arises essentially from the single point, noted earlier in figure 9.2, representing the high volatility after the Crash of 1937 and the relatively low margin requirement of 40 percent set by the Federal Reserve in an attempt to revive a moribund stock market. Thanks to the high persistence in both volatility and margins, however, the single point in figure 9.2 becomes a heavily weighted cluster of points, as can be seen from figure 9.4, which shows the scatter of the Hardouvelis regression of table 9.1.

Table 9.3
First difference regressions of volatility on margins
October 1935 to December 1987

Independent variables	Dependent variable: $\Delta\sigma_{y,t}$
Constant	0.000032
	(0.0002)
ΔM_t	-0.0035
	(0.0058)
R^2	0.0006
$D.W.$	1.93
Autocorrelation coefficients of residuals:	
Lag 1	0.0367
2	0.0538
3	0.0411
4	-0.0073
5	0.0068
6	0.0024
7	-0.0209
8	0.0587
9	0.0272
10	-0.0018
11	-0.0401
12	-0.3107

Hardouvelis was certainly aware that his variables and his regression residuals were highly autocorrelated and he took what he thought were the standard precautions. But he appears to have underestimated the seriousness of his autocorrelation problem so that his elaborate corrections proved to be inadequate.

Fortunately, a simple alternative procedure for dealing with highly autocorrelated series is available and can easily be checked for conformity with the requirements for valid inferences in regressions. That method is just to run the regression in the first differences of the variates rather than their levels. The results of regression in difference form are shown in table 9.3. Note first the diagnostics. The Durbin-Watson statistic and the serial correlations of the residuals are no longer sending alarm signals. The coefficient of the margin variable has now dropped substantially in size from that in the levels regression of table 9.1 and cannot reliably be distinguished from zero. The lack of any strong relation between the two variables shows up clearly in the scatter presented in figure 9.5.

Conclusion

Recent claims that the Federal Reserve's authority to set margin requirements give it a potentially powerful tool for controlling stock market volatility, and by extension, speculative excesses, have been shown to be unsubstantiated. The claims appear to rest on misinterpretations of the statistical record, and in particular on an insidious problem known as "spurious regression." When the necessary statistical precautions are taken, no relation between margins and volatility can be detected. That the Federal Reserve System has made no change in margin requirements since 1974 suggests that the System has long since anticipated this statistical finding.

This chapter is based on a paper presented at a seminar co-sponsored by the University of Munich and the Bayerische Verein Bank in Munich, Federal Republic of Germany, June 13, 1989; and on a paper coauthored with Professor David Hsieh, also of the Graduate School of Business, University of Chicago, and published in The Journal of Finance 44, *March, 1990.*

References

Hardouvelis, G.A. "Margin Requirements and Stock Market Volatility." *Federal Reserve Bank of New York Quarterly Review*, 1988a.

Hardouvelis, G.A. "Margin Requirements, Volatility, and the Transitory Component of Stock Prices." Unpublished manuscript, Columbia University, 1988b.

Officer, R.R. "The Variability of the Market Factor of the New York Stock Exchange," *Journal of Business* 46, 1973.

Figure 9.1. Monthly volatility and initial margin requirement

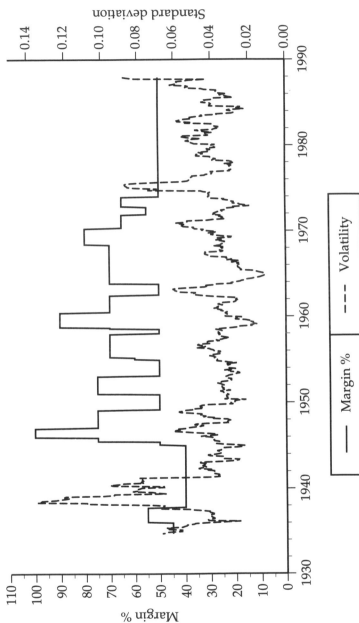

Figure 9.2. Average volatility during the margin periods

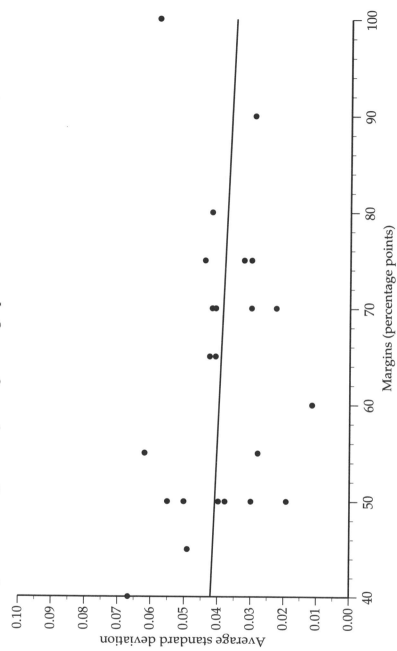

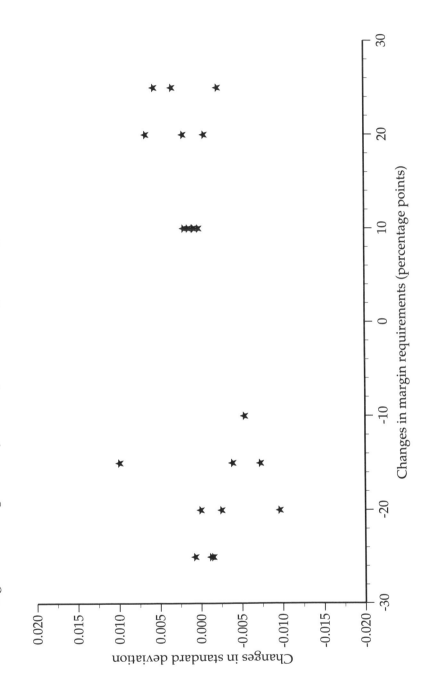

Figure 9.3. Changes in daily volatility versus changes in margins

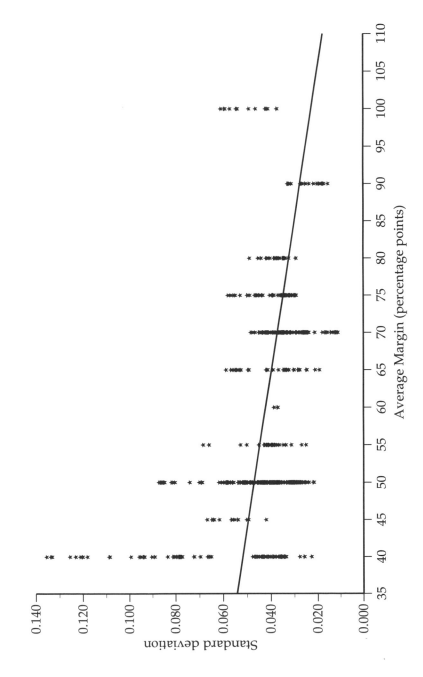

Figure 9.4. Monthly volatility versus average margins

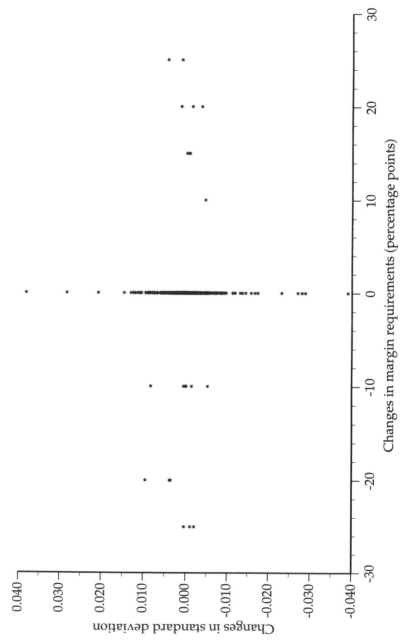

Figure 9.5. Monthly volatility changes versus margin changes

10 Should Short-Term Trading Be Taxed?

Senators Dole and Kassebaum of Kansas have jointly introduced a bill (S.1654) entitled "The Excessive Churning and Speculation Act of 1989." The Act places a 10 percent tax on gains realized by pension funds on assets held less than thirty days, and a 5 percent tax on assets held less than 180 days. Placing higher taxes on short-term than on long-term gains is nothing new in US tax law, of course. But the tax in S.1654 differs from past practice and from other current proposals for capital gains taxes with multiple holding periods by allowing no netting out of capital losses. Given the likely plentitude of short-term losses in the large and widely diversified equity portfolios of pension funds, the normal allowance for losses would have turned S.1654 into little more than a minor nuisance (and one that might actually have increased short-term trading). Even so, the Act does exempt "hedge" transactions so that most of the old taxpayer tricks (like buying straddles or selling-against-the-box) that convert short-term gains into long-term gains can still be used by fund managers to avoid the tax. But the supporting documents for S.1654 profess no great concern for the likely low revenue yield of the proposed new tax. The purpose of the tax is educational; by raising the cost of trading it directs the attention of plan sponsors to unnecessary churning by their portfolio managers.

What new facts about brokerage expenses plan sponsors will glean from filling out their tax forms is far from clear, however. (Perhaps they may learn that even passively managed index funds can have short-term, and hence presumably taxable, gains.) But it would be a mistake to dismiss S.1654 as just another ill-considered attempt at behavior modification by the nanny state in Washington. Sooner or later someone in Congress, perhaps even the Act's original sponsors, will surely note a better way of accomplishing the stated objectives of S.1654: just put an excise tax of a mere 1 to 2 percent on *all* transactions, rather than some big number like 5 percent to 10 percent only on gains. A flat excise or turnover tax can be shown to give roughly the same tilt against short-term trading and in favor of long-term holding as the capital gains tax with rate differentials, but without the lock-in effects and the incentives those lock-in effects generate to engage in unnecessary, tax-avoidance transactions. And, of course, unlike S.1654, a transactions tax would actually raise serious money!

So many, in fact, are the seeming advantages of a transactions tax over a capital gains tax that the real puzzle is why a transactions tax has not long ago been introduced. The answer may lie perhaps in the death-kiss that any proposal for new taxes brings these days to the legislators and the political parties initiating them. That may also explain why S.1654 uses the familiar language of already-existing capital gains taxes and why it is narrowly targeted to pension funds. Pension funds, as the beneficiaries of government largesse via tax exemption (or at least tax deferral) are in no position to complain too loudly. And even if they do complain, they are few, they don't vote, and they have managed to antagonize some of those who *do* by seeming to side with the raiders against local interests (spurred on by incumbent managers) in some recent takeover battles.

How long before the political taboos now blocking a general securities transactions tax will crumble is hard to say. But changes in climate can already be seen in the concern by the press as well as by Congress and the administration that an obsessive focus on current stock prices, induced by pressures to meet the short-term return goals of institutional investors, is leading US businesses to neglect research and generally to pass up projects with large, but long-deferred, payoffs. This corporate myopia theory of supposed recent US economic deficiencies has achieved cliché status in only a few short years. But the evidence offered tends to be anecdotal, selective, and often self-serving, as when embattled managements block stockholders from accepting huge takeover premiums by appeals for patience and forbearance–appeals reminiscent of those directed by Messrs Gorbachev and Honecker to their own particular constituents. Many of the myopia anecdotes, moreover, seem to neglect the ancient truth that time is money. A dollar five years from now is *not* worth a dollar given up today. In fact, if your cost of equity capital is 14 percent–surely not an unreasonable guess these days–then even *two* dollars five years from now is not worth a dollar today!

The currently fashionable view of so many of today's elderly decision makers and opinion molders that our investment horizons have been shortening may thus signify only that current real capital costs are high by the standards they remember. When government bonds were selling to yield 4 percent, and when inflation, in peace time at least, was running at never more than 1 to 2 percent a year, planning horizons of twenty to thirty years made perfect sense. But not at current, and much higher, real costs of capital.

When real costs of capital are high, a shortening of investment horizons should actually be welcomed, not deplored. Capital in short supply–and that, after all, is what an unusually high cost of capital (plus an unusually heavy inflow of foreign capital) signifies–is more effectively employed from society's point of view in projects that generate their payoffs quickly and thus help relieve the shortage. When domestic capital is plentiful, however, as seems to be currently the case in Japan (and as was the case in the USA in the past when it was a major capital exporter), the pressures to economize on it are correspondingly reduced.

Even if corporate managers really were more myopic than their high capital costs required, transactions taxes on their stockholders and other investors would only make things worse. Such taxes will, as intended, reduce the liquidity of shares as a way of holding wealth. The less liquid the security, the higher the returns required by investors, or, what amounts to the same thing, the higher the cost of capital to firms issuing the securities. Unlike the current vague charges of corporate myopia, moreover, the higher yields associated with the reduced liquidity of securities have been amply documented. A particularly striking example is offered by so-called "letter stock," which typically sells at discounts of 20 to 30 percent or even more below the prices of unrestricted shares in the same company!

In sum, transactions taxes, even at seemingly low rates, can have large and far-reaching consequences. Let us hope that S.1654 is just a reflex expression of frustration–Kansas shaking a figurative fist at Wall Street, so to speak–and not the opening gun in a war to be waged by Congress and the administration against market liquidity.

This chapter is based on a statement prepared for the annual survey of current issues by Institutional Investor, *December 1989.*

11 Index Arbitrage and Volatility

Few issues divide academic finance specialists from some of their practitioner counterparts as sharply as the social value of stock-index arbitrage. To academics, index arbitrage is essentially a benign institution serving to enforce the "law of one price." Any economist can and, with the slightest encouragement, will explain how correcting persistent violations of that law leaves everyone better off, or at least leaves some better off and no one worse off. Many practitioners believe, however, that index arbitrage leaves the arbitrageurs better off, but everyone else worse off because index arbitrage makes stock prices more volatile.

The term volatility in this context has proved unfortunate because the critics of index arbitrage and the academic defenders use the word in different senses. Hence we have had a classic dialogue of the deaf. The academics are concerned mainly with the risk an investor assumes in holding some particular class of assets such as equities, bonds, or real estate. To approximate risk in this portfolio sense, they focus on the variability or volatility of rates of return on assets over reasonably long holding-period intervals, though for reasons of statistical efficiency, they often compute volatility over shorter intervals such as months or even days and then aggregate to get estimates of variability over longer horizons. The tabulations of rates of return on equities by the academics show that volatility in the years since index futures and options contracts were introduced has not been notably high by past historical standards except perhaps for the temporary surges on October 19, 1987, and again on October 13, 1988. That the large price moves on those October days might actually have been caused by index arbitrage, as one so often reads in the financial press, is a charge no academic researcher takes seriously. Arbitrage transactions, with a buy side in one market and a sell side in the other, can have no substantial *net* effect on the price level. Nor do the observed variations in day-to-day volatility seem to be much related to changes in the intensity of program trading. The academics have thus tended to dismiss the recent torrent of complaints about index arbitrage and volatility as mostly hysteria.

For the practitioner critics of index arbitrage, however, the statistical tabulations by the academics of annual, monthly, or even day-to-day volatility are largely beside the point. By volatility of prices the critics are expressing their concern with the trading, not the holding, of stocks. They really mean the *velocity* of prices, in the sense of the very rapid, minute-to-minute (sometimes even second-to-second) sequences of price moves that the sudden triggering of index arbitrage programs often brings in its wake. These periodic bursts of very short-term velocity are held to be damaging to the market, whatever may be happening to longer-term volatility. The critics of index arbitrage might thus perhaps have had a more receptive hearing from the academic defenders had they avoided the statistical term volatility altogether and tried to explain instead who specifically they believe is harmed by the velocity of index arbitrage.

At first sight, of course, the victims may seem easy enough to identify. The critics might argue that, in principle, *anyone* who trades with an arbitrageur loses. An arbitrageur sells stock and buys futures because he *knows* the current stock price is too high relative to the futures and is soon to fall. (Strictly speaking, of course, the arbitrageur knows only that intermarket *spread* must fall, which could happen, conceivably, even if stock prices rose after the arbitrageur's sale. But to give the critics the benefit of the strongest possible case, let us suppose, throughout, that arbitrage buying of futures and selling of stock always causes prices on the stock leg to fall.) Were it only a matter of public market orders crossing against the arbitrageur's trades, the presumed damage from arbitrage would hardly be of major social concern. No one likes to lose, of course, but on average, a random liquidity-motivated market order is as likely to be on the same side as the arbitrageur as on the opposite side. The critics could argue, however, that one group of market participants does systematically lose to the arbitrageurs, namely, the market makers, broadly construed to include both the specialist and those who enter limit orders on his book. These market makers provide liquidity or immediacy to market-order traders by committing themselves to trade, at least for some stipulated sizes, at prices announced in advance. They give the market-order traders a free option, so to speak.

That the holder of a public limit order might be vexed indeed when an arbitrageur exercises that free option is easy to understand. Consider a resting limit order bid at 29-7/8 when the last trade was at 30. Suddenly an index-arbitrage sell program sweeps in. The bids at 29-7/8 are all hit; then, in succession, those at 29-3/4, at 29-5/8 and so on, down perhaps to 29-1/2. When the dust has settled a few minutes later, the limit order bidder at 29-7/8 finds himself with a confirmation at that price. The electronic data handling systems of the NYSE do get that good news to him quickly. But they also tell him the bad news, to wit: that he has just suffered an immediate loss of about 1-1/2 percent on the confirmed trade (the equivalent currently of about forty points on the Dow).

Limit order buyers must be presumed to know that these adverse hits can occur. They expect that over a long series of transactions their gains from better than average execution prices on their limit orders will more than balance out the occasional bad hits. The critics may be arguing, however, that the average *frequency* (and perhaps also the average size) of these adverse hits to the market makers has increased in recent years because of index arbitrage. More frequent hits would have a social, and not just a private, cost to the extent that they lead market makers and limit-order customers to protect themselves by widening their average spreads, by reducing the size of the orders to which they are prepared to precommit, and, perhaps in some cases, by abandoning limit orders altogether. (In point of fact, limit orders have fallen substantially relative to market orders in recent years, though other factors, including the Exchange's fee structure, may also have contributed to the decline.) The real case against index arbitrage might thus be not that it increases volatility in the standard academic sense of that term, but that by increasing the risks and hence costs of market making, it effectively imposes an excise tax on market liquidity (though with the arbitrageurs and not the government collecting the revenues).

The market makers themselves, however, must assume some blame for their troubles. Their quotes simply do not adjust to macro news shocks and sentiment shifts as rapidly as do prices on the futures exchange. The lag in stock quotes creates the opportunity that the arbitrageurs exploit.

That the slowness in adjusting quotes on the NYSE is the real source of the pain inflicted by arbitrage is suggested by the absence of complaints about intermarket arbitrage in the many other futures and options markets currently operating. When a government bond dealer looks at the appropriate window on his quote screen and sees that the futures price has fallen significantly below his own quotes, he doesn't wait around for the arbitrageurs to arrive. He immediately marks down his quotes. *Potential* rather than actual arbitrage thus is the main enforcer of the law of one price in the dispersed, multi-dealer settings typical of most spot markets.

The specialist on the NYSE, however, does not have the freedom of a dealer to jump his quotes up or down merely because he sees a big move in the S&P futures price on the screen above his booth. The specialist's price continuity obligations rule that course out. The retail limit order holders can, in principle, pull their lagging quotes, but unless they are continually monitoring their screens (that is, unless they are behaving like professional dealers), they are unlikely to be able to move fast enough. Nowadays, thanks to the Super DOT, the arbitrageurs are almost sure to get there first.

The Exchange has so far sought to equalize this race between the arbitrageurs and the market makers mainly by slowing the arbitrageurs with sidecars, collars, circuit breakers, and, most recently, by proposing virtually to ban program trades on big-move days. Steps of that kind not only delay the return to price uniformity but are unnecessary. The simpler and more socially efficient approach is to look in the opposite direction and speed up the adjustment of the limit orders! A new class of orders could be introduced, for example, to be called perhaps "contingent limit orders," permitting standing limit orders to be marked up or down automatically by a prespecified percentage whenever a certain specified movement in the futures market occurred. The specialist, relieved of his obligation to walk the price down an eighth at a time, need then only see that single transaction is made at the new, contingency-adjusted limit price level to force the computed index value (which is always based on the last transaction price) into closer conformity with the futures price. Both the potential gains to the arbitrageur and the potential losses to the limit order holders would thereby largely be removed, but with no violation of the law of one price and hence no reduction in market efficiency.

Automatic adjustment of limit orders need not be restricted to movements in futures prices, of course. Thanks to the wonders of electronics, the limit order book can now be programmed to handle a wide variety of new kinds of customer contingency orders (all for an appropriate fee, of course). The NYSE, by the nature of its basic product, can never hope to match the futures and options exchanges in introducing new investment vehicles. But with some relatively simple and straightforward updating of its rules, it could mitigate the impact of intermarket arbitrage, give new encouragement to the use of limit orders and create valuable new investment-strategy options for its retail customers.

This chapter appeared as Appendix G3 in the report of the New York Stock Exchange's Special Panel on Market Volatility and Investor Confidence, June 1990.

12 International Competitiveness of US Futures Exchanges

Futures exchanges are business organizations providing transaction services and associated clearing and settlement services in a wide variety of products ranging these days from agricultural products (corn, soybeans, beef cattle) to precious metals (gold, silver, platinum) to petroleum products (heating oil, gasoline) and, most important currently, to financial instruments (stock indexes, Treasury bonds, foreign currencies).

Although often dubbed "commodity exchanges," the futures exchanges trade not physical commodities, but *contracts,* which are similar in many respects to "insurance policies" where the "hazard" being insured is the change in the price of the underlying commodity over the life of the contract. Because the terms of settlement between the parties to the contract depend on the price of the underlying commodity at the time of settlement, futures and options contracts are often called "derivative instruments." That term can be misleading, however, if it suggests, as some critics of futures and options markets intend it to, that the market for the underlying commodity is the only "real" market, in the sense of the place where value is actually determined. In fact, however, whenever a strong and active futures market exists the true value of the commodity is much more likely to be "discovered" in the futures market than in the underlying spot market. The lower transactions costs and higher liquidity on the futures exchanges make those markets the more natural entry port for price-relevant information. Precisely why the costs might be lower and the liquidity higher on futures markets than on spot markets will be explained in due course. Suffice it to say at this point that the costs of trading and settlement are lower on the futures exchanges because the essential business strategy of those exchanges is to keep them lower. The futures exchanges are the "discount stores" of the financial services industry.

A breakdown of the futures exchange industry by location and type of product traded for 1980, 1985, and 1990 is presented in table 12.1.

Table 12.1: Number of futures exchanges

	1980	1985	1990
Commodity			
United States	9	10	10
Rest of world	14	13	13
Financial			
United States	4	6	6
Rest of world	1	6	16

Source: Research Division, Chicago Mercantile Exchange.

The US futures industry is by far the largest in the world at the moment. The Chicago Mercantile Exchange (hereafter CME), for example, currently the second largest exchange in terms of volume, as conventionally measured, traded over 100 million contracts last year, mostly in financial instruments and foreign currencies. Multiplying the number of contracts by the nominal value of each–one S&P 500 contract, for example, has a face value of about $175,000 currently and one Eurodollar contract a face value of $1 million–yields impressive dollar totals. The nominal dollar value, so computed, of the S&P 500 contracts traded daily would surely equal or exceed the dollar value of shares traded on the NYSE. But these purely notional totals can be seriously misleading. The actual *cash* changing hands in a day's trading in S&P 500 contracts at the CME can never be more than a small fraction of the cash flow at the NYSE for reasons that will become clear later.

A better indicator of the true economic weight of the industry therefore may be not a flow measure like contract volume, but a stock measure like market value of the enterprise. Exchanges in the USA of course, do not formally issue common stock. US law insists that exchanges be organized not as the profit-making corporations they really are, but essentially as country clubs, with those privileged to trade directly on the floor constituting the "members." The posted prices for those memberships can thus constitute one measure, at least, of the franchise values that an exchange embodies. In the case of the CME, for example, whose full membership seats currently sell for $500,000 or so, the combined worth of the stake of the 2,800 or so members of various classes comes to nearly $800 million. That size would put the CME roughly among the lower fifth of the firms listed on the NYSE in terms of capitalization. By comparison, the franchise value of the NYSE is on the order of $500 million. The franchise value of the entire US futures and options industry was about $2.0 billion in mid-1989, and that of all overseas exchanges might come to perhaps a fifth of that.

The customer clientele base of the US futures industry is primarily domestic, but the foreign presence is also substantial, running perhaps to 20 percent or more for such internationally relevant contracts as petroleum, gold, and Eurodollars, as well as US Treasury bonds and stock index products. US customer purchases of foreign contracts are still much smaller than foreign purchases of US contracts, but the outflow has grown substantially in recent years, particularly since the introduction of stock index futures and option products in the Tokyo market. A noticeable rise in US customer use of foreign markets, primarily London, has also occurred recently in the special case of so-called "exchange for physicals" (EFPs) in connection with the CME's S&P 500 index contract. The London-based EFPs, which will be discussed in more detail later, currently amount to somewhere between 1 and 1.5 percent of the S&P 500 contract volume.

Some estimates of the relative market shares in financial futures of US and foreign exchanges are presented in table 12.2 for 1980, 1985, and 1990. Note the rapid rise in foreign share, in terms of contract volume, since 1980. In 1980 the futures industry was almost entirely–and in financials, literally entirely–a US phenomenon. By 1990, however, the rest-of-the-world share in financial contracts had risen to a substantial 37 percent.

Table 12.2: Financial market share

	1980	1985	1990
United States	100%	94%	63%
Other	—	6%	37%

Source: Research Division, Chicago Mercantile Exchange.

That trend in market shares can be expected to continue apace in the years ahead. The essential technology for exchange-based trading of futures and options is no secret and, in the technology of electronic or screen-based trading of options and futures, some overseas competitors may even be somewhat ahead of the USA . In fact, in the normal course of industrial evolution, the US dominance might well have ended long since, save for the enormous advantage that inevitably attaches to all "first movers" in an exchange setting. So great apparently are the economies of scale in liquidity that the trading demand for any contract quickly gravitates to a single exchange. Even a new competing contract that is better designed can rarely hope to win away the business of a contract that is well established at another exchange. The savings in transaction costs and especially in market impact costs in the more liquid market often more than counterbalance the contracts' defects.

US exchanges will continue to enjoy this advantage on its contracts that are already well established assuming, of course–and it is by no means a comfortable assumption to be making these days–that heavy-handed regulatory interventions do not undermine the liquidity of those contracts. But growth in this industry has typically proceeded by the introduction of new contracts that respond to the new pockets of price volatility that turn up, often so unexpectedly, as the domestic and world economies evolve. The 1960s had their pork bellies, the 1970s had their foreign currencies, interest rates, and petroleum contracts, and the 1980s had their stock indexes. As we look ahead to the 1990s no one knows what the hot new products will turn out to be. But they stand as much chance of making their first appearance abroad as in the USA.

The competitiveness of the US industry involves much more, however, than facing off against foreign futures and options exchanges. Exchanges both in the USA and abroad must contend with the powerful competition of "off-exchange" or "over-the-counter" products, like "swaps," that are equivalent in many essential respects to exchange-traded futures and options, but subject to very different forms of regulatory supervision. If the futures exchanges are the discount stores (or, perhaps better, the "one-size-fits-all" stores) of the industry, the producers of some of these equivalent products, mostly the large international banks, are the top-of-the-line firms, offering "tailor-made" services to their customers. And, of course, thanks to the wonders of electronic networking, the customers are increasingly able to deal with each other directly, by-passing both the exchanges and the banks.

To forecast where the eventual boundaries will be drawn between these competing segments is at least as difficult for the derivative products as for any other industrial area. Who in 1979, after all, could have predicted the enormous retreat of the US automobile industry in the face of Japanese competition? A better approach to forecasting the competitive future of the US futures exchanges is to focus in on their technology and cost structure, highlighting in the process those areas in which the US futures industry might reasonably hope to maintain its edge over its many rivals at home and abroad. That search must begin with a clear understanding of how and why exchange-traded futures contracts differ from off-exchange, negotiated forward contracts. That subject is taken up next, followed by an appraisal of the competitive strengths of the overseas exchanges. The paper concludes with some speculations about the impact on futures trading of governmental regulation–the wild card in the competitiveness equation.

Exchange-Traded Futures Contracts: Demand, Supply, and Technology

To those unfamiliar with how futures work, transactions in them may well smack of witchcraft. Imagine, if you will, a magician displaying an ingot consisting of 1,000 ounces of 99.9 percent pure silver at a time when silver sells for $7.00 an ounce. The magician announces that by uttering certain magic words he will transmute this silver ingot not into gold–because that sort of alchemy is so old-fashioned–but into US Treasury bills. The magic words he then pronounces are: "Sell silver futures." And sure enough, the Treasury bills suddenly appear in place of the ingot.

"How did he do it?"–the audience gasps in wonder. For the answer, take a closer look at the terms of the futures contract. It obligates the magician to deliver 1,000 ounces of silver three months from today at a price of $7.15 an ounce. But silver today is selling for only $7.00 an ounce. Has the magician perhaps found a patsy to pay him the extra fifteen cents in Treasury bills?

Not at all. Look again at the contract, this time from the point of view of a buyer who will need 1,000 ounces of silver three months from now. He could, if he chose, buy the silver immediately at $7.00 an ounce and store it for ninety days. That, however, would involve two kinds of costs: first, storage costs at, say, $0.01 per ounce, and second, the opportunity cost of the funds needed to buy the silver. After all, if he didn't buy the silver, he could have invested the money in safe Treasury bills, yielding currently, say, 8 percent annually or 2 percent per quarter. Two percent on the $7,000 investment comes to $140 or $0.14 an ounce. Hence the buyer should be indifferent between buying the spot silver now at $7.00 and buying a futures contract obligating him to buy the silver three months from now at $7.15 an ounce. And by the same token, the seller-magician should be indifferent between selling the three-month futures contract for $7.15 an ounce or selling the silver immediately for $7.00, saving the $0.01 storage cost and *investing the $7,000 in Treasury bills*. The effective purchase of the bills is already taken care of, as it were, in the price stipulated in the futures contract.

This parable of the magician transforming silver into Treasury bills is merely a verbal transcription of the so-called "cost-of-carry formula" that defines the equilibrium price of a futures contract in terms of the current spot price of the commodity. In its simplest form, the cost-of-carry can be expressed by the equation:

$$f_{0,T} = P_0\left(1 + r(T) + s(T) - d(T)\right)$$

where $f_{0,T}$ is the price today (that is, at time 0) for a unit of the commodity to be delivered T days from now; P_0 is the current spot price of the commodity; $r(T)$ is the cumulative interest opportunity cost over the T days; $s(T)$ is the cumulative storage cost; and $d(T)$ is the cumulative "convenience yield" from holding the commodity over the T-day interval. The latter term was left out of the parable to simplify the story. But its role becomes important when we turn to consider why people choose to buy and sell futures contracts at all. If it is bills they want, why not just buy them directly and be done with it?

Because the firms and individuals holding (or planning to hold) inventories of commodities or securities, who constitute the primary clientele of the futures exchanges, want to have their cake and eat it too, so to speak. They want the convenience of having adequate inventory on hand to meet customer or production needs, but they don't want to face the risk that the value of that inventory may suddenly drop on them. To avoid that risk they can "hedge" by mimicking our magician and selling futures against their inventory position.

That selling the futures contract will in fact dispose of the price risk is easily seen by extending the previous example. Suppose that the spot price of silver were to fall over the next three months from its current level at $7.00 an ounce to $5.00 an ounce. Even a magician might be understandably disconcerted by this hit of 28 percent, or $2,000 on his silver holdings. But remember that he has a contract counterparty who has agreed to take the silver off his hands at the end of the three months for $7.15 an ounce. Our hedger has the choice of going ahead with that delivery of the silver, which will bring in $7,150, or of keeping the silver and buying back his contract (or one equivalent to it) which will then be selling for $2.15 an ounce (that is, the $5.00 value of the silver on the delivery date minus the delivery price of $7.15). Or, if silver futures were a so-called "cash settled" rather than a "delivery settled" contract, the hedger would keep the silver and merely accept a check from the counterparty for $2,150. In all three cases, the hedgers' net worth at contract expiration would be $7,140, exactly as if the hedger had put his original $7,000 into riskless Treasury bills.[1]

That the hedgers can insulate themselves from risk by selling futures should be clear enough by now. But where does that risk go? Is the whole futures industry anything more than just a gigantic game of "hot potato?"

The answer offered in many conventional descriptions of futures markets is that the risks are assumed by a special class of investors dubbed "speculators" whose steady nerves make them better able than the hedgers to face the specter of falling prices. But speculators are only part of the risk-transfer story. (And risk-bearing is only part of their function in the grand scheme of things. Speculators, lured by the prospect of trading gains, also help speed the incorporation of new information into prices; and by their trading activity, even when they guess wrong, help to defray the overhead costs of the exchanges.) In practice, much of the downside risk feared by hedgers like our magician gets shifted to firms and individuals more worried by *upside* risk (as, for example, a manufacturer committed to selling its output of photographic film under fixed price contracts, and now concerned about a possible rise in the cost of a key raw material). Both sides of the trade, in other words, are often business firms using futures contracts not for the pleasures of gambling, but to manage the risks of their inventory positions. And, as profit-oriented business firms, they can be presumed to be managing those risks at the lowest cost possible, a fact that is crucial for weighing the competitive prospects of the futures exchanges.

Those exchanges, of course, are by no means the only alternative open for firms in their efforts at risk management. Rather than hold silver in inventory, for example, a "short hedger" (like our magician and so called because he sells and hence takes a short position in the futures)

---

[1]The net worth is $7,140 and not the $7,150 of the contract price because we must net out the storage costs. Those costs are in the futures price, it is is true, but they were also incurred by the hedger. The same netting out applies to the convenience yield. On that score, note that if the hedger were actually to draw down the inventory during the three months, the original hedge would no longer be exact, but a riskless position could be restored by "lifting" (that is to say, buying back) futures contracts in the amount of the inventory sold.

might switch to a Japanese-style "just-in-time" inventory strategy. And a "long hedger" like our film manufacturer might abandon selling under fixed price contracts and shift the price risk to his customers. Or the two hedgers might contract with each other directly via expressions of interest on computer bulletin boards and then negotiate a forward contract that fully meets their individual needs. Or, as is particularly likely these days for foreign exchange risks and interest rate risks, they may each find a bank willing to take the opposite side of their risks, either directly as a principal or as a broker, by arranging for them to "swap" their positions. Given these and other alternatives always available to the firms, what leads them to do it with futures? The answer is, of course, that under certain conditions, though certainly by no means always, risk management with futures happens to be the cheapest way.

When and why futures exchanges may be cost effective[2]

The parties entering any forward arrangement, whether an exchange-traded futures contract or an over-the-counter forward contract, face the costs of protecting against contract default by the other party (and, of course, also incur the substantial costs and uncertainties of legal redress when a default does occur). Tales surface after every market crash of losers unwilling or unable to fulfill their contractual obligations. Even mere rumors of such defaults by major market traders can lead to self-protective withdrawals from the market by other traders. Such rumors circulated at the height of the panic on October 19, 1987; and similar difficulties arose again more recently, when potential buyers of the assets of the then still technically free-standing brokerage subsidiaries of Drexel Burnham Lambert refused to deal with them after the parent company filed for bankruptcy.

Forward markets and credit monitoring. One way of reducing vulnerability to contract default is to obey the ancient dictum: know thy

---

[2]Two excellent academic studies of the cost effectiveness of futures trading are those of Carlton (1984) and Telser and Higginbotham (1977).

counterparty and check his credit-worthiness thoroughly before signing the contract. And keep checking it thereafter throughout the life of the contract, because a firm's credit-worthiness can deteriorate dramatically even in the short span of three months. This time-tested route of credit monitoring is precisely that followed in the huge interbank foreign-exchange and swap markets. It works there as well as it does because the market is essentially an exclusive club with a small number of wealthy and well-known players, each of whom, moreover, has considerable expertise in checking the credit, not only of each other as counterparties, but also of their underlying corporate customers who place the orders.

A drawback of the system, however, is its less-than-complete flexibility when, for any of a number of sound business reasons, one of the bank counterparties or one of the underlying corporate customers wants to withdraw from the agreement before the contract expires. In principle, of course, the relevant parties to a forward contract are free to renegotiate the original terms, and in practice they frequently do. The party wanting out, however, would surely prefer not to be constrained to deal solely with the original counterparty, but rather to be able to deal with any third party willing and able to assume the obligations of the original counterparty over the remaining life of the contract. Finding a "willing" third party is often easy enough; but verifying the "able" part requires a new round of credit checking both by the party wanting out, who would presumably have to reassume the obligation if the third party defaulted, and probably also by the original counterparty as well. Rechecking credit worthiness in this fashion every time a contract obligation is transferred is feasible really only when all players already know each other and when they deal in contract sizes large enough to spread the fixed costs of credit checking and negotiation.

Assuring contract performance in future markets: the role of the clearinghouse. For the rest of the universe of firms and contract sizes not meeting these conditions, the futures markets have developed an alternative approach that greatly economizes on the amount of credit checking (and of legal pursuit) that might otherwise be needed to assure performance both of the original forward contract and of any subsequent transfers of its obligations. The futures markets do it by setting up a "clearinghouse" as the counterparty to *both* sides of every contract. Technically, the forward contracts bought or sold on the exchanges are all contracts with the clearinghouse–an arrangement that not only permits an efficient solution of the credit problem, as we shall see below, but that has other important advantages relative to forward contracts negotiated directly between the parties. With only a single issuer, contract terms can be standardized so that any seller can get out of his original obligation simply by "offsetting" it with the purchase of any other and fully equivalent contract. His accounts on the books of clearinghouses would then be in balance at zero and his obligations to the clearinghouse to fulfill the original contract are effectively ended. Yet the original buyer need have no concern at that point, or earlier, about the seller carrying out the contract's obligations. The clearinghouse, and not the original seller, whoever that might happen to be, is the contract counterparty to whom the buyer looks for satisfaction of the contract's terms.

The clearinghouse, as the counterparty to both sides, thus relieves the credit-risk anxieties of the contracting parties to the trade by substituting its own credit for theirs. But what makes those promises by the clearinghouse credible enough to permit bargains to be routinely struck on the floor of the exchange between complete strangers? The answer lies in an ingenious multilevel, defense-in-depth strategy, long recognized as the hallmark of futures-market trading.[3] The first line of defense for the clearinghouse consists of the initial "margins" or good faith deposits it requires in advance in cash or cash equivalents from each side of every trade. The initial margins are set high enough to absorb possible trading losses by either party on any days except those with extraordinarily large price changes. The second line of defense is

---

[3]The system can be traced as far back as the rice futures market in the Tokugawa Japan of the 1730s (Schaede, 1988) and was presumably rediscovered independently by the Chicago grain markets in the 1860s, though the destruction of records in the great Chicago Fire of 1871 makes any exact dating almost impossible. For an economic analysis of the margin system, see Telser (1981).

a daily settling up of the accounts. Recall that our cost-of-carry for-ward price of $7.15 was appropriate when spot silver was $7.00 an ounce. Should the futures price of silver have risen during the trading day to $7.25–as might happen, say, if the spot price rose to $7.10–anyone who sold silver futures yesterday at $7.15 has already incurred an obligation to pay $100 (that is, the ten-cent price change times 1,000 ounces) to the buyer at contract expiration, and possibly much more than $100 if the price of silver were to keep rising. To allay any concerns the buyer might have about the satisfaction of his claims (as well as to make sure that the clearinghouse remains a zero-balance clearinghouse and not a bank), the clearinghouse "marks to market" each trader's position at the end of the trading day. The gains and losses of each side to the contract are tabulated and the winners may withdraw their gains in cash if they so choose–drawing it, in effect, from the loser's margin deposits. Losers desiring to hold their positions must deposit more cash if their margin account has dropped below its "maintenance margin" level. Should the shortfall in the margin account not be rem-edied by the start of the next day's trading, the account will immediately be closed out by offsetting the position in the trading pit at the prevailing price. The same fate can be meted out to losers if they fail to meet intraday margin calls on days with exceptionally large price moves.[4] The clearinghouse defense system, in short, seeks to solve the problems of customer credit risk and of maintaining the credibility of its own guarantees by minimizing the amount of credit in the system. The futures markets aim to be not merely "cash on delivery" markets, but "cash before delivery" markets.

Behind these frontline clearinghouse defenses, the futures exchanges have erected still others to dampen the impact of any failures to meet obligations within the clearing mechanism itself. Customer margin accounts must be "segregated." They are not a source of borrowed funds to any brokerage firm, and hence are insulated from any brokerage firm

---

[4]As a further precaution against overextended customers, the exchanges (spurred on by the regulators) also impose "position limits." The exchange margins, moreover, are only the minimums. Brokers frequently require some customers to post additional initial margins.

failures. Each so-called "clearing firm" that constitutes the membership of the clearinghouse must also guarantee the contract performance of the brokerage firms and individual members for which it chooses to serve as clearing agent and support that guarantee with margin deposits and frequent intraday margin calls. The clearinghouses also have guarantee funds (sometimes called "security deposits" or "clearing corporation stock"), parent corporation guarantees for the trading of clearing member subsidiaries, and substantial committed bank lines of credit to provide emergency liquidity on short notice. The clearing firms themselves are jointly and severally responsible for each other's failure to perform, and the financial integrity of the clearinghouse itself is sustained ultimately by the full wealth of all the members of the exchange.

That this combined system of defenses is effective is evident in the oft-quoted boast of the CME and the Chicago Board of Trade, the two largest exchanges, that no customer of theirs has ever suffered from a contract default.[5] But, of course, there are no free lunches. The system of margins-cum-daily settlements, in particular, does impose costs on the market users and, to that extent, reduces their demand for trading services. Balancing the conflicting needs for transaction volume on the one hand, and clearinghouse security on the other, is a major part of every exchange's business strategy and helps explain their very hostile reaction to calls for government control over margins–a subject to be taken up later.

Thanks to their system of bonding traders with margins, the futures exchanges have carved out and maintained a zone of comparative advantage in their competition with directly negotiated forward contracts. But for a wide range of transaction sizes, the trading floors of the exchanges provide another equally important competitive edge.

---

[5]On two of the smaller exchanges, however, clearing-member defaults have in fact occurred within the past twenty years–Chicago Discount Brokers on the Mid-America Exchange and Volume Investors on the Commodity Exchange (COMEX). In the latter case, all customers were ultimately made whole, but only after some delay.

Transactions costs and the floor-trading system

Although transaction sizes on futures exchanges are an order of magnitude or more smaller than in the interbank forward foreign exchange market or the dealer Treasury bond market, the differences in *ad valorem* costs of actually effecting transactions in the two market settings are nowhere near as large. The bid-ask spreads in the Chicago Board of Trade's Treasury bond pit, for example, are typically 1/32nd or three one-hundredths of one percent on a contract size of $100,000, with perhaps another one-hundredth of one percent or so additional in direct commissions. Large customers can sometimes better that in the spot market, but not always. And the futures market offers an at least partially compensating advantage in the form of its transparency; transactors can see the prices at which trades are actually taking place.

The particular technology that US futures markets use to provide their customers with low-cost and transparent transaction services is that of a centralized "open-outcry" market with competing market makers. Orders flow from the customers to "floor brokers" or "order fillers" who then auction these orders publicly to the "floor traders" or "locals." The locals, by and large, are not long-term "value buyers" but short-term intermediaries whose trades serve to offset the inevitable lack of perfect synchronization between the arrival of buy orders and sell orders. They provide the users with "immediacy" and that can be a most valuable service indeed to someone seeking to hedge an inventory, often heavily financed with short-term loans, of an underlying commodity or financial instrument subject to great price volatility.[6] The compensation the market makers expect to receive for supplying this immediacy is the expected difference between the prices at which they buy and resell on the one hand, and the costs they incur in the process.

These costs for the locals are of two major kinds, over and above the direct record-keeping and paper-shuffling costs inevitably incurred in

---

[6]"Immediacy" is closely related to, but not quite synonymous with "liquidity." A market is said to be liquid if it not only provides immediacy, but does so for reasonable quantities at little change in price. The futures markets provide liquidity as well as immediacy by having many locals on hand to compete for all or part of each incoming customer order.

any financial transaction. The first is simply the mirror-side of the same exposure to an adverse price move that the customer gives up by trading with a market maker rather than waiting for the ultimate counterparty to arrive. The market makers may well have greater tolerance for this risk than the individual customer, as noted earlier, but that is only one reason the arrangement remains viable. In a competitive, open-outcry market, the delay risk is a shared risk. The larger the population of traders in the pit, the lower, on average, the costs to each assuming the temporary price risks–an example, once again, of the kinds of economies of scale so critical in determining a market's ability to stay competitive.[7]

Why then does not the number of floor traders increase to the point where the unit cost of bearing the temporary price risk becomes effectively zero? The answer lies in the second major, and all too often neglected, cost of market making, to wit: the opportunity costs of the financial and human capital necessary to sustain a continuous market presence. Given these costs, the supply of market makers can be expected to adjust until, in equilibrium, the net expected market returns (after adjustment for risk) of the marginal market maker just equal his cost of maintaining a continuous market presence. The higher the costs of maintaining that presence, the fewer the market makers in equilibrium and hence the higher the effective costs of immediacy to the customers. In the limit, when the number of market makers that can recover their fixed costs becomes sufficiently small, the market ceases to be viable.[8]

---

[7]The delay risk discussed here blends into another risk, to wit: the adverse selection risk in which the market member is disadvantaged by trading with people who have inside, or at least markedly superior, information to his. Risk of this kind is probably more acute in the case of individual stocks, say, where it has been the focus on much study, than for the much less idiosyncratic "commodities" traded on the futures exchanges. The substantially lesser vulnerability of stock index futures to insider information is another reason why market spreads for the futures are substantially smaller than on the separate stocks that make up the index.

[8]For a fuller account of the equilibrating process, see chapter 2 in this volume.

Recognizing these essentially fixed costs of market making and the adjustments in the supply of market makers they induce can help illuminate both the history and the business strategy of the US futures exchanges. They make clearer, for example, why the futures exchanges found their first natural niche in agricultural commodities. The long chain of handlings and processings of farm commodities on the road to their ultimate consumers creates a continuing demand for *trading* as the processors successively hedge and unhedge their inventories. By contrast, the highly publicized Consumer Price Index futures contract of the Coffee, Sugar, and Cocoa Exchange never found a place, even though many firms had substantial contractual cost-of-living commitments that they might well have wanted to hedge. But those commitments apparently did not change often enough to generate the steady flow of orders needed to sustain the continuing presence of market makers on the trading floor of an exchange.

The overhead costs of maintaining market presence create not only economies of scale but economies of scope as well. Floor trading skills are not strongly contract-specific. Hence futures exchanges have always had many contracts trading simultaneously, giving their market makers more chances to trade enough to meet their overhead expenses. The same inexorable logic of overhead costs also underlay the diversification of the US futures exchanges in the early 1970s beyond their original, and at that time somewhat stagnant, niche in agricultural products to foreign exchange contracts, options, and financial futures generally.

In the course of the twenty years during which the US futures exchanges were diversifying from agriculturals to financials they have achieved economies of scale that, at first sight, might make them seem impregnable to direct competition in their successful contracts either from foreign futures and options exchanges or from the off-exchange, forward markets. And, indeed, they probably *would* be impregnable in those contracts, if everything could stay the same. But, of course, it can't. New technology has been developed and new regulatory initiatives have been proposed that could lead to a dramatic redrawing of current competitive boundaries.

The Competitive Threat from Overseas Futures Exchanges

The major threat from overseas to the currently dominant position of US futures markets is probably a technological one: the development and perfection of electronic screen trading. Decentralized electronic screen trading, if it can be made to work efficiently, could undercut the main source of the scale economies and hence the current comparative advantage of US futures exchanges, to wit: the large pool of highly skilled and experienced floor traders. Foreign competitors would need many years, if not generations, to put comparable populations of market makers on their trading floors. But with successful electronic screen trading, the very centralized trading floor itself becomes dispensable, as the example of the post-Big Bang London Stock Exchange so vividly demonstrates.[9]

Electronic trading systems are of two basic kinds at the moment, though inevitably with some overlap. At the one extreme are dealer-quote screens or "bulletin boards" like those of NASDAQ in the USA or SEAQ in London. Execution of small orders at a dealer's posted price is usually guaranteed, but larger orders must be phoned in and negotiated. Some such systems are fully transparent in the sense of reporting all recent transaction prices along with the current dealer quotes, but on many others the reporting of large negotiated transactions done off-screen can be delayed until the end of the trading day or even longer. At the other extreme to the dealer bulletin boards are the more recently developed "order matching" systems in which the screen serves essentially as a visible "limit order" book. Those with access to the network enter their bids and offers subject to a well-specified set of time, price, and size priorities. The posted limit prices are then matched by the computer and when a valid trade is possible, it is executed (and confirmed) directly without need for additional telephone calls. Since the computer executes all trades, the system can easily be made fully transparent,

---

[9]Still another example is the fully electronic New Zealand Futures Exchange (NZFE). For a sparsely populated country with no single dominating financial center, a computer network made much more sense than any centralized exchange.

though the use of separate windows on the screen for trade reporting makes for the kind of crowded and busy picture that seems user friendly only to members of the current Nintendo generation.

That electronic market systems of either of these types could win a head-to-head competition with active, high volume contracts like the Chicago Board Options Exchange's Treasury Bond pit or the CME's Eurodollar pit, either currently or in the foreseeable future, is far less likely than many computer enthusiasts seem ready to believe. A pit with several hundred locals offers far faster–indeed, virtually simultaneous–transaction-handling capacity. Nor is it simply a matter of waiting until computer technology improves, as it someday surely will, to the point where several hundred simultaneously bidding locals can actually be accommodated on the screen. The problem is not so much technology as motivation. In a screen trading environment, the floor trader loses his "edge" in the sense of the information advantage he draws from being present on the floor and able to observe the incoming order flow. By having to post his quotes in advance on the screen, he must now offer, in effect, a free option to all other traders and thus runs a greater risk of being picked off by someone with better or more up-to-date information. Screen trading systems, in sum, particularly of the order-matching kind, thus are unlikely to attract the services of large numbers of competing market makers and hence to offer levels of immediacy and liquidity comparable to those of the currently most active trading pits.[10]

Barring regulatory upheavals, the US exchanges are likely to feel the competitive impact of overseas screen trading not so much in their main and firmly established markets as in the markets for new products and low-volume products. They might also have faced competitive inroads in the form of screen trading even of their established products in after-hours trading, had not both the CBOT and the CME taken steps to counter such entry–the former by holding additional, after-

---

[10]Screen networks, if big enough, may not *need* market makers in the traditional sense, however. Big networks may come close to the Walrasian ideal market in which *all* potential buyers and sellers are present and ready to trade.

normal-hours pit trading sessions and the latter by planning a screen-based order-matching system of its own (Globex) for after-hours trading. Nor, once an overseas exchange has successfully launched a new screen-traded contract, can a US exchange automatically hope to capture the business by introducing the contract or a close substitute on its own trading floor. The "first-mover" advantage in this industry is too strong.[11]

Given its economies of scale, floor trading in an already established contract may well have cost advantages over screen trading. But if a successful screen trading contract comes on the scene first, the floor may never attract enough volume to get up to speed.

The emphasis here has been on the possible competitive impact of overseas exchanges on the US industry. But competition runs both ways. And, subject, as always, to the important qualification, "regulation aside," the US futures exchanges could also reasonably be expected to increase their penetration of overseas markets.[12] The view, once treated as axiomatic, that each country had a natural and largely un-beatable advantage in the trading of its own domestic instruments can no longer be taken for granted now that more shares of Volvo, to pick one conspicuous example, trade in London than in Stockholm. Deriva-tive instruments are, in the nature of the case, even less firmly tied to any particular country. Any exchange, wherever it happens to be lo-cated, can create a futures or option contract on any underlying object, even the Rock of Gibraltar, provided only that the object change in some reasonably objectively measurable dimension. Physical delivery has never really been essential to futures contracts. Until the passage of the CFTC Act in 1974, the possibility of delivery served merely as

---

[11]A first-mover advantage also exists for screen trading computer networks because the cost of developing a worldwide network is high and because bro-kerage firms face both space and financial limits on the number of separate computer consoles they can handle. Hence the recently announced decision of the Chicago Board Options Exchange to join Globex rather than continue its attempts to set up a competing after-hours electronic network of its own.

[12]The Nikkei 225 stock index futures contract, now screen-traded in Japan, may some day provide an interesting test case. The US futures exchanges, for reasons to be noted later, have not so far chosen to offer such a contract.

little more than a legal technicality to keep some state courts from treating commercial futures contracts as unenforceable gambling debts. Very little delivery ever actually took place, though the very possibility of making or taking delivery may have helped to assure the convergence of the futures price to the spot price at the expiration date. The 1974 Act, however, made cash settlement legal for futures contracts, and that has been the route to settlement taken in most, though by no means all, of the new contracts introduced since that time. Not only is physical delivery thus not critical for a viable futures contract, but neither is the possibility of direct intermarket arbitrage, although arbitrage, by tying the price of the derivative more closely to that of the underlying object, certainly makes the contract more useful to potential hedgers.

The tabulation in table 12.3 of foreign-source contracts being traded in 1980, 1985, and 1990 shows that the process of trading contracts involving nondomestic underlying objects is already well under way.

Table 12.3: Trading other country's products

	1980	1985	1990
United States	—	—	Diffs (CME)
			ECU (NYCE)
Other	—	Eurodollar (LIFFE)	Euromark (LIFFE)
			German Bund (LIFFE)
			Yen Bond (LIFFE)
			Eurodollar (LIFFE)
			Euromark (MATIF)
			US Dollar (NZFE)
			Eurodollar (SIMEX)
			Eurodollar (TIFFE)

Source: Research Division, Chicago Mercantile Exchange.

Particularly noteworthy is the German Bund contract traded not in Frankfurt, but on the London International Financial Futures Exchange

(LIFFE). Equally interesting, though not shown in table 12.3, is the Nikkei Stock Index Futures contract, first introduced on the Singapore International Monetary Exchange in 1988 and taken over by the Osaka Stock Exchange in 1989. Nor is the competition in cross-border products a matter of the futures exchanges only. Derivative contracts much in the news recently are the Nikkei warrants (essentially long-term put and call options) traded over-the-counter and on the American Stock Exchange.

Given the ease nowadays of effecting cross-border financial transactions (for most sophisticated customers nothing more is usually involved than pushing a button or two), trade in futures and options in a totally free and unregulated environment could be expected to flow to the cheapest market. And the US industry, given the economies of scale and scope that it has already achieved, would be a formidable competitor indeed. But no industry, and certainly not this one, operates internationally in a totally free and unregulated environment. Protectionism, both direct and indirect, is as much a fact of life in financial services as anywhere else. Many of the key issues in international and intermarket regulation have been covered by former SEC Commissioner Grundfest (1990) and need not be repeated here. The concern instead will be with some seemingly purely domestic regulatory policy proposals that would raise the cost of trading on the exchanges, and to that extent would weaken their competitiveness both internationally and relative to their domestic rivals.

Regulation and Competitiveness: the Case of Stock Index Futures Margins

Regulation, in practice, affects an industry's competitiveness mainly by lowering it. Regulation, by its very nature, makes costs of production higher than they otherwise would be. Circumstances can always be imagined, of course, in which regulation might actually *improve* an industry's viability on balance. Instituting the SEC in 1934 may perhaps have helped restore confidence in the US stock market to investors demoralized by the Crash of 1929. The same investor-confidence argument is being invoked currently to justify costly new trading regulations for the futures exchanges in the wake of the FBI's sting operation disclosed in January 1989. But the relation of regulation to confidence can easily be oversold. The exchanges themselves have the strongest of commercial motives to maintain the confidence of their customers, but not to overinvest in it. The regulators and Congressional overseers face no such cost/revenue tradeoff and thus inevitably overreact to any appearance of scandal. As one wag put it: when a Congressman says that his constituents are losing confidence in the market, he really means that his constituents are losing confidence in him!

To say that regulation raises costs of production is not to suggest, of course, that such cost increases are never justified. Externalities, such as pollution, do exist; and imposing compensating costs on those who cause it, and thereby reducing their combined output of product plus pollution, is often clearly in the public interest. But the presumption of social benefit from the added regulatory costs requires a more careful balancing of all the gains and losses, direct and indirect, than our political mechanisms can seem to supply. The result of our efforts to correct for externalities has all too often found the direct costs plus the unintended side consequences of the regulatory intervention substantially outweighing the benefits actually achieved. The proposed transfer to the SEC of margin authority for index futures can serve, perhaps, as an instructive example of how such an imbalance could easily arise despite the best of intentions on the part of the regulators.

Mandated margins for index futures: the presumed benefits

Proposals to transfer the authority over stock index futures margins from the private-sector exchanges to public-sector regulators first surfaced in earnest, as is so often the case with calls for regulation, after a specific event, in this instance the great market break of October 19 and 20, 1987. The Brady Commission in its post-mortem study of the Crash made "harmonization" of stock and futures margins a key recommendation. While the term harmonization was nowhere defined, their call for harmonization was everywhere regarded, and was presumably so intended by the Brady Commission, as a code word for federal control over index futures margins. The call by the Brady Commission was taken up subsequently by both the former and the current Chairmen of the SEC and, of course, their Congressional overseers. A bill transferring index futures margin authority to the SEC has, in fact, been introduced, with Administration backing.

In the period immediately after the Crash of 1987 the main emphasis of those calling for federal regulation was on the dangers to the safety and integrity of the entire payments system posed by the massive flows of cash margin funds from the losers to the winners after a major market move. The force of this argument was largely undercut, however, by the very fact that the financial system did manage to survive despite the biggest one-day move in US stock market history. The system survived, moreover, despite the almost complete absence at the time of any contingency planning for such emergencies on the part either of the banks or of the monetary authorities. Such contingency plans have since been put into place, and so effectively, apparently, that the much discussed mini-crash of October 13, 1989–a market break of more than 6 percent–produced virtually no visible signs of strain on the payments system.

Proponents of federal regulation have thus tended to put less stress recently on systemic strain and more on the supposed contribution of low futures margins to market volatility. The high leverage in a futures position is said to encourage excessive speculation in the futures market, causing erratic and unwarranted price moves that then flow from there via index arbitrage to the stock market in damaging bursts of "episodic volatility."

To review in detail the enormous (and still rapidly growing) literature on market volatility and its proximate causes would clearly not be appropriate in a paper of the present limited scope. Suffice it to say that the Administration's strongly stated views on the contribution of index futures to market volatility find little support in the serious academic literature on the subject. The Administration's arguments, in fact, are little more than modern-dress versions of the charges that have long been raised against futures markets generally, not merely stock index futures markets.

The charge that the futures markets are roiling the spot markets always seems plausible on the surface because the lower cost and greater liquidity of trading futures makes the futures market the natural entry-port for new information. The news–once "discovered" or revealed in price changes for futures–flows from there to the cash market by the arbitrage process. In most cash markets, only minor arbitrage flows are actually needed to restore the price relations required by the cost-of-carry formula. Spot market dealers typically "price off the futures." That is, they observe the current futures price and mark their own quotes up or down accordingly. But in the case of stock index futures, the spot market is not a dispersed dealer market, but another exchange, and one, moreover, whose official rhetoric stresses the price continuity delivered by its franchised specialist and by the public limit-order book he manages. That very continuity, however, by slowing the adjustment of prices, created both tempting opportunities and much public notoriety for the index arbitrage in the early years of the index contract. As the NYSE adjusted to the new realities, prices there have adjusted faster, substantially reducing thereby the profitability of intermarket arbitrage. True arbitrage, never anywhere near as large as the public's perceptions of it, has accordingly diminished substantially. But its notoriety lingers on.[13]

The notion that "news" and not futures trading is responsible ultimately for the large price changes in the spot market has also been resisted by many because specific "smoking guns," as it were, can so rarely be tied to big market moves. But news, in the relevant economic sense, is not just "news events," like assassinations or military defeats. The pricing of stocks involves more than merely appraising current and

---

[13]For evidence on the speeding up of price adjustment in the NYSE relative to futures prices see Froot, Gammill and Perold (1990). Rough calculations of the gross and net profitability of index arbitrage suggest, as one would expect, that truly riskless arbitrage operations under current conditions would just barely match the nominal riskless rate of return on Treasury bills. Much of what the NYSE currently classifies as "index arbitrage" must therefore presumably represent similar-looking, but actually highly risky strategies such as "legging," in which the futures and offsetting cash legs are not set simultaneously, but with one or the other deliberately lagged.

near-term dividends and earnings. Required also are projections of growth rates and risk-adjusted discount rates for earning power far into the distant and highly uncertain future. Thanks to the highly nonlinear way that these growth rates and discount rates enter into prices, even small changes in the perception of what might be called the future economic climate can lead investors to rethink their previous decisions about the proper allocation of their wealth between equity and fixed income securities. When a sufficiently large number of them choose, more or less simultaneously, to reduce their equity proportions substantially, then, given the fixity of the supplies of equity and debt securities in the immediate short run, equilibrium can be restored only by a drop in equity values substantial enough to restore the desired equity exposure. Large, economic climate-related readjustments of that kind appear to have occurred in October 1929, October 1987 and, on a smaller scale, in October 1989 (although, in that case at least, the failure of the United Air Lines (UAL) buyout can be identified as a specific event that triggered the reappraisal of future buyout prospects more generally). Which October, or perhaps even which May, will see the next major readjustment of equity proportions no one, of course, now can say. But happen someday it surely will, no matter what the regulatory structure.

Federal margin regulation and the costs of futures trading

No amount of regulation in general or of "oversight" can keep major price moves from taking place when circumstances demand. Even closing down a market altogether will merely shift to another market the volatility flowing from perceived changes in the underlying fundamentals. In the particular case of the regulation of stock market margin requirements by the Federal Reserve System, moreover, a mountain of academic studies testifies to the almost complete absence of any detectable causal relations between the Fed's mandated minimum initial margin requirements and subsequent stock market volatility.[14] Nor is this judgment about underlying market volatility likely to be altered in

---

[14]See among many others Schwert (1990), Kupiec (1989), and Hsieh and Miller (1990).

any way if the authority to set index futures margins were transferred from the exchanges either to the Fed (which doesn't want the responsibility) or to the SEC (which very much does). Federalizing control over futures margins will simply raise the cost of trading index futures and lower the quantity of futures contracts traded.

That such must be the case is almost axiomatic. Futures exchanges, as seen earlier, set their margins according to standard business "profit-maximizing" conditions. When they consider raising margins, they weigh the gains from reducing the risks of contract default against the loss of business from customers deterred by the opportunity costs of posting higher margins. No outside regulator can be presumed to set margins in the same way; if they did, why bother with regulation at all? And even if the regulators sought to find the profit-maximizing balance, they are hardly likely to be better at that task than the exchanges themselves. The result in either case must be a departure from the (constantly changing) optimum margin level.

How far the public-sector determined margins will deviate from the exchange's optimum will depend, of course, on the particular objective function followed by the regulators in setting margin levels. That objective function, whatever its precise form, must inevitably be highly asymmetric, in the sense that an active regulator invites heavy criticism for the few bad market days but receives little praise for the many uneventful ones.[15] The indicated strategy under those circumstances appears to be that followed by the Fed in setting initial stock-market margins over the past sixteen years: set the margin level high and keep it there! That way, the regulator can never be blamed either for precipitating a crash by raising margins sharply when the market is surging, or for causing the market to overheat by having set margins too low on the upside. The very fact that the margins had to be raised to

---

[15]Nor, of course, do the regulators derive the same kind of financial benefits that the exchanges do from increases in the volume of contracts traded, though the regulators might conceivably do so indirectly if user fees or charges were levied to defray the regulatory expenses. Otherwise, they feel pressures to expand volume only indirectly via the pressures that the exchange members can bring to bear on the Congressional overseers of the regulators.

stop the overheating, moreover, will be taken by the public and by Congressional overseers as *prima facie* evidence that the margins had been set too low in the first place.

The pressures on the SEC–currently the leading candidate for regulator of index futures margins–to follow the high-and-stable margins policy will be even greater than those that led the Fed to that policy. Unlike the Fed, the SEC (and the Treasury Department) really seem to believe that "excessive speculation" in index futures causes market crashes for which they may be held responsible once they win their highly publicized fight for margin authority. And the SEC, in its long-standing role as guardian of what it sees as the main market, can hardly be expected to be acutely sensitive to any drops in trading volume that high margins might cause in one of the merely derivative markets newly brought under its mantle.

But while index futures margins would thus surely rise under any public-sector regulatory authority, the effective increase in trading costs that results will depend considerably on how the new rules would apply to the various categories of traders. Initial "speculative margins"–in the sense of margins for accounts that do not qualify for the lower "hedger margins"–are currently $20,000 or about 11 percent on a contract with a nominal value of $175,000. Raising these margins to $87,500 to match the 50 percent level currently in force for common stocks–an equalization often suggested by critics of index futures–would make index futures prohibitively expensive for this class of traders. With futures marked to market daily, the five-day (or longer) settlement period for stocks would make them a better buy. Loss of these accounts would represent about 20 percent of the current open interest at the CME. If initial speculative margin levels were to be set not at 50 percent, but at only 20 percent ($35,000) as some on the SEC have hinted, then most of the purely retail portion of the accounts, currently running between 5 and 7 percent of the open interest, would likely still be lost. The nonretail remainder, consisting mainly of commodity pools, can also be expected to reduce participation in index futures substantially, though some of the trading activity might well be shifted to other futures contracts, at the CME or elsewhere, where the opportunity costs of the margin requirements would be lower.

The institutional hedging accounts that make up the bulk of the open interest pose additional problems for the regulators. Some critics interpret the call for harmonization of margins to mean that the special status of hedging margins (currently $6,000 per contract or a bit more than 3 percent of nominal value) be eliminated altogether. After all, no such exemptions apply to margined long or short positions in common stocks. Special exemptions from margin requirements do exist, it is true, for broker-dealers and other stock market professionals, but they must meet capital requirements which have much the same effect. Those capital requirements, which apply to both long and short stock positions, would be equivalent to margin requirements of 20 to 25 percent. If, in the name of harmonization, futures margins for hedgers were to be raised to the same level, the drop in volume for the contract would be virtually total, despite the often-heard claim that margins don't really have a cost to the pension funds and other big institutional traders. True, those institutions *could* post billions of dollars of Treasury bills with a clearing firm as collateral rather than posting cash on which no interest is earned, or posting bank letters of credit on which fees must be paid. But holding bills has an opportunity cost in the form of lower yields, and even if it did not few such institutions would be prepared to give up custody of any major portion of their assets under current customer account-segregation rules. The segregation requirement applies only to a broker's customer accounts taken as a whole; any individual customer would still be exposed to a default by another customer, even if not, perhaps, to a failure of the brokerage firm itself.[16]

Some have argued that the basic goal of harmonization might be achieved in less drastic fashion by restricting the hedging exemption to short hedgers only, that is, to those who actually hold the underlying stocks and propose to sell futures against them. The long hedgers, or anticipatory hedgers as they are sometimes called, who now represent a third or so of the open interest would be subject to the speculative

---

[16]In this connection see Jordan and Morgan (1990).

margins. The benefits to the long-run viability of the market from this seemingly less restrictive definition of hedging are much less, however, than they might seem at first glance. The short hedgers will indeed still be able to sell. But, as the old Wall Street joke goes: "to whom?"

Transferring control over index futures margins from the private sector to the public sector will thus occasion a sizeable drop-off in the volume of contracts traded. The drop-off would range from a minimum of perhaps 20 to 25 percent if the increase in margins is confined to so-called speculative margin accounts, to as much as 100 percent if the higher levels were applied also to hedgers (short and long), to floor traders (most of whom now face no margin requirements as such since they typically zero out their positions by the end of the day), and to the margins that clearing firms must maintain with the clearinghouse. Many have considered the disaster scenario unlikely on the grounds that the SEC, having obtained the margin authority on the promise of being a responsible regulator, would hesitate to be caught murdering the futures market in public. But, in a world where the chairman of the SEC's Congressional oversight committee has likened index futures to cockroaches, not even this possibility can safely be ruled out. One way or another, then, the volume of business in index futures will surely contract. Where the lost business is likely to go is the final question to be considered.

Federal margin controls and international competitiveness

The Eurodollar and Eurobond markets today stand as vivid reminders of how heavy-handed interventions by US regulators can shift the locus of activity in the financial services sector. Federal regulation of margins on index futures will induce similar shifts in trading patterns, though perhaps less dramatically so, at least in the immediate short run. The Euromarkets, after all, are markets only in a generic sense. Their business is basically carried on by separate broker-dealer firms and banks dispersed over virtually the entire world, or at least that part of it beyond US regulatory jurisdiction. Index futures, by contrast, are traded currently on centralized exchange markets with very specific locational ties. Moving whole business complexes from one location to another is certainly not unthinkable, as is clear from such past examples as the community of skilled glass workers who migrated *en masse* from Charleroi, Belgium, to found Charleroi, Pennsylvania, in the 1880s. Another example is the more recent displacement of the diamond-cutting industry from the Netherlands to New York and to Israel. But no such dramatic translations can be expected in an industry whose products are as generic as index futures even though, as emphasized earlier, the size and skills of its body of trading locals are a major source of its competitive comparative advantage.

The shift in business will take place rather in separate tranches, with the first slice almost certainly going to London. London, as noted earlier, has already made inroads on the CME's S&P 500 index futures contract, thanks to two particular features of US regulatory laws governing stocks and securities. The CFTC Act and related statutes currently allow negotiated, off-exchange transactions in futures only for the transfer of a futures contract in return for delivery of the underlying commodity itself (hence the term exchange-for-physicals, or EFPs). At the same time, the SEC-mandated trading rules prohibit the short-selling of stock on any exchange under its jurisdiction except on an uptick. The SEC also prohibits dealers from crossing blocks or portfolios of stocks without first exposing those trades to the floor. The CFTC rules on negotiated block trades are even more restrictive. The consequence: those seeking either to short-sell a portfolio of S&P 500 stocks without violating the uptick rule or to undertake a negotiated transaction in stock index futures do so in London with an EFP after regular US trading hours.

In the normal course of competitive give and take, the CME could surely have been expected to propose counter moves that might win back at least some of the after-hours block business lost to London, for example, by petitioning the CFTC (as it has in fact recently done) to loosen its current restrictions on large-order transactions negotiated off-exchange. That the CME's ability to respond to competitive challenges will be weakened directly by the higher levels of margins mandated by the SEC has already been established. But the SEC could also damage even further both the CME and the NYSE by heeding those urging it to rein in the London EFPs now used for bypassing the uptick rules. Such steps, if successful, would give additional impetus to the direct trading of large-cap US stocks in London, and as the spot market there becomes more liquid, the introduction of a London-based US index futures contract for after-US hours trading becomes a very real possibility.[17]

Meanwhile, at the other end of the world's time zone in the Far East, the weakened position of the CME would open opportunities for after-hours trading of US index futures that might well be picked up first by SIMEX in Singapore. That exchange, after all, was first off the mark in Japanese stock index futures when the Japanese markets were hobbled by their own regulators and while the efforts of the US exchanges to fill the gap were still being delayed by the SEC and the CFTC.[18] The SIMEX Japanese index contract, for a variety of reasons, never achieved critical mass and the business was eventually absorbed by the immensely strong financial service industry in Japan proper. The same evolution might well be repeated for an after-US hours contract on the US S&P 500 or similar contract.

As after-hours index futures contracts in London and the Far East become rooted and grow more liquid, the overseas exchanges will certainly be tempted to expand into the prime-time hours of the newly high-margin, high-cost US index futures markets. Is it possible that some exchange not under US jurisdiction, but still in the US time zone, might get there first? Toronto might seem the natural candidate, judging by some reactions to its recently introduced Canadian Index Participation Security (IPS)–a contract often cited these days by the

---

[17]Given the large-cap stocks from so many countries currently trading in London, that city is also the likely home of the first international stock index future when and if it is ever traded. Enactment of the transaction tax recently trial-ballooned in Washington would greatly increase the likelihood of a successful US index futures product in London. The tax would not only accelerate the trading of US stocks in London, but, unless very carefully drawn, might kill the competing US index futures industry altogether.

[18]Despite having since received approval from US regulators to offer Japanese index products, both the CME and the CBOT have hesitated to begin trading, mainly because they fear that too few large-cap Japanese stocks trade in the USA (thanks to the reluctance of Japanese firms to meet the stringent SEC registration requirements).

SEC and the Treasury as the kind of innovative hybrid futures security supposedly driven abroad by the lack of a unified US regulatory structure. These glowing references to the Toronto IPS by the Treasury and the SEC can be dismissed, however, as merely another case of "negative campaigning" by those agencies against the CFTC from whom they seek to wrest jurisdiction over index futures. The index participation certificates traded in Toronto are essentially fully collateralized warehouse receipts. They do not have the features that led the courts to classify as futures contracts the products of the same name introduced and later withdrawn by the American Stock Exchange and the Philadelphia Stock Exchange.[19] In principle, of course, the Toronto Stock Exchange could choose, at any time, to expand its product line and contest for market share against a weakened US futures industry. Its much-praised computerized trading system, however, appears better suited for the low-volume trading of individual stocks and retail-sized stock baskets than for the high-volume, large-size transactions in futures contracts by institutional investors. Should those institutional customers seek trading alternatives to futures during US trading hours, they are unlikely to find them in Toronto.

Four other possibilities they might turn to come immediately to mind: three are already on stream and one is only a gleam in the eye of some enterprising financial engineers. Some of the business lost to the futures exchanges will flow back to the NYSE either directly in program trades or as block trades negotiated in the upstairs market and subsequently crossed on the floor. Some of the business will be picked up in off-exchange trades with so-called third market block traders like Jefferies, and some to fourth market crossing networks like Instinet or POSIT. And some will flow to the index options exchanges. Those exchanges have run, until recently, a far distant second to index futures

---

[19]The Philadelphia and America products were withdrawn not because they could not legally be traded, but because trading them would have forced the Philadelphia and American Stock Exchanges to met the requirements of two separate regulators, the CFTC as well as the SEC. The irony of this complaint by the exchanges has apparently been lost on the SEC, however, which has made the IPS experience a major part of its case to impose the same double burden on the futures exchanges.

thanks to the very low position limits imposed by the SEC, which has the regulatory jurisdiction over options on stocks. Those limits have now been raised to the point where institutional investors can, and do, seriously consider options an effective substitute for futures in hedging strategies. But that effectiveness of options as a substitute for futures traces in no small part to the ability of options market makers to hedge their own positions quickly and cheaply on the futures exchanges. Without that protection, spreads and commissions in the options market are likely to be forced to levels far larger than institutional investors have become accustomed to paying.

Sooner or later, then, one such disgruntled institutional investor will surely approach the risk-management division of a world-class bank with the following proposition: "You currently swap dollars for yen and swap fixed rate debt for floating rate debt. Can you do a three-month swap for me of, say, $100 million in an indexed portfolio of stocks against $100 million in Treasury bills? I realize that you might have to put up additional bank capital against the swap under the new BIS capital rules, but I will compensate you for that by posting collateral with you up front and adding to it (or subtracting from it) periodically over the life of the agreement as your risk exposure changes."

The operation described is, of course, a contract equivalent to an index futures contract in every essential respect but one: it would trade in the interbank forward market and not on an exchange where margins were set by the SEC. No one yet can say which banks in which countries are best positioned to pick up the stock swap business (and ultimately the commodity swap business) that the US futures exchanges lose. But if size of bank offers any clue, the flow of business is surely much more likely to be out than in.

This chapter is based on a paper prepared for the Conference on International Competitiveness in Financial Services, American Enterprise Institute, Washington, DC, May 31 to June 1, 1990. The author is indebted to the Chicago Mercantile Exchange's Research Division for compiling the volume estimates presented at several points in the text and to the division's chief economist, Todd Petzel, for helpful comments on an earlier draft. Thanks are due also to George Benston, Fischer Black, John P. Davidson, Kenneth French, and Alan Meltzer.

References

Carlton, Dennis. "Futures Markets: Their Purpose, Their History, Their Growth, Their Successes and Failures." *Journal of Futures Markets* 4, 3, 1984.

Froot, Kenneth A., James F. Gammill Jr and Andre F. Perold. "New Trading Practices and the Short-Run Predictability of the S&P 500 Index." Working paper, Harvard Business School, 1990.

Grundfest, Joseph A. "Securities Markets in International Perspective." Paper presented at the Conference on International Competitiveness in Financial Services, sponsored by the American Enterprise Institute, Washington, D.C., May 31-June 1, 1990.

Hsieh, David, and Merton H. Miller. "Margin Regulation and Stock Market Volatility." *Journal of Finance* 44, March, 1990.

Jordan, James V., and George L. Morgan. "Default Risk in Futures Markets: The Customer-Broker Relationship." *Journal of Finance* 45, July, 1990.

Kupiec, Paul. "Initial Margins Requirements and Stock Returns Volatility: Another Look." *Journal of Financial Services Research* 3, December, 1989.

Schaede, Ulrike. "Forwards and Futures in Tokugawa-Period Japan: a New Perspective on the Dojima Rice Market." Working paper, Universitaet Marburg, May, 1988.

Schwert, G. William. "Stock Market Volatility." *Financial Analysts Journal*, 1990.

Telser, Lester, and Harlow Higginbotham. "Organized Futures Markets: Costs and Benefits." *Journal of Political Economy* 85, October, 1977.

Telser, Lester. "Margins and Futures Contracts." *Journal of Futures Markets* 1, 1981.

13 Volatility, Episodic Volatility, and Coordinated Circuit Breakers

Every country must surely have a proverb or folk tale in which unhappiness actually comes from having one's wishes granted. Such indeed seems to be the predicament of governmental overseers of the financial markets, particularly in the USA. Twenty years ago, they complained that archaic and high-cost (often monopolistic) financial market structures were seriously impeding the flow of domestic savings to productive investment. But all that has changed. Thanks largely to the dismantling of cartelized commission structures, and especially also to the development of new financial instruments and new information-processing technologies, the liquidity and efficiency of the US capital markets have increased far beyond anything imagined in the late 1960s and early 1970s. Yet, complaints are still being heard. The charge now, however, is that the markets have become *too* liquid. The call these days is for ways to raise the cost of trading and to slow markets down–back, presumably, to what they were before the regulators' wish for greater efficiency had been granted.

The case *for* market liquidity and against these attempts to "throw sand into the gears" was a major theme in my Keynote Address at the Pacific-Basin Finance Conference in Taiwan in 1989 (chapter 6 of this volume), and I will not repeat the arguments here. Instead, I shall turn to another class of complaints of much concern at the moment to our regulators and to the pundits of our financial press, namely that excessive market liquidity in the form of futures-related program trading in general, and index arbitrage activity in particular, has greatly increased market volatility, to the detriment both of individual savers and business investors. So deeply ingrained has this perception become that merely appealing to the data on volatility is likely to be of little avail, though a very brief review of the salient facts will dutifully be attempted. The major focus instead will be on one of the solutions currently being explored by the exchanges and their regulators for mitigating the problems, real and perceptual, posed by episodes of extreme volatility, such as those on October 19 and 20, 1987, or October 13, 1989. That solution, proposed originally by the Brady Commission and endorsed recently by the Securities Industry Association (the trade association of the brokerage industry) and by the New York Stock Exchange Special Panel on Market Volatility and Investor Confidence, calls for coordinating existing circuit breakers into a single, integrated system of trading halts during periods of great market stress. The case for installing circuit breakers, whether separately or in concert, will be reviewed and the prospects for achieving further integration of existing circuit breakers will be appraised.

Index Futures and Stock Market Volatility

The widespread view, expressed almost daily in the financial press (and now reinforced by similar sentiments in the Japanese press or, at least, in the English-language Japanese press) is that stock market volatility has been rising in recent years and that the introduction of low-cost speculative vehicles such as stock index futures and options has been mainly responsible. The evidence, however, fails to support either part of the charge.

Contrary to the public perception, volatility, whether measured as the variance of rates of return over monthly, weekly, or even daily intervals is only modestly higher than during the more placid 1950s and 1960s, but substantially below levels reached in the 1930s and

1940s.[1] Even the 1950s and 1960s had brief, transitory bursts of unusually high volatility with a somewhat longer lasting major burst of volatility occurring in the mid-1970s. The number of large one-day moves (that is, moves of 3 percent or more in either direction) has indeed been higher in the 1980s than in any decade since the 1930s, but almost entirely thanks to the several days of violent movement in the market during and immediately following the Crash of October 19, 1987. Increased day-to-day volatility seems to accompany every major crash (as the Japanese stock market is all too plainly been showing at the moment). In fact, the tendency of volatility to rise after crashes and fall during booms is one of the few well-documented facts about the time-series properties of volatility. These bursts of post-crash volatility typically die out within a few months, and that has been basically the case as well for the Crash of 1987.[2] The 1930s were different because the high levels of post-1929-crash volatility persisted so long into the next decade.

The failure to find evidence in the statistical record of a rising trend in volatility suggests that the public may be using the word volatility in a sense different and less technical than in academic research. By volatility the public seems to mean primarily the Crash of 1987 itself and other days when large market movements, particularly down moves, occur. These precipitous, market-wide price drops cannot always be traced to specific news events. Nor, as I have argued in chapter 6, should this lack of a smoking gun be seen as in any way anomalous in markets for assets like common stock whose values depend on subjective judgments about cash flows and resale prices in the highly uncertain future. The public, however, takes a more deterministic view of stock prices: if the market crashes, there must have been a specific reason. In thrashing around for an explanation of price falls, important segments of the retail brokerage community, the financial press, and the regulatory authorities have fastened on computerized program

---

[1]For a comprehensive survey, see Schwert (1988).
[2]See Nelson (1989).

trading and especially that form of program trading known as index arbitrage.

Index arbitrage: the new villain

Why index arbitrage should have acquired its unsavory public reputation is far from clear.[3] Unlike portfolio insurance, which can in principle be destabilizing (particularly if its presence as an informationless trade in the market is not fully understood), intermarket index arbitrage is essentially neutral in its market impact. The downward pressure of the selling leg in one market is balanced by the equal and opposite buying pressure in the other. Three recent and extremely thorough studies of intraday moves (Neal and Furbush, 1989; Duffie et al., 1990; and Harris et al., 1990) also report no tendency for cash market prices to reverse after episodes of index arbitrage. The cash market's behavior after program trades was found to be entirely consistent with the view that prices are being driven by information, not mere speculative "noise" originating in the futures market–as critics have so often charged.

Nor should these findings be considered in any way remarkable. The low cost of trading index futures makes the futures market the natural entry port for new information about the macroeconomy or for changes in sentiment by investors, particularly by large well-diversified institutional investors, about the appropriate portion of their portfolios to maintain in equities rather than bonds. The news or sentiment change, if big enough to push prices through arbitrage bounds, is then carried from the futures market to the cash market by the program trades of the arbitrageur.[4] Thanks to the electronic order routing systems of the NYSE, the delivery of the news from the futures market may well seem

---

[3]I assume here and throughout that index arbitrage is so familiar to likely readers as to require no further definition or elaboration. A detailed description of the mechanics is in chapter 7, "Equilibrium Relations Between Cash Markets and Futures Markets," in this volume.

[4]Sometimes, of course, the flow of significant news runs in the other direction as on the mini-crash of October 13, 1989, following the announcement that the UAL takeover deal had fallen through.

fast by past standards. But arbitrage is still merely the medium, not the message.[5]

That so much recent criticism has been directed against the index-arbitrage messenger rather than the message itself may reflect the negative connotations always attaching to the term arbitrage. Let me save those speculations about arbitrage for another occasion, however, and turn instead to one of the institutional reforms currently being proposed for dealing with the problems, real or imagined, of "episodic market volatility"–to use the currently fashionable euphemism for events like those on October 19, 1987, and October 13, 1989.

Circuit Breakers as a Response to Episodic Volatility

The Brady Commission recommended "circuit breakers" (in the sense of pre-programmed trading halts) as one constructive way of coping with the kind of market breakdowns that occurred during the Crash of 1987. Trading halts, by themselves, of course, are nothing new. No exchange, after all, yet operates 24 hours a day. All exchanges do interrupt trading at least once every day, at the closing bell, and sometimes more frequently, as in the case of US Treasury Bond futures at the Chicago Board of Trade, where a second, after-hours trading session is held on most evenings during the week. These normal and regularly scheduled trading halts are everywhere taken for granted. But intraday programmed trading halts of the kind recommended by the Brady Commission have generally been greeted with scorn by most economists.

These economists point out that the market had ample chance over the weekend of October 17 and 18, 1987, to "pull itself together" and "catch its breath" following Friday, October 16, when the market fell by a substantial 6 percent. The two days of cool reflection, however, seemed only to intensify the selling panic that took place when the

---

[5]I have argued in chapter 11, "Index Arbitrage and Volatility," in this volume that index arbitrage might conceivably disadvantage the market makers (specialists plus limit order holders) at the NYSE. But these wounds would be essentially self-inflicted and easily remedied by the use of contingent limit orders that permitted pricing off the futures, as is routine in other spot markets.

markets reopened on October 19. In fairness, however, the panics of major concern to some supporters of circuit breakers were those that seemed to have occurred on October 19 and especially on October 20 long *after* the opening, as word spread of the steadily falling prices on the trading floor.

But the affirmative case for circuit breakers rests on more than these psychological (or perhaps pseudo-psychological) bases. A case–weak, perhaps, but not entirely frivolous–can be made for circuit breakers in terms of more or less standard micro-market structure theory. And an even more compelling case can be made in terms of the organizational imperatives confronting the exchanges (and their governmental over-seers) once the exchanges are seen not just as "markets" in the economist's general sense, but as "business enterprises" following well-considered business strategies in selling transaction services to their customers.

Circuit breakers from a micro-market structure perspective

The micro-market structure case for intraday circuit breakers starts from the proposition that the Walrasian market of standard welfare economics is an ideal that can only be approximated by any feasible, real-world market. The continuous, two-sided markets now offered by the Chicago futures markets and the NYSE differ substantially from each other in important ways; and both differ in turn from discrete batch or call-auction markets (such as the London gold fixing) or the current opening market for stocks on the NYSE. No reason exists to suppose that any one of these micro-structures is necessarily the closest approximation to the Walrasian ideal under all circumstances, any more than to suppose that one type of transportation, whether it be automobile, boat, plane, or train, is always the best way to travel.

In particular, the continuous market offered by the NYSE is designed to operate efficiently these days up to a maximum transaction volume of perhaps a billion shares a day, assuming those trades are spread more or less evenly throughout the day. Peak loads exceeding those levels can be handled only at steeply rising costs and subject to consider-able "rationing," formal and informal. (In chapter 4 of this volume I warn of the chaotic floor conditions likely to accompany a major order imbalance.) The effective capacity of the NYSE was much smaller in October 1987 and the system suffered then what amounted to a "brown-out" when hit with a transactions demand that surged to a rate of 500 million shares for the day. Kleidon (1990) points out, for example, that in October 1987 most incoming limit orders were routed not directly to the specialists, but first to special card printers and then delivered manually to the specialists. The limited capacity of the order-card printers (plus the inevitable breakdowns) led to a massive queue of limit orders waiting for execution throughout most of the day.[6] Kleidon argues that the delays in executing the backlog of limit orders (compounded by problems in the software for cancelling limit orders) meant that the actual transaction prices reported on the tape were "stale," that is, they actually reflected the information of anywhere from thirty minutes to an hour earlier. Since the nature of the delay was not fully appreciated at the time, the tape was thus sending out a misleading signal of the true state of supply and demand.

No one can say for sure, of course, whether the volume on October 19 might have been handled more effectively had the exchange been able to switch to one, or perhaps a series of single-price call auctions during the day. But the proposition is certainly arguable, as is the proposition that the market participants might have voted for just such a switch in a plebiscite, had one been possible, even though they clearly prefer continuous markets on most other, and less hectic, trading days.

In a related micro-structure argument Greenwald and Stein (1989) note that *all* potential buyers and sellers are assumed present and ready to participate in a Walrasian market. In real-world securities and futures markets, by contrast, sellers, say, may bring their orders to market before the ultimate counterparty buyers actually assemble. The transactions of the early arriving sellers are made with intermediary market makers who hold the orders in inventory until the ultimate buyers eventually do arrive. In some micro-structure models of this

---

[6]In the two and a half years since the Crash, the NYSE has upgraded the system so that most limit orders are now routed electronically directly to the specialist's screen.

transfer process, like that in Grossman and Miller (1988), the focus is on the immediate pricing decisions of the market makers. The eventual transfer of the sell orders from the market makers to the ultimate buyers is taken as proceeding smoothly in an essentially Walrasian way. But, as Greenwald and Stein emphasize, such a straightforward and simple unwinding of this second stage cannot always be taken for granted.

The potential buyers in a real-world market, whose market makers are confronting an unexpectedly large surge of sell orders, cannot always be sure of the price at which their market orders to buy will, in fact, be executed. This transaction price uncertainty, they show, may lead the buyers in turn to reduce the size of their orders, or to cancel them altogether until the range of execution uncertainty narrows.[7] Such transfers of the security as do occur during these intervals of great transaction price uncertainty are hardly likely to meet the Walrasian welfare conditions, and the transfers may have to be reversed in subsequent rounds of trading.

Something very much like this seems to have happened, Greenwald and Stein would argue, about noon New York time on October 19, 1987, when transaction price uncertainty reached what we can only hope was its all-time high. As can be seen from figure 13.1, the futures price, rather than being at its normal premium to the index, was actually at a huge discount to the index. Why was this seeming profitable arbitrage opportunity not exploited? Partly, we now know, because the staleness of the NYSE prices made much of the gap itself essentially an illusion, and partly because, with the chaos on both floors, no one could be sure of being able to exercise either leg at the indicated prices, let along both legs close to simultaneously. During this interval of three hours until the close, prices of stocks fell by nearly 10 percent (and of futures by nearly 12 percent) only then to reverse almost completely when the markets reopened to heavy buying volume on the morning of October 20 (see figure 13.2). That a trading halt or equivalent circuit breaker

---

[7]The stale price phenomenon described in the previous footnote might also entice additional market order sellers to enter the market in the mistaken hope that they can execute at those temptingly high prices.

imposed at 1:00 p.m. or so EST in New York might have obviated this sequence of huge fall at heavy volume, followed by offsetting rise at equally heavy volume, is a proposition–Greenwald and Stein would insist–that surely cannot be dismissed out of hand.[8]

Circuit breakers from a futures market perspective

Circuit breakers, in the form of daily maximum permissible price moves (in either direction) from the previous day's close, have long been a standard feature in US futures markets. Once the down limit is hit, say, that price becomes the permissible low for the rest of the day, though trades above the limit are permitted. Trading resumes on the next trading day with new limits. The price limits appear to be the natural (in the sense of least-cost) institutional response by the industry to two problems that large sudden price changes pose for its particular trading, clearing, and settlement technology.

In a futures market, unlike the stock market, no one has responsibility for maintaining price continuity. When sentiment changes abruptly, the bids and offers in the trading pit can jump immediately to the new equilibrium. The jump may well be fast enough and far enough to sweep through a floor broker's entire "deck" of resting limit orders and stop orders, taking the broker effectively out of the game as it were. The trading halt that occurs when prices hit the limit gives the broker time to get back to the customers for revised and updated instructions to be followed when the market resumes trading. The customers might, in principle, of course, have issued instructions in advance to their brokers about how to change their original bids and offers in the event of a large change in the market parameters. But spelling out (and enforcing) the responses to every future contingency would be impossibly costly under present or any likely foreseeable technology. The trading pause at the limit is a simpler and cheaper way of making sure that the bids, offers, and executed transactions do

---

[8]The uncertainties discouraging transactions on October 19 were further compounded by rumors that some brokerage firms and possibly even some exchanges might fail. Circuit breakers, some have argued, might at least have given some time to get out the denials.

accurately express the considered preferences of the customers when trading is eventually resumed.

The price limits of commodity exchanges are, to this extent, very much in the spirit of Greenwald-Stein circuit breakers. They serve as well, however, to deal with a second, subtler and much less widely appreciated problem of futures-style pit trading.[9]

Price limits, clearing firms, and floor traders. The floor population of market makers in the "open-outcry" trading pits consists primarily of "locals" trading for their own account, but whose settlements are guaranteed by a "clearing firm," that is, by a member of the exchange's clearinghouse. Should a local suffer trading losses beyond his or her capacity to pay, the clearing firm must make up the difference.

The concern of the clearing firms over large sudden price moves is thus easily understandable. Thanks to the zero-sum nature of futures trading, every large price move, whether up or down, leads to substantial losses for something on the order of half the floor population. As guarantors the clearing firms protect their interests, as do creditors generally, by imposing capital requirements on their locals sufficient to cover, and typically to more than cover, a normal day's potential trading losses. Large sudden more-than-normal moves, however, not only can blow away this protection for the clearing firm, but may create additional incentives for the locals that are adverse in the extreme to the clearing firm's interests. A local already wiped out has nothing more to lose and potentially much to gain from "double-or-nothing" strategies with what amounts to the clearing firm's money. The price limit, once hit, however, gives the clearing firm time to remove potentially insolvent traders from the floor before they accumulate further losses.

----

[9]On this point especially, but by no means only, I have benefited greatly over the years from discussions with my sometime colleague and co-author, Sanford Grossman. His distaste for circuit breakers is so intense, however, that I hesitate even to mention his name in this context. But I will mention one of his oft-repeated objections to them, viz, that the prices revealed in a market, even one highly stressed, offer a better inducement for counterparties to assemble than do any "reopening indications" issued during the trading halt.

In principle, of course, the clearing firm could protect itself even without formal price limits and associated trading halts. But continuous monitoring of trader positions would be far too costly, if indeed possible at all under present, trade-recording technology. And requiring traders to maintain higher precautionary levels of equity cover, though certainly feasible, would be costly for the traders and reduce the number of those who clear through the firm. Price limits, blunt instruments that they may be, thus seem to be cost effective for controlling clearing firm exposure, and, by their evident satisfaction of the survivorship principle, are arguably also the most efficient solution.[10]

Why then, one wonders, were index futures the first (and still virtually the only) major contract for which price limits did not apply? Perhaps the exchanges underestimated the fatness in the tails of the distribution of stock returns. The early and middle 1980s were relatively placid ones for the stock market. The bond market in those years was the high volatility market, and the Treasury Bond futures contract of the Chicago Board of Trade *did* have a daily price limit. Calls for installing a price limit on stock index contracts began to be heard at the futures exchanges in late 1986 and early 1987, but none of the exchanges then offering the product wanted to give its actual and potential competitors an edge by moving first.[11]

Circuit breakers from a stock market perspective
The NYSE, like the famed Windmill Theatre in London during the Blitz, has always boasted: "We never close!" Actually, of course, the NYSE suspends trading frequently; not in all stocks at once to be sure

---

[10]Price limits can sometimes be hit for several days in succession. To keep such occasions infrequent, the rules of most exchanges widen the limits after each triggering. In some cases, however, such as the silver crash of 1980, even those successive enlargements may be unable to get trading restarted for up to a week or more. Note also that limits do not apply in the contract close-out month.

[11] The CME did retain, however, some discretionary power to restrain order imbalance by limiting the number of contracts that large traders could sell during any half-hour bracket during the trading day and did, in fact, invoke this "bracket rationing" at several points during the Crash of 1987. (See Chapter 4 in this volume.)

(except perhaps in cases of presidential heart attacks or assassinations) but in single stocks and at times in large batches of stocks. Sometimes, moreover, the Exchange may not be closed, technically speaking, but it's not exactly open either. On October 19, 1987, for example, some of the Exchange's largest and most important stocks, such as IBM, did not begin trading until nearly an hour and a half after the opening bell sounded. The Exchange, in sum, has always had circuit breakers. They differ in form from those of the futures exchanges mainly because the basic business strategies of the exchanges differ.

A key element in the long-successful marketing strategy of the NYSE is the notion of "price continuity." The potential customer can look at the ticker tape, observe the price on the last trade and be confident of making a (small) trade at that price or within an eighth of it either way some 90 percent or more of the time. Transaction price uncertainty, in sum, is effectively eliminated.

No reason exists to believe, however, that the underlying time series of equilibrium stock prices is itself smooth and continuous. Indeed, the analysis of other markets suggests that speculative prices are highly discontinuous, if only because the news and sentiment changes that drive prices will themselves come in discrete packets and because the mapping of news into prices is highly nonlinear. (See Mandelbrot, 1963.) How then can the NYSE successfully market an inherently lumpy product as if it were smooth? The answer is that they "have a little man in there," so to speak. The Exchange gives each of its "specialists" an exclusive franchise to trade a particular stock in return for the specialist's commitment to maintain the continuity of the transaction price series for the stock—trading as a principal on his own account where appropriate and interacting as a broker with the limit order book and with the floor brokers according to an elaborate set of priority rules.

Most of the time, of course, the system *does* accomplish its design objective of maintaining price continuity. But when a really big news item hits or a major change in sentiment occurs, orders pour in on one side of the market. Any attempt by the specialist to keep the price from changing, or even to walk the price to its new equilibrium value an eighth at a time will quickly blow away the specialist's capital (and clean out all the resting limit orders as well). Since continuity cannot be maintained in any event, why not just let the specialist jump the price to its new equilibrium value and be done with it? Because the key decision as to where the new maintainable trading price really lies cannot be left to the specialist's judgment alone. The specialist, after all, is a privileged market insider, often with a large inventory position accumulated perhaps from earlier unsuccessful attempts to smooth the price transition. The Exchange's oft-cited policy of granting primacy to public orders demands, therefore, that the new price level be determined by a more objective procedure such as a call auction of essentially the same kind used to open the day's trading. Even this call auction is not completely objective, of course. The specialist and the relevant floor governors still must decide how long to keep the auction open in the hope of narrowing the price jump by seeking more counterparties before banging the hammer and resuming the flow of transactions (and commissions). Over time, of course, as in any other business, a body of tradition and experience can be expected to develop that best balances the organization's costs and benefits from trading halts and delayed openings.

Circuit breakers: problems of intermarket coordination

Circuit breakers, in sum, seem to meet organizational needs in both futures markets and the NYSE and have been, in fact, a feature of both markets (except for the index futures contract) since well before the Crash of 1987. That crash merely added new sets of rationalizations for circuit breakers, some stressing the need to mitigate the adverse consequences of the great transaction price uncertainty that discourages potential buyers during a crash and some merely hoping that "time-outs" might help calm a jittery public and discourage panic selling. But while both markets have circuit breakers, the differences in the way they work raises questions about whether they should be more closely coordinated; and if so, how.

The case for coordination is most starkly illustrated by the distressing events, not so much on October 19, 1987 (bad as that day was), but on the even more chaotic day following. That day opened, as noted earlier, substantially higher than the close of the day before, and for a while all seemed headed back to normal (see figure 13.2). Around noon New York time, however, a new selling wave suddenly struck both markets. In Chicago futures prices plunged while in New York circuit breakers, in the form of trading delays and halts, struck many of the large-cap stocks in the S&P 500 index. So many halts were occurring, in fact, that the managers of the CME, upon learning that the Board of Directors of the NYSE was about to hold an emergency meeting, feared that all trading in New York might well be about to close, leaving the CME to face the flood of sell orders alone.[12] With no offsetting arbitrage buying demand coming in, the CME's floor traders would have little hope of unwinding the long positions they had already assumed on the way down and no way of absorbing more of the selling wave sloshing over from New York. Prices might well collapse so far as to threaten the solvency of the floor traders and the clearing firms responsible ultimately for their losses. Prices would snap back the next day, of course. But for the CME and its floor population, there might *be* no next day!

Fearing just this kind of irreversible catastrophe, the managers of the CME closed that exchange at about 12:15 p.m. New York time. By one of the many ironies of that fateful day, that closing came only minutes before the cavalry came riding to the rescue in the form of substantial buy orders from the so-called Tactical Asset Allocators and, even more conspicuously, from a wave of announced corporate share repurchases. The CME shutdown thus turned out to have been unnecessary, but only just barely, and still leaving the CME with the nightmare of someday having to stand alone when the New York market was closed.

The post-crash circuit breakers. The close call on October 20, plus the strong recommendation for circuit breakers by the Brady Commission, led both exchanges early in 1988 to formalize their procedures for intraday closings. The CME emerged with a three-step series of price limits.

---

[12]The Chicago Board Options Exchange had already closed because its rules stopped trading in index options whenever 50 percent of the stocks in the index, by value weighting, were not trading.

The first step applies only to the day's opening. The S&P 500 futures contract may not open more than five S&P 500 points (currently about one and a half percent) up or down from the previous close. This opening limit continues for ten minutes or until the market trades off the limit. If the market remains at the limit after ten minutes, trading halts for two minutes and a new opening range is established. The CME replays the down, so to speak, giving the customers a chance to "recontract" by sending new and updated instructions to their floor brokers.

The second limit is a down limit only, at twelve S&P 500 points (about three and a half percent currently) from the previous day's close. The contract may not trade lower for thirty minutes or until 2:30 p.m. Chicago time, whichever comes first. The third limit applies when the market moves thirty points above or below the previous close. The contract cannot trade beyond this limit for one hour after the limit is reached; and if that point is reached after 1:30 p.m. Chicago time, the limit applies for the rest of the day.[13]

The NYSE has a two-step circuit breaker procedure, apart from certain additional "side-cars" and "collars" to be noted later. If the Dow Jones average declines by 250 points (a bit over 9 percent currently) from the previous close, trading in all stocks is halted for one hour. If, after reopening, the Dow Jones average falls by another 150 points (that is, by another 6 percent or so), all trading is halted for two hours. Nothing is specified beyond 400 points down; everyone, presumably, would be too dazed by then to care.

The circuit breakers and the market break of October 13, 1989. By June 4, 1990, the NYSE's 250-point and 400-point circuit breakers had never been engaged and the CME's twelve-point and thirty-point price limits

---

[13]Shortly after the mini-crash of October 13, 1989, the CME filed rule proposals with the CFTC inserting a twenty-point down limit between the current twelve-point and thirty-point limits. Approval of the new rules by the CFTC was granted on June 18, 1990, and the CME has since instituted them on a trial basis.

have both been hit on only a single day, October 13, 1989.[14] A closer look at the events of that day may thus throw some useful light on the benefits and costs of existing circuit breakers. Admittedly, this is only a sample of one; but a sample of one is at least better than a sample of zero.

Figure 13.3 shows the S&P 500 cash price and the S&P 500 futures price minute by minute on October 13, 1989. Figure 13.4 shows the volume of trading at each exchange minute by minute over the same interval. Note that the futures contract hit its first-step, twelve-point down limit at 3:06 p.m. New York time. Unrestricted trading resumed at 3:30 p.m. and futures prices plunged more or less steadily thereafter until the second-step, thirty-point limit was hit at 3:51 p.m. New York time. The market then remained locked limit-down for the rest of the trading day, with a few brief up-blips just before 4:00 p.m. The NYSE maintained its regular trading through the entire day, though a number of individual stocks (particularly in the airline industry) experienced substantial trading halts in the period shortly after 3:00 p.m.

A frequently voiced objection to circuit breakers has been that the trading halt might become a self-fulfilling prophecy as traders rush to avoid being locked into their positions when prices come in range of the trigger point. The surge in the volume figures for futures just before the limit kicks in is certainly consistent with such a "magnet" effect. But a major news story also was breaking at the same time–the collapse of the UAL buyout deal–and that story might well have loosened a flood of orders because of its negative implications for other airline take-overs, and indeed, for corporate takeovers generally. The volume data are also consistent with a "spillover" effect from futures to the cash market, though again, some substantial rise in cash market trading would have been expected on the basis of the news.

Between June and August, 1990, no less than four separate studies of the October 13, 1989, mini-crash appeared. Three of these were by

---

[14]The CME's twelve-point limit was also triggered on October 24, 1989, following an unusually large foreign sell order. The price quickly bounced back above its limit, however, and normal trading resumed. During the summer of 1990, the twelve-point limit was hit on two separate occasions.

government regulatory agencies–the SEC, the CFTC, and the General Accounting Office (GAO), which was called in to mediate the dispute between the other two over who or what was responsible for the price break. The GAO, not happy at being called on to take sides in the acrimonious battle over jurisdiction for index futures, concluded, not surprisingly, that more research was needed before any firm judgment could be made.

The fourth study, by Henry McMillan of the SEC's Office of Economic Analysis, was a very thorough and detailed econometric investigation of the impact of the circuit breakers on October 13. McMillan finds that price dispersion (measured by distributions of the absolute value of successive price changes) increased after circuit breakers were lifted on October 13, and by noticeably more than it does on regular market openings. He also found substantially more price dispersion on October 13 than on October 16, 1987, another Friday on which the market fell by about 6 percent, but with no circuit breakers in place. He concludes that circuit breakers may well have impaired price discovery on October 13 rather than aided it as Greenwald and Stein would have hoped. McMillan also finds in the path of prices just prior to the triggering of the circuit breakers some patterns of runs that strongly suggest a magnet effect.

All in all, and despite some minor signs of stress, the most striking feature of this episode on Friday, October 13, may well have been its aftermath, or perhaps absence of aftermath. Recall that the earlier crash episode, Friday, October 16, 1987, was a down day every bit as bad as this one, and was followed by the catastrophe when the markets reopened after the long weekend on Monday, October 19, 1987. This time, however, no such disaster occurred. Monday, October 16, 1989, was an unremarkable day.

Can the circuit breakers that cut in this time on Friday the Thirteenth (or the putative ones that might have cut in on Monday) be credited for the difference in outcomes? Or should the credit go to some of the other lessons learned from the previous crash–especially the realization that a 6 percent drop in the market in a single day, though hardly pleasant or cheering, does not mean that the economy is about to plunge into an abyss as deep as the 1930s? The monetary authorities, moreover, this time issued their comforting reassurances first thing Monday morning, not on Tuesday after the market had already gone into shock.

But while we may never know for sure what role, if any, the post-1987-crash circuit breakers played in fending off a Monday disaster in 1989, we do know one respect at least in which the circuit breakers failed to live up to the hopes of some of their more enthusiastic original proponents. In the face of a 6 percent drop, the mere presence of circuit breakers did nothing to convince Congress, the public and the financial press that the markets were in fact under control. The press, after the event, made virtually no reference to the safety nets the exchanges had installed.[15] Criticism of the markets, particularly of the index futures market and index arbitrage, mounted to a new intensity.

The Securities Industry Association/NYSE panel proposals for coordinated circuit breakers. That the critics and competitors of the index futures exchanges would use the mini-crash of October 13 as a "border incident" in calls for war against the index futures industry was only to be expected. The call for volunteers in the war had already been sounded, in effect, by the Securities and Exchange Commission in the ritual denunciations of "speculation fueled by low futures margins" that the Commission issued during and immediately following the episode, even before its staff had time to review the events of the day in detail.[16] The Commission, of course, had long been regretting its abdication of jurisdiction over broad-based index futures in the Shad-

---

[15]The tide may have turned, however. Press accounts after the CME's twelve-point limit was triggered on July 24, 1990, were highly favorable on the whole to the circuit breakers. But the market did happen to bounce back that day after trading was resumed. A better test of public acceptance will come when the market next breaks through the twelve-point limit and falls to the twenty-point and thirty-point limits.

[16]The Commission's staff did, as noted, eventually (June 1990) present a report on the mini-crash that, not surprisingly, confirmed its earlier position. The SEC's analysis and conclusions in that report were challenged, however, in reports by the Commodity Futures Trading Commission.

Johnson accords of 1981. In the immediate aftermath of the Crash of 1987, the then SEC Chairman David Ruder had called for the ending of the accord and for the restoration of jurisdiction over index futures to the SEC. But he had been rebuffed by the Presidential Working Group on Capital Markets–an inter-agency coordinating group formed after the crash of 1987. The members were the SEC Chairman, the CFTC Chairman, the Chairman of the Board of Governors of the Federal Reserve System, and the Secretary of the Treasury, with the latter serving as Chairman. By 1989, however, the chairmanship of the Working Group had passed to the new Secretary of the Treasury, Nicholas Brady, who had earlier chaired the Presidential Task Force on Market Mechanisms (the Brady Commission). For Secretary Brady, the mini-crash of October 13, different in most respects as it may have been from the maxi-crash of two years earlier, served nevertheless as an occasion to remind all concerned that the Brady Commission's four-point policy agenda (unified regulatory jurisdiction, harmonized margins, unified clearing, and coordinated circuit breakers) had yet to be implemented. He called on (sometimes literally) the members of the US investment community and the corporate power structure to join him in a crusade to rein in the index futures industry once and for all.

In the congressional battles that followed Secretary Brady's call to arms–battles still being fiercely contested at the time of this writing (August 1990)–the Brady Commission's agenda items of margin authority and of agency jurisdiction over index futures have received virtually all the attention. Circuit breakers appear to have figured hardly at all in the testimony of Secretary Brady or of the current SEC Chairman Breeden before any of the congressional committees with a stake in the outcome of the fight for jurisdiction over futures. The exchanges themselves, and the professional investment community more generally, rather than the Treasury or the SEC, have now become the main proponents of the kind of coordinated intermarket circuit breakers that had figured so prominently in the earlier Brady Commission report. In fact, the Securities Industry Association, the trade association of the US brokerage and investment banking community, after dutifully endorsing the principle of harmonized margins and other regulations, made an elaborate set of coordinated circuit breakers the center piece of the recommendations in a widely publicized press release on program trading. An even more detailed and elaborate set of circuit breakers, strongly influenced by the Securities Industry Association's proposals, was also the first and most prominent recommendation of the Special Panel on Market Volatility and Investor Confidence commissioned by the New York Stock Exchange in January 1990.

The NYSE Special Panel, chaired by Roger Smith, Chairman of General Motors Corporation, had nineteen members covering most of the NYSE's many constituencies. Seven members, including Chairman Smith, were chief executives of major US corporations who were also serving as members of the NYSE's governing Board of Directors. An eighth was Donald Stone, Vice Chairman of the NYSE and a principal of one of its leading specialist firms. Six other members were the chief executives of major securities firms covering investment banking along with both national and regional retail brokerage firms. Most of the securities industry representatives also served on the Securities Industry Association panel mentioned earlier. The remaining five panelists consisted of two large institutional investors, one representative of an organization of individual investors, another the charismatic Special Counsel of the CME, Leo Melamed, and one academic (the present writer).

Given the diversity of the NYSE Special Panel and the intense emotions attaching to terms like "volatility" and "investor confidence," the degree of consensus reached in the main body of the Special Panel's report (though not its recommendations) is quite remarkable. Much credit is due to the NYSE's staff economists who skillfully and patiently led the panel members through the now vast academic research literature on volatility and program trading. The overwhelming weight of that research suggests, as noted earlier, that no substantial recent surge in statistical volatility has in fact occurred, and certainly none that can be traced causally to index arbitrage. The contrary view, so often and so vehemently expressed by the critics of index futures (including several of the NYSE Special Panel members) appears to be less a matter of volatility in any precise sense of that term than of the all-too-unpleasant fact that even a not unusually volatile stock market *will* fall some of the time; and when it does happen to fall substantially, that fall, like any other out-of-the-ordinary event, is bound to command headlines. Even so, an investor survey commissioned for the Panel by the NYSE turned up surprisingly little anxiety in the investing public over either program trading or volatility. Rather, the main concern of individual investors seemed to be the honesty of their brokers!

Though the analysis and conclusions in the main body of the NYSE Panel's report differed substantially in tone and substance from those of the earlier Securities Industry Association report, many of the specific recommendations turned out to be the same (not entirely surprisingly given the overlap in membership). Both panels dutifully endorsed unified regulation and harmonized margins (though with dissents from two members of the NYSE Special Panel). And both gave top priority to the installation of multi-tiered, coordinated circuit breakers.

The NYSE Special Panel's proposal was the more elaborate of the two and involved no less than five distinct stages. For the first stage, the CME would retain its current opening ten-minute price limit of five S&P 500 points (up or down). The subsequent four stages are as follows, with price changes measured from the previous day's close:

Stage	CME	NYSE	Duration
	(up or down)	(up or down)	
1	12 S&P points	100 Dow points	60 min.
2	24 S&P points	200 Dow points	90 min.
3	36 S&P points	300 Dow points	120 min.
4	48 S&P points	400 Dow points	120 min.

If the price of the S&P futures contract moves in either direction by the amount specified, the CME is to invoke a *price limit* at that level, not a *trading halt*. For the NYSE, however, the corresponding Dow point limits (set so that the CME limits will normally cut in slightly before those of the NYSE) will trigger an across-the-board trading halt in all NYSE stocks lasting for the time listed. During the trading halt, the exchange's specialists will disseminate information about order imbalances and will frequently post "indications" of likely price ranges when trading resumes. The trading will resume using the NYSE's regular opening procedure.

Because large imbalances may prevent some stocks from reopening at the scheduled time, an additional safety valve is provided for the futures markets. When the trading halt expires, the index futures (and options) markets would follow their normal opening procedures, but would not reopen unless 50 percent (by market capitalization) of the stocks in the S&P 500 index were open and trading. Such a procedure, had it been operative on October 19, 1987, might well have dispelled the confusion surrounding the supposed "billboard" effect of the huge opening futures discount on that day (see figure 13.1). That gap, perhaps more than any other single factor, was responsible for the still-lingering view in our financial press that the futures market was the Judas goat that led the unsuspecting stock market sheep to the slaughter on October 19. The gap, of course, was mere illusion. Both markets were hit simultaneously by the accumulated selling pressures that had built up over the weekend. The futures price dropped immediately to its new trading level on the open. The NYSE's computed S&P index, however, did not. As noted earlier, many of the leading large-cap stocks, including such key ones as IBM, did not begin trading until an hour or more after the opening. But the prices used for compiling the S&P Index are the prices of the last recorded *transaction* which, in the case of the nontrading stocks, were the hopelessly obsolete prices from the close on Friday, October 16, 1987. As more stocks eventually opened at their lower current trading prices, the index and the futures price moved closer together. The eventual convergence of the two series, in short, was simply the lagging stock market prices finally adjusting to reality. The NYSE Special Panel may have done a real service in dispelling further confusion on this point by also recommending that an S&P index of average quote indications be constructed and widely disseminated, with the indications gradually replaced by actual transaction prices as individual stocks reopen and resume trading.

Note finally the pattern of durations for the sequence of trading halts, or trading pauses, as proponents of circuit breakers prefer to call them. Cumulatively, they come to six and a half hours–virtually the entire length of the trading day. We know, therefore, that once these circuit breakers are instituted, we need never fear a repetition of the nightmare experience of October 19, 1987, when the market fell by 508 Dow points in a single day. Trading for the day will have been halted by the time the fall has hit 400 points!

Whether the ambitious set of coordinated circuit breakers proposed by the NYSE Special Panel will ultimately be instituted we have, at this time, no way of knowing. The CME, for its part, has committed to adopting the Special Panel's proposal, provided all other major stock and options exchanges do the same. If they don't, the CME proposes to make permanent its own current pilot program for price limits at twelve, twenty, and thirty S&P points. The NYSE has not so far filed the implementing rule changes with the SEC, its regulator, even though the exchange sponsored the Panel and has endorsed its report and recommendations. Rather than striving for intermarket coordination, the NYSE seems to have opted instead for intermarket *separation* in the form of its new Rule 80A.

Collars, side-cars and Rule 80A. The new Rule 80A is merely the latest in a long series of steps taken by the NYSE since the Crash of 1987 to restrict institutional program trading and index arbitrage in the interest of its retail customers–or, at least, as it interprets those interests. The first steps were the so-called "collars" introduced in January 1988 which called on member-firm program traders to refrain voluntarily from entering program orders on the electronic Super-DOT order-routing system whenever the market moved in either direction by seventy-five Dow points. The collar was lowered to fifty Dow points in February 1988 and with SEC approval was made mandatory in April 1988. The Super-DOT collars were triggered some seven times between

April and September 1988, five on the upside and two on the down.[17] Neither index arbitrage nor other program trading stopped during these collared intervals, however. The trades were simply executed manually–at a higher cost and subject to more risk and tracking error than usual–by those firms with direct access to the floor. The effects on market volatility of introducing this form of inefficiency appear to have been negligible; and, to no one's regret, the collars were allowed to die in October 1989, when the NYSE adopted both its still-untriggered 250 and 400 Dow point circuit breakers and its "side-car" proposal.

The side-car cuts in when the S&P 500 contract has dropped twelve S&P points (approximately ninety-six Dow points) below the previous day's close. For the next five minutes, retail orders have priority over program trades on the Super-DOT system; and for the rest of the day (save for the last thirty-five minutes) new stop and stop limit orders are banned except for individual orders of 2099 shares or less. This deliberate tilting of the exchange rules against institutional customers was intended to counter some of the complaints that the market nowadays is "rigged against the small investor," to use the characteristically colorful language of one former Secretary of the Treasury. The small investor, however, appears to have been unimpressed.

The NYSE and some of its large member firms known to be active program traders hoped for a bigger and more positive reaction from the newly introduced Rule 80A. The rule generalizes and extends the familiar "uptick" rule, under which short sales may be made only on a plus tick (that is, at a price higher than the previous price) or on a zero-plus tick (that is, at a price equal to the previous price, but which price was itself higher than the price previous to it). Under Rule 80A, whenever the market moves down by fifty Dow points, index arbitrage sell orders, even if not short sales, can be executed only on a plus tick or a zero-plus tick for every component share; and, if the market moves up by fifty points, index arbitrage buy orders can be executed only on a minus or zero-minus tick.

---

[17]For a fuller account of experience with the collars, see the Report of the NYSE Special Panel, especially Appendix E.

The NYSE submitted its proposed new Rule 80A to the SEC for approval in February 1990 before its own Special Panel had really begun its deliberations. As noted earlier, the Securities Industry Association report endorsed the new rule, as eventually did the NYSE Special Panel (though with strong dissent by the academic member and by the special counsel of the CME). The SEC has recently given its formal assent to the rule and it is now in force, though technically only on a one year trial basis.

The economic rationale for the new Rule 80A is not entirely clear. The rule's proponents stress that it is intended not to ban index arbitrage, but merely to ensure that the arbitrage is "stabilizing" rather than destabilizing. But that explanation is merely self-serving "body English" of the kind legislators often use to title their bills (as in the recent proposal to tax the short-term capital gains of pension funds, S.1654, titled by the introducing senators as "The Excessive Churning and Speculation Act of 1989"). The supporters of Rule 80A, some of whom, as noted, are currently among the exchange's largest program traders, must surely be aware that when the trigger-point is reached, Rule 80A will almost certainly make index arbitrage infeasible. The qualification "almost certainly" could be omitted if index arbitrage of the S&P 500 contract literally required dealings in 500 separate stocks. The probability is infinitesimal that all 500 stocks would meet the tick requirements simultaneously. In practice, however, arbitrage programs typically involve no more than fifty of the largest stocks, and sometimes even fewer. The MMI index contract, moreover, involves only twenty stocks. Thus, some small probability does exist that index arbitrage might occur even after a fifty-point market move; but the tracking-error risk would be so great that little arbitrage activity could be expected.[18]

---

[18]Note that the 80A restrictions on index arbitrage are asymmetric in the sense that they prevent buy-futures/sell-stock arbitrage after a fifty-point drop, but not buy-stock/sell-futures if the market subsequently should happen to turn around after reaching, say, minus 100. Once the market bounced back to minus 25, Rule 80A is suspended until such time as it again hits fifty points, plus or minus, from the previous day's close.

Perhaps the supporters may believe that giving up the index-arbitrage business on those relatively rare big-move days–fifty-point moves (currently one and seven-tenths percent) have been occurring recently at an average rate of a bit more than one per month–is a reasonable price to pay for avoiding public and congressional charges that their program trading activities had caused a crash. Or, perhaps, they may be cleverer yet. They may believe that while Rule 80A greatly increases the risk of intermarket "spreading"–which is a better term under the circumstances than arbitrage–it also increases the rewards to those few well-positioned firms who can bring it off successfully either directly (perhaps with a small subset of stocks) or indirectly via off-exchange or off-shore transactions.

Postscript on Rule 80A. The Rule 80A cut-off at fifty Dow points was triggered for the first time on Friday, August 4, 1990, after the Iraqi invasion of Kuwait was announced and again on Monday, August 6, 1990, after a major embargo (if not actually a blockade) of Iraqi oil shipments seemed imminent. If the original sponsors of Rule 80A hoped to contain the price falls to fifty points, they were disappointed. On both days the price fall continued unchecked all the way down to the CME's twelve S&P point down-limit (about 100 Dow points). Early press accounts suggest that CME volume and liquidity were markedly reduced after the Rule 80A restrictions came into play. Bid-ask spreads and successive-transaction spreads on the CME were substantially larger than usual and the premium of the futures over index fluctuated erratically around its normal level. The results of these first two days are suggestive, but judgment must be reserved because both triggerings occurred at the open. Delayed openings and stale prices at the NYSE would have limited index arbitrage and widened spreads on those days, as they did at the open on October 19, 1987, even if Rule 80A had not been operative. The real test of 80A will come when the price break occurs in the middle of the trading day, as it did on October 13, 1989.

Unsettling as these two August days may have been, a small silver lining can perhaps be detected among the clouds. Witness, for example, the following from the August 7, 1990, column by Floyd Norris, a featured writer in *The New York Times* business section and not normally a strong supporter of index futures. Noting that Rule 80A was operative on August 4 and August 6, Norris concludes:

> For the stock market, an important lesson of the past two trading days may be that prices can plunge even if the index arbitrageurs are legislated out of the market. Stock index futures now make it much easier for traders to try to slash their stock positions quickly. When many try to do so at once, a price fall can result quickly, and be felt in the stock market whether or not the index arbs are trading. That was true in 1987, and it is true in 1990.

Conclusion

The mini-crash of October 13, 1989, though far smaller than the maxi-crash of October 19, 1987, has spawned almost as many reports and commissions. Notable among these has been the New York Stock Exchange's Special Panel on Market Volatility and Investor Confidence (chaired by Roger Smith of General Motors). The Smith panel's major recommendation for dealing with periods of episodic volatility, like those of the October market breaks, was an elaborate set of coordinated circuit breakers that would simultaneously close down temporarily, and then reopen, both the index futures markets and the stock market when large changes in the broad market indexes were occurring. Coordinated price limits and trading pauses along these lines had also been recommended earlier by the Brady Commission, though in much less specific detail. In one important respect, however, the Smith panel broke with the Brady Commission. The Brady Commission report had emphasized that the most chaotic market conditions on October 19 and 20, 1987, had occurred when the futures market and the cash market had become disconnected. The Smith panel, by endorsing the NYSE's proposed Rule 80A, had voted, in effect, to disconnect the markets by severing the arbitrage link between them whenever the price level moves by fifty Dow points (roughly one and seven-tenths percent at present levels).

The SEC has now approved Rule 80A, though technically only on a one-year trial basis. The CME, which had earlier adopted a multi-level set of price limits much like those proposed for the futures markets by the Smith panel, may thus be led to reconsider its posture on circuit breakers. That the CME would turn away completely from price limits is unlikely, however. Daily price limits have long been a standard feature of futures contracts for reasons related to the efficient functioning of the exchange. Only by historical accident was a limit not in place for the S&P 500 contract on the fateful day of October 19, 1987, and its absence is still regretted by many of the CME's leading members. They continue to believe that the welfare losses of customers from being unable to trade on October 19 would have been less than the welfare losses of trading in markets as inefficient, both informationally and technically, as those during the great Crash of 1987.

Whatever the balance on welfare account–and the essential empirical work on this score still remains to be done–the likelihood is small that a price limit on index futures would have deflected the torrents of criticism directed at the futures markets after the Crash of 1987. That much is clear from the aftermath of the mini-crash of October 13, 1989, during which price limits *were* in operation. Subsequent triggerings of the price limit have indeed received a more positive reception from the financial press, though perhaps only because the market seemed to bounce back after hitting the limit, as indeed the market usually will, given the truism that larger price falls are rarer than smaller ones.

Large price breaks may be rare, but they will surely happen. Price limits and trading pauses can spread the falls out over time; but neither circuit breakers nor more drastic steps (such as banning index futures altogether) can prevent major changes in price levels from occurring whenever a sufficiently large fraction of investors seek to reduce the proportion of their wealth they hold in equities. The best to be hoped is that as the public becomes more aware of circuit breakers, their triggering during a fall might alleviate what opinion pollsters have identified as a major concern during recent crash episodes: the fear that computer-driven markets are thrashing about, like some mad Golem, totally out of human control. Unless and until this sense of control has been restored, the index futures markets, as the most recent arrivals on the scene, will remain vulnerable to political attack.

This chapter is based on a keynote address given at the Second Annual Pacific-Basin Finance Conference, Bangkok, Thailand, June 4 to 6, 1990. Helpful comments on an earlier draft were received from Allen Kleidon and Andrei Shleifer.

References

Duffie, Gregory, Paul Kupiec and Patricia White. "A Primer on Program Trading and Stock Price Volatility: a Survey of the Issues and Evidence." Working paper, Board of Governors, Federal Reserve System, 1990.

Greenwald, Bruce C., and Jeremy C. Stein. "Transactional Risk, Market Crashes and the Role of Circuit Breakers." Working paper, Harvard Business School, 1989.

Grossman, Sanford, and Merton H. Miller. "Liquidity and Market Structure." *Journal of Finance* 43, 3, July, 1988.

Harris, Lawrence, George Sofianos and James E. Shapiro. "Program Trading and Intraday Volatility." NYSE Working Paper 90-03, 1990.

Kleidon, Allen W. "Arbitrage Nontrading and Stale Price." Research Paper No. 1091, Graduate School of Business, Stanford University, May, 1990.

Mandelbrot, Benoit. "The Variation of Certain Speculative Prices." *Journal of Business* 36, 3, October, 1963.

McMillan, Henry. "The Effects of the S&P 500 Futures Market Circuit Breakers on Liquidity and Price Discovery." Office of Economic Analysis, US Securities and Exchange Commission, June, 1990.

Miller, Merton H. *Financial Innovations and Market Volatility.* Mid America Institute for Public Policy Research, Chicago, 1988.

Neal, Robert, and Dean Furbush. "The Intraday Effect of Program Trading on Stock Returns: Some Preliminary Evidence." Working paper, Department of Finance, University of Washington, 1989.

Nelson, Daniel B. "Conditional Heteroskedasticity in Asset Returns: a New Approach." Working paper, Graduate School of Business, University of Chicago, 1989.

NYSE Special Panel on Market Volatility and Investor Confidence (Roger Smith, Chairman). New York, June, 1990.

Presidential Task Force on Market Mechanisms (Nicholas Brady, Chairman). Washington, DC, March, 1988.

Schwert, G. William. "Business Cycles, Financial Crises and Stock Volatility." Working paper, William E. Simon Graduate School of Business, University of Rochester, 1988.

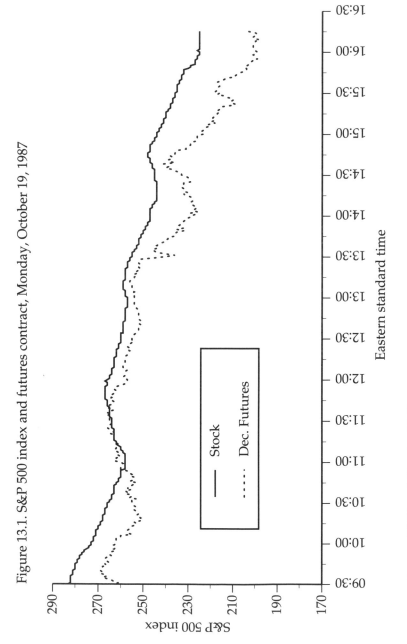

Figure 13.1. S&P 500 index and futures contract, Monday, October 19, 1987

Source: CME and Standard & Poors.

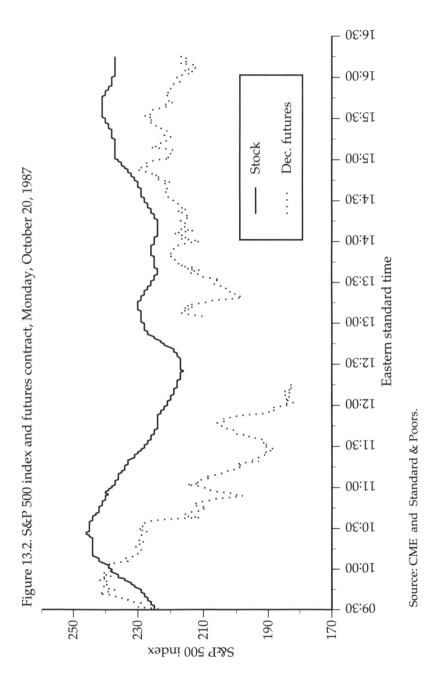

Figure 13.2. S&P 500 index and futures contract, Monday, October 20, 1987

Stock

Dec. futures

S&P 500 index

250

230

210

190

170

09:30   10:00   10:30   11:00   11:30   12:00   12:30   13:00   13:30   14:00   14:30   15:00   15:30   16:00   16:30

Eastern standard time

Source: CME and Standard & Poors.

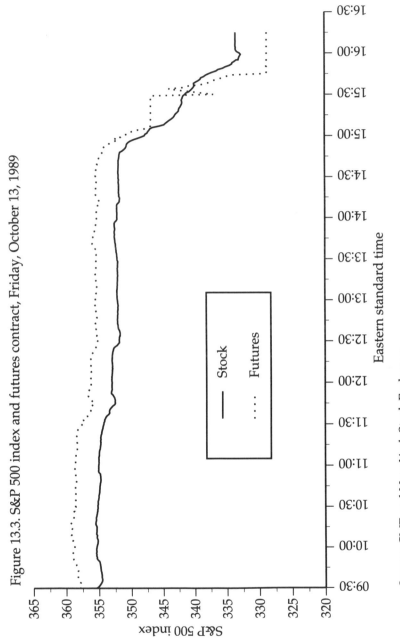

Figure 13.3. S&P 500 index and futures contract, Friday, October 13, 1989

Source: CME and New York Stock Exchange.

Figure 13.4. S&P index and futures contract, October 13, 1989
Minute-by minute

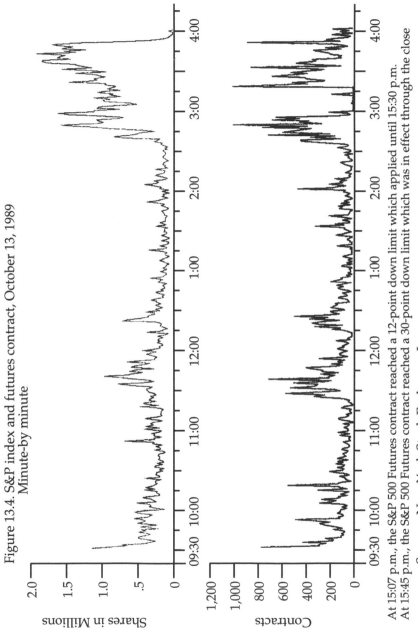

At 15:07 p.m., the S&P 500 Futures contract reached a 12-point down limit which applied until 15:30 p.m.
At 15:45 p.m, the S&P 500 Futures contract reached a 30-point down limit which was in effect through the close

Source: New York Stock Exchange, Inc.

Part IV

The Academic Field of Finance

14 The Academic Field of Finance: Some Observations on Its History and Prospects

This occasion is doubly gratifying to me: to be receiving an honorary degree, and to be receiving it from a university with which I have so many cherished links, both personal and professional. I was among the very first foreign visitors some twenty years ago to the university's then newly formed Center for Operations Research and Econometrics–a center which has become one of the leading (and, in Europe, certainly *the* leading) focal point of research in mathematical economics. During that year-long stay I also inaugurated the professorial part of the interchange between the Graduate School of Business at Chicago and the department of applied economics in Leuven–an interchange that has now gone to the third generation, involving not just my own students but the students of my students.

But in another sense my ties of affection for the Katholieke Universiteit te Leuven go back much further yet. On the wall of the library there is a plaque commemorating the school children of Boston, Massachusetts, who contributed pennies from their lunch money to help rebuild the library after its destruction in the First World War. I was one of those children. A penny may not seem very much these days but at the time it represented 20 percent of my weekly allowance. And, as we've all come to learn with some regret, the dollar and its pennies went a lot farther in those distant times.

A nomination for an honorary degree proposed by a business school or department of applied economics is likely, I am sure, to be as much or more a recognition of the field as of the person. Six years ago, Leuven's nomination of Harvey Wagner reflected not only his own substantial scholarly contributions to the field of management science, but the critical role of management science itself in initiating the changes in teaching methods and research emphasis that have come to characterize management education in a university setting. It was the example of management science, in fact, in the 1940s and 1950s that established, once and for all, that management could be a subject with serious intellectual and scholarly content. (Certainly, in my own case, the chance to work with Abraham Charnes and William Cooper–those pioneers of mathematical programming–was a major factor in attracting me and other young economists to the Graduate School of Industrial Administration at Carnegie Tech in Pittsburgh where so much of the new-model business study was being developed.)

But if management science was *the* field of the 1940s and 1950s, my field, finance, surely became *the* field in the 1960s and 1970s. By the late 1970s the finance courses were far and away the most heavily enrolled in virtually every leading business school. The graduating students were pouring into the major financial centers and institutions and applying both their lessons learned and their own inventiveness to new financial instruments and new ways of measuring managerial performance. In fact, as a field of study, finance may have succeeded too well; a problem facing many US business schools today is how to keep their finance faculties from following their students to Wall Street!

What gave the academic field of finance its great impetus in the 1960s and 1970s was a powerful and almost unique interaction of theory and empirical research. Management science surely had as much or more sophisticated theorizing; marketing had its mountains of statistical material. But neither had quite the reinforcing action of the two that can produce the almost explosive, cumulative growth of a new field of study. This growth in finance undoubtedly still has a way to go. But the first signs–certainly not of senescence, but at least of maturing in the field–are already beginning to appear. And it is natural to begin to speculate about what may be recognized, say, in the year 2006, as *the* field of the 1980s and 1990s.

I have some thoughts about the field from which the man or, nowadays, with increasing likelihood, the woman candidate may be chosen, but perhaps the best way to convey them may be first to review briefly some of the developments in finance over the past twenty years or so that have spurred its growth and that may provide some clues about where the main current growth direction seems to be pointing. I hasten to add that this review is not intended as a complete, and certainly not as an unbiased, history. The record is far too long, the subject matter too diverse, and I am too close to its many still lingering controversies.

My review can at least serve as a reminder, if one were needed, that the path of progress, whether in academic fields or the broader world of affairs, has a large element of the unanticipated and often of the completely unintended.

Certainly, the first major breakthrough in modern finance had such consequences. By first, I am not referring to the Modigliani-Miller propositions; they too did have unexpected consequences that I will get to in due course. But they were not first. That honor belongs to the mean-variance portfolio selection model of Harry Markowitz first presented in article form in the early 1950s–the more detailed and elaborate book treatment not actually appearing until the end of the decade.

The Links to Management Science and Mathematical Statistics: Harry Markowitz and the Theory of Portfolio Selection

In the early 1950s Markowitz was not a member of any finance faculty but a doctoral student with an interest in mathematical statistics. His work was presented as a thesis in the Economics Department at Chicago–there being, at that time, no formal statistics department at the university.

The theme of the thesis was diversification. The concept was one that, at the intuitive level at least, was well understood by practitioners in insurance and portfolio management. The random variations of the returns on individual securities would tend to cancel out as more securities were added to the portfolio–hence the gains from diversification. But the gains would be limited by an positive correlation of the individual outcomes with each other, as a fire insurance company, say, might find to be the case for a group of insured houses on the same street in the same town. Drawing on his field of mathematical statistics, Markowitz formalized these notions of the gains (and limits) of diversification and showed how an optimally diversified portfolio could be achieved–in the sense of one bearing the lowest risk for any given level of expected return–once the mean returns, variance and co-variance of the component elements were specified.

Markowitz not only described the optimum portfolio, but actually developed an efficient computational algorithm for finding it–so-called quadratic programming, in contrast to linear programming. I stress this programming solution as a reminder that for Markowitz himself, and for many others at the time, the contribution of the work was in management science, rather than finance or economics. They saw the model as actually being implemented by individuals and financial institutions to select optimal portfolios. That selection process was indeed the main thrust of Markowitz's later book. And for all I know perhaps someone, somewhere, may actually have tried to select a portfolio his way. But if that had been the model's sole, or even major, accomplishment it would have long since sunk without a trace for reasons amply discussed by David Durand in an early and rather scathing review of Markowitz's book.

Markowitz's portfolio model, however, found another life as an economists' or "observers'" model rather than as the management scientists' or "doers'" model originally intended. Financial economists were concerned with the relative prices (or, more accurately, the relative expected rates of return) of different securities. To construct the relevant demand curves for securities they needed a model of a representative investor balancing return against risk. The Markowitz mean-variance, constrained-optimum model fitted the bill perfectly. In the hands of such economists as James Tobin, William Sharpe, John Lintner and Eugene Fama, the Markowitz model quickly grew into that theory of equilibrium valuation known as CAPM–the Capital Asset Pricing Model–the model which, perhaps more than any other, directly and

indirectly underlay the huge upsurge of empirical research in finance
that began in the middle 1960s.

The Link to Economics: the Modigliani-Miller Propositions

If the Markowitz model of portfolio choice turned out to be the indispensable building block from which the theory of the demand for risky
securities could be constructed, that role on the supply side of the
market for corporate securities was played by the Modigliani-Miller
models of capital structure choice and dividend policy choice. The
profession took much longer, however, to see the Modigliani-Miller
propositions as steps on the road to sectorial supply functions rather
than primarily as descriptive or prescriptive micromodels.

The Modigliani-Miller articles are difficult to describe briefly if
only because they covered so wide a range–and by present-day standards, certainly too wide a range–of topics. The 1958 paper, entitled,
"The Cost of Capital, Corporation Finance and the Theory of Investment," for example, not only discussed all three components of the title
at length but opened with a general survey of problems of characteriz-
ing and valuing random income streams, and went on to establish the
paper's central result with an arbitrage proof so vivid that many
mistakenly identified it with the proposition being proved. (I should
add that, fortunately, many were not confused, among them Fischer
Black and Myron Scholes who used a similar line of reasoning in
building their option-pricing formula, as did Stephen Ross for his arbitrage pricing theory.) The paper then turned to the relation between
risk and return on levered shares, presented some of the first empirical
tests of the Modigliani-Miller capital structure propositions, and
closed with a discussion, later found to be wrong, of the effect of
corporate income taxes on capital structure decisions.

The second Modigliani-Miller paper, entitled "Dividend Policy,
Growth and the Valuation of Shares," was only slightly less far-
ranging. The topics covered, over and beyond the basic dividend proposition and proof, included a variety of valuation formulas, dividend
information effects, the meaning of the term "growth stocks," some

problems posed by speculative bubbles, plus the inevitable tax complications—all subjects that appeared and reappeared regularly in subsequent research and controversies.

How difficult it is to summarize briefly the contribution of these papers was brought home to me very clearly after Franco Modigliani was awarded the Nobel Prize in Economics in part—but, of course, only in part—for the work in finance. The television camera crews from our local stations in Chicago immediately descended upon me. "We understand," they said, "that you worked with Modigliani some years back in developing these Modigliani-Miller theorems and we wonder if you could explain them briefly to our television viewers." "How briefly?" I asked. "Oh, take ten seconds," was the reply.

Ten seconds to explain the work of a lifetime! Ten seconds to describe two carefully reasoned articles each running to more than thirty printed pages and each with sixty or so long footnotes! When they saw the look of dismay on my face, they said: "You don't have to go into details. Just give us the main points in simple, common-sense terms."

The main point of the first, or cost-of-capital, article was, in principle at least, simple enough to make. It said that in an economist's ideal world of complete and perfect capital markets, and with full and symmetric information among all market participants, the total market value of all the securities issued by a firm would be governed by the earning power and risk of its underlying real assets and would be independent of how the mix of securities issued to finance it was divided between debt instruments and equity capital. Some corporate treasurers might well think that they could enhance total value by increasing the proportion of debt instruments because yields on debt instruments, given their lower risk, are, by and large, substantially below those on equity capital. But, under the ideal conditions assumed, the added risk to the shareholders from issuing more debt will raise required yields on the equity by just enough to offset the seeming gain from use of low cost debt.

Such a summary would not only have been too long, but it relied on shorthand terms and concepts, like perfect capital markets, that are rich in connotations to economists, but hardly so to the general public. I thought, instead, of an analogy that we ourselves had invoked in the original paper. "Think of the firm," I said, "as a gigantic tub of whole milk. The farmer can sell the whole milk as it is. Or he can separate out the cream and sell it at a considerably higher price than the whole milk would bring. (Selling cream is the analog of a firm selling low yield and hence high-priced debt securities.) But, of course, what the farmer would have left would be skim milk, with low butter-fat content, and that would sell for much less than whole milk. (Skim milk corresponds to the levered equity.) The Modigliani-Miller proposition says that if there were no costs of separation (and, of course, no government dairy support program), the cream plus the skim milk would bring the same price as the whole milk."

The television people conferred among themselves for a while. They informed me that it was still too long, too complicated and too academic. "Have you anything simpler?" they asked. I thought of another way that the Modigliani-Miller proposition is presented which emphasizes the notion of market completeness and stresses the role of securities as devices for "partitioning" a firm's payoffs in each possible state of the world among the group of its capital suppliers. "Think of the firm," I said, "as a gigantic pizza, divided into quarters. If now, you cut each quarter in half into eighths, the Modigliani-Miller proposition says that you will have more pieces, but not more pizza."

Again there was a whispered conference among the camera crew and the director came back and said, "Professor, we understand from the press release that there were two Modigliani-Miller propositions. Maybe we should try the other one."

He was referring, of course, to the dividend invariance proposition and I know from long experience that attempts at brief statements of that one always cause problems. The term "dividend" has acquired too great a halo of pleasant connotations for people to accept the notion that "the more dividends the better" might not always be true. Dividends, however, as we pointed out in our article, do not fall like manna from heaven. The funds to pay them have to come from somewhere—either from cutting back on real investment or from further sales (or reduced purchases) of financial instruments. The Modigliani-Miller dividend proposition offered no advice as to which source or how much to tap. It claimed, rather, that once the firm had made its real operating investment decisions, its dividend policy would have no effect on shareholder value. Any seeming gain in wealth from raising the dividend and giving the shareholders more cash would be offset by the subtraction of that part of their interest in the firm sold off to provide the necessary funds. To convey that notion within my allotted ten seconds I said: "The Modigliani-Miller dividend proposition amounts to saying that if you take money from your left-hand pocket and put it in your right-hand pocket, you are no better off."

Once again whispered conversation. This time, they shut the lights off. They folded up their equipment. They thanked me for my cooperation. They said they would get back to me. But I knew that I had somehow lost my chance to start a new career as a packager of economic wisdom for television viewers in convenient ten-second sound bites. Some have the talent for it; and some just don't.

These simple, commonsense analogies certainly do less than full justice to the Modigliani-Miller propositions; crude caricatures or cartoons they may be, but they do have some resemblance. So much, in fact, that looking back now after more than twenty-five years it is hard to understand why they were so strongly resisted at first. One writer–David Durand, the same critic who had so strongly attacked the Markowitz model–even checked out the prices for whole milk, skim milk and cream in his neighborhood supermarket. He found, of course, that the Modigliani-Miller propositions didn't hold exactly; but, of course, empirical relations never do. A good theory, by its very nature, must be a drastic simplification. Whether its empirical discrepancies lead to a rejection depends on the alternative theories available. There simply were none in the middle 1960s, or at least none that could be reconciled with the main body of economics as it had developed over the years.

By the late 1960s, then, a definite turning away occurred from what was being seen as fruitless empirical testing of the Modigliani-Miller propositions against vaguely specified or downright unacceptable alternatives. The focus shifted to the specific changes in assumptions needed to match the model's predictions more closely to the model's observations.

In this matching of theory to the data, the word most used these days–and in finance at least almost certainly over-used–is "anomalies." Once an anomaly has been declared, the researchers in the profession swarm around like sharks in a feeding frenzy. We seem to have more than our quota of them in finance–a factor certainly in the earlier noted remarkable surge of research in the field over the past generation. They range from the merely strong (like the Monday effect or the January effect) to the seriously challenging, like the small-firm effect or like the major class of anomalies that began to dominate research on the Modigliani-Miller models as the decade of the 1970s began.

That some extended discussion of this particular class of major Modigliani-Miller anomalies would find its way into these remarks comes as no surprise to my Belgian ex-students. In speculating with one of them a while back as to what might be an appropriate theme to speak on, he suggested: "Why not talk about the Belgian favorite sport?" "Do you mean bicycle-riding?" I asked. (During my visit in 1966 I knew that I had Eddie Merckx among the neighbors in my commune. I am also perhaps one of the two or three Americans who can recognize the name of Rick van Looey.) "No," he said. "The Belgian national sport is tax avoidance." But that's the United States's national sport too! And for basically the same reasons. Our governments persist in trying to apply nineteenth century tax concepts to a world with twentieth century (and soon to be twenty-first century) capital markets.

The Tax Anomalies and the Search for the Equilibrating Costs

The details of the tax systems in the USA and Belgium differ somewhat, particularly after the latter's recent corporate tax reforms, but the essentials are roughly the same, as indeed they are in most of the developed countries of the world. The systems have two major sets of income taxes: one is a graduated tax (sometimes a very steeply graduated tax) on personal incomes; the other, an essentially flat rate tax on corporate profits. Why are the personal income tax rates graduated? Because widely accepted standards of social justice call for the burdens of maintaining the common weal to be distributed according to "ability to pay," and because so many nineteenth and early twentieth century social reformers and economists (with the notable exception of the great American economist, Irving Fisher, whose work underlies so much of modern finance) believed that something called "income" was the best measure of that ability to pay. And, indeed, if all personal income took the form of wages and salaries, perhaps they might have been right (or, at least the errors in their view might have had few serious practical consequences). But, of course, wages and salaries are not the only sources of income. Income in the form of dividends, interest or rentals can be earned on capital funds saved or inherited. Profits can be made either in regular business operations or merely from buying something at one price and reselling it for more. And it is that last possibility, the possibility of capital gains and losses, that directly or indirectly creates most of the problems.

To keep the wheels of commerce from grinding to a complete halt, the steeply graduated rates of the personal income tax cannot be applied with full force to capital gains. But if the rates on this form of income are reduced relative to other forms, the tax system develops the equivalent of an enormous internal voltage pressure. Incentives are created to transform high-taxed forms of capital income such as interest or dividends into lower-tax capital gains. And since the distinctions among these forms are matters of legal and accounting definitions rather than of economic fundamentals, such transformations can be confidently expected. The corporate business form is a particularly efficient engine for these and related transformations; hence the separate additional corporate income tax in most Western countries imposed, at least in part, as a deliberate counterweight or "franchise fee" for the tax-saving potential of the corporate form of business. (The policymakers, of course, are also well aware that corporations do not vote; and the view that corporate shares are owned only by the rich is widely held even among workers, many of whose nest-egg pension funds are invested in corporate stocks).

Contemplating tax systems of this kind in the middle 1960s, with the original Modigliani-Miller leverage and dividend propositions then becoming more widely understood and appreciated, one conclusion seemed inevitable: these patched-up tax systems with their substantial rate differentials among forms of receiving capital income cannot long survive. The restructuring of financial flows by firms and investors will occur until all income from capital is taxed at the same uniform rate (which might well eventually become zero as Myron Scholes and I speculated in our article "Dividends and Taxes" of a few years back.)

Consider, for example, the Modigliani-Miller leverage proposition and recall that it implies, among other things, that all sources of capital have the same cost to the firm. True, their specific terms and standings in terms of priority may differ. But these and other differences in their relative risks are reflected in their relative yields; the firm gets what it pays for (and pays only for what it gets). This economic equivalence, however, is not recognized in the accounting conventions underlying the tax law. Interest payments on that part of a firm's capital funds obtained from suppliers who qualify as legal creditors are treated as a cost of doing business, and can be deducted from earnings in computing taxable profits. At tax rates on corporate profit in the neighborhood of 50 percent (which has been the case in the USA for the entire forty years since Second World War), the deductibility of interest could amount to a subsidy of as much as fifty cents on each dollar of debt capital raised by the firm.

This is where one of the glaring Modigliani-Miller anomalies I mentioned earlier was clearly visible. For despite these seemingly huge subsidies, US firms did not resort particularly heavily to debt financing. Even by the late 1970s, when the substantial on-going price inflation was probably interacting with other elements of the tax code to further increase the advantages of corporate debt financing, corporate debt ratios were only marginally higher than in the lower-taxed 1920s. For some large, and clearly otherwise well-managed corporations, such as IBM, the debt ratio was actually negative. They held more interest-bearing securities as taxable assets than they had issued as interest-deductible liabilities. Firms also seemed content to pour out billions of dollars in fully taxable dividends each year despite the availability of financial strategies along Modigliani-Miller lines that would have converted those dividends into tax-favored capital gains.

Faced with long-persisting, seeming disequilibria of this kind, economists almost instinctively look for some "cost" whose presence off-sets what would otherwise appear to be unexploited profit opportunities. Sometimes, of course, these presumed equilibrating costs may seem little more than giving a name to our ignorance as in the oft-invoked, unspecified "costs of adjustment" or the "long and variable lags" so popular with monetarist macro-forecasters. But in the case of debt financing there were surely a number of well-known and very real kinds of costs to appeal to. Most conspicuous, of course, and first to be systematically brought into the discussion of the Modigliani-Miller tax anomaly were the costs of bankruptcy or more generally of the costs of reorganizing the firm and renegotiating contracts after an actual or threatened failure to meet obligations to creditors. Under US law and custom, the reorganization and/or liquidation proceedings can be very lawyer-intensive and hence very expensive, particularly when many separate creditors are involved. The indirect costs of reorganization proceedings can sometimes loom even larger—the loss of key employees, the alienation of customers and suppliers and, above all, the diversion of management time and energies from more productive activities. For all that, however, neither empirical research nor simple common sense could convincingly sustain these presumed costs of bankruptcy as a sufficient, or even as a major, reason for the failure of so many large, well-managed US corporations to pick up what seemed to be billions upon billions of dollars of potential tax subsidies.

Attention then shifted inevitably from these highly visible terminal costs of debt to others of a more subtle, more pervasive and on-going kind. The reference here, of course, is to what has come to be called "agency theory" and which, though certainly much stimulated initially by the Modigliani-Miller anomalies, has since spread widely, and fruitfully, throughout finance and economics. Agency theory in its most general sense stresses the differences in knowledge and incentives that the various parties bring to a contract and especially the limitations that such differences impose on the ability of the parties to extract the maximum benefits possible from their coming together. That contracts between debtors and creditors should be particularly subject to these limitations will hardly seem surprising to anyone who has ever had a chance to look through the fat volume of procedures and suggested contract provisions in the loose-leaf manuals that banks and insurance companies typically supply to their loan officers. (And behind each paragraph there is a story, as a loan officer once told me.) But that contracting costs of these kinds could account for the major tax anomaly (or for the wide variations in financial practices among otherwise similar companies) seems hardly credible, particularly in view of the amazing ingenuity in the design of securities shown by our lawyers and investment bankers in recent years. Any lingering doubts should be dispelled by the great surge in so-called leveraged buyouts and associated high-yield "junk bond" financings since 1980. When the tax benefits are large enough–supplied in the LBO case by a combination of inflation and of fast capital write-off provisions that made it profitable to shift old properties to new hands–appropriate vehicles will spring up for catering to them.

The Debt and Taxes Model: Additional Paths to Equilibrium

The converse proposition holds as well. If otherwise well-managed firms with access to ingenious investment bankers are failing to pick up huge tax savings by adapting existing financial instruments or developing new ones, then perhaps the presumed tax benefits may not really be as large as they seem from a literal reading of the tax statutes. Tax subsidies do indeed share the essential property of government subsidies generally; they lead to greater production of the commodity subsidized. But unlike the more typical commodity subsidies, the government does not stand ready to buy up the excess supply. Where the government *does* buy, equilibrium can be restored and the further flow of supply can be shut off only when marginal production costs have been driven up to the support price. But where the government does *not* buy the subsidized output, as it generally does not for its tax subsidies, another automatic shut-off mechanism can come into play, namely the fall in market prices received on sales of the subsidized commodity.

It was to this, all-too-easily overlooked additional price-adjustment mechanism in the debt market that I sought to direct attention in my "Debt and Taxes" paper of some ten years back. Somebody, after all, must buy the bonds that US corporations want to sell. And if the demand for those bonds behaves like that of any normal commodity, the extra supply induced by the tax subsidy can only be taken up by lowering the price, or in the reverse way we use in discussing bonds, by raising the interest rate offered. The supply-demand analogy can be pushed further yet. Just as the most eager buyers of a subsidized but not price-supported commodity will benefit from the fall in market price of the subsidized commodity, so too will the most eager buyers of bonds. In this category, I am happy to say, are college professors, like myself, whose soon-to-be received pension funds are heavily invested in these tax-subsidized instruments. The main losers in the subsidy game are, of course, bond issuers who must pay the high interest rates but do not qualify for the subsidy; and, by a delicious irony, that turns out to be our own deficit-ridden federal government which caused the whole problem in the first place.

The taxable corporations that are of major concern here do qualify for the subsidy, of course. That, after all, is what gave rise to the anomaly. But the expanded "Debt and Taxes" model had one even more delicious irony left. Under some extreme, but not wholly implausible conditions, the tax subsidy of interest deduction under the corporate income tax can be shown to be exactly offset by the tax penalty on interest inclusions under the personal income tax. We would be back once again to something like the original Modigliani-Miller world in which all sources of capital, this time even with taxes, would have the same cost to the firm. Although that rather startling special case has, not unnaturally, been the main focus of much subsequent controversy, it was not, and was not intended to be, the main contribution of the "Debt and Taxes" extension. That contribution, rather, was the restoring of a sense of proportion to discussions of capital structure decisions by keeping the tax effects from crowding out virtually everything else that might be brought to bear on the choice. No stars are visible when the sun is shining. And similarly here.

Until the demand side of the market and the level of interest rates had been brought into the equilibrating process, the direct and indirect costs of debt finance—the costs and wastes of separating the cream from the milk as it were—could not be easily and plausibly integrated with the basic Modigliani-Miller framework. Marginal equalities of costs and benefits could not be met without having to imagine mechanisms driving costs of debt finance to levels that would have been as anomalous in their own right as the anomalies they purported to eliminate.

A somewhat similar evolution has been taking place for the dividend tax anomalies. There the missing costs that prevented the tax gains from being reaped were even harder to imagine than for the debt subsidy. So much so, in fact, that many in the profession were beginning to despair that even the gross facts of corporate dividend behavior could be explained without bringing in persistent irrationalities of a kind invoked nowhere else in finance. But new supply-adjustment models have been proposed recently for dividends along lines very similar in spirit to the "Debt and Taxes" model. Like that model, the newer models leave much smaller tax discrepancies to be explained, and hence make it much less urgent for researchers in finance to seek solutions outside the standard paradigms of economics.

The Emerging New Streams of Research

The increased attention being devoted to formal models of market equilibrium with taxes does suggest, however, that the Modigliani-Miller perfect-world models have finally become assimilated. Like their counterparts in physics, they have served to define the boundary limits within which acceptable solutions are constrained to lie. With the outlines in place, the emphasis is shifting to filling in the rest of the puzzle.

Considerable progress has, in fact, already been made; some highly colored or strongly patterned pieces have already begun to be fitted together, ready for later insertion into the full design. One thinks immediately in this connection of the agency theory literature of which I spoke earlier, particularly if broadly construed to encompass the work in the area of information economics as well. Information economics is where the bright young theorists are flocking these days. Their models and concepts have already begun to alter our way of looking at markets and market prices which, after all, lie at the center of our concerns as economists. It is from this emerging new stream of research in economics and finance that I predict the degree candidate for the year 2006 will be selected. I only wish I could be there to help make the occasion for him (or her) as memorable as you have made it for me.

This chapter is based on an address delivered on the occasion of receiving an honorary doctorate from Katholieke Universiteit te Leuven, Leuven, Belgium, May 15, 1986.

Index